AF598898

DRAWING AND PAINTING Beautiful Flowers

Discover Techniques for Creating Realistic Florals and Plants in Pencil and Watercolor

Kyehyun Park

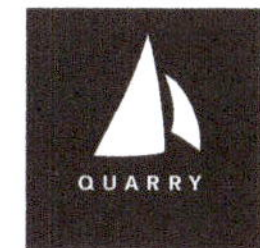

Quarto.com

© 2022 Quarto Publishing Group USA Inc.
Text and images © 2022 Kyehyun Park

First Published in 2022 by Quarry Books, an imprint of The Quarto Group,
100 Cummings Center, Suite 265-D, Beverly, MA 01915, USA.
T (978) 282-9590 F (978) 283-2742

All rights reserved. No part of this book may be reproduced in any form without written permission of the copyright owners. All images in this book have been reproduced with the knowledge and prior consent of the artists concerned, and no responsibility is accepted by producer, publisher, or printer for any infringement of copyright or otherwise, arising from the contents of this publication. Every effort has been made to ensure that credits accurately comply with information supplied. We apologize for any inaccuracies that may have occurred and will resolve inaccurate or missing information in a subsequent reprinting of the book.

Quarry Books titles are also available at discount for retail, wholesale, promotional, and bulk purchase. For details, contact the Special Sales Manager by email at specialsales@quarto.com or by mail at The Quarto Group, Attn: Special Sales Manager, 100 Cummings Center, Suite 265-D, Beverly, MA 01915, USA.

ISBN: 978-0-7603-7330-9

Digital edition published in 2022
eISBN: 978-0-7603-7331-6

Library of Congress Cataloging-in-Publication Data is available.

Design: Kate Barraclough
Page Layout: Megan Jones Design

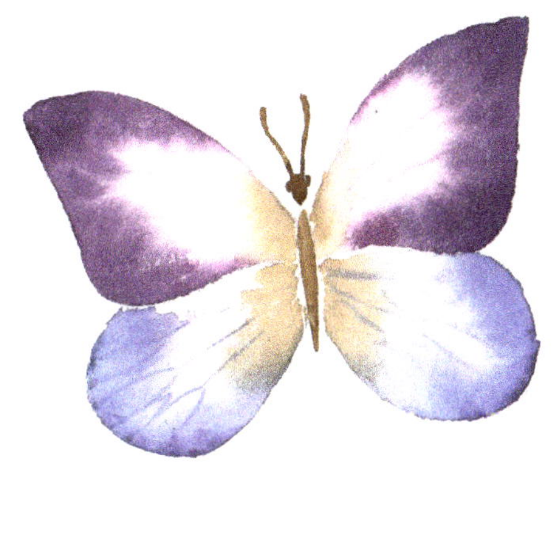

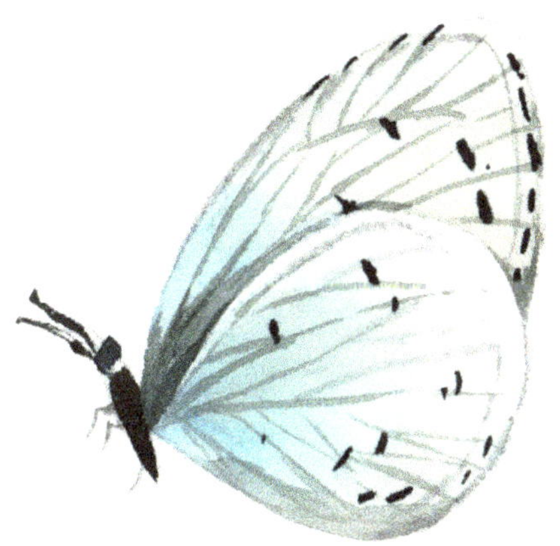

I dedicate this book to everyone who wants to learn how to draw flowers, my daughter Jia, husband Hoonju, family members living in Korea, and friends.

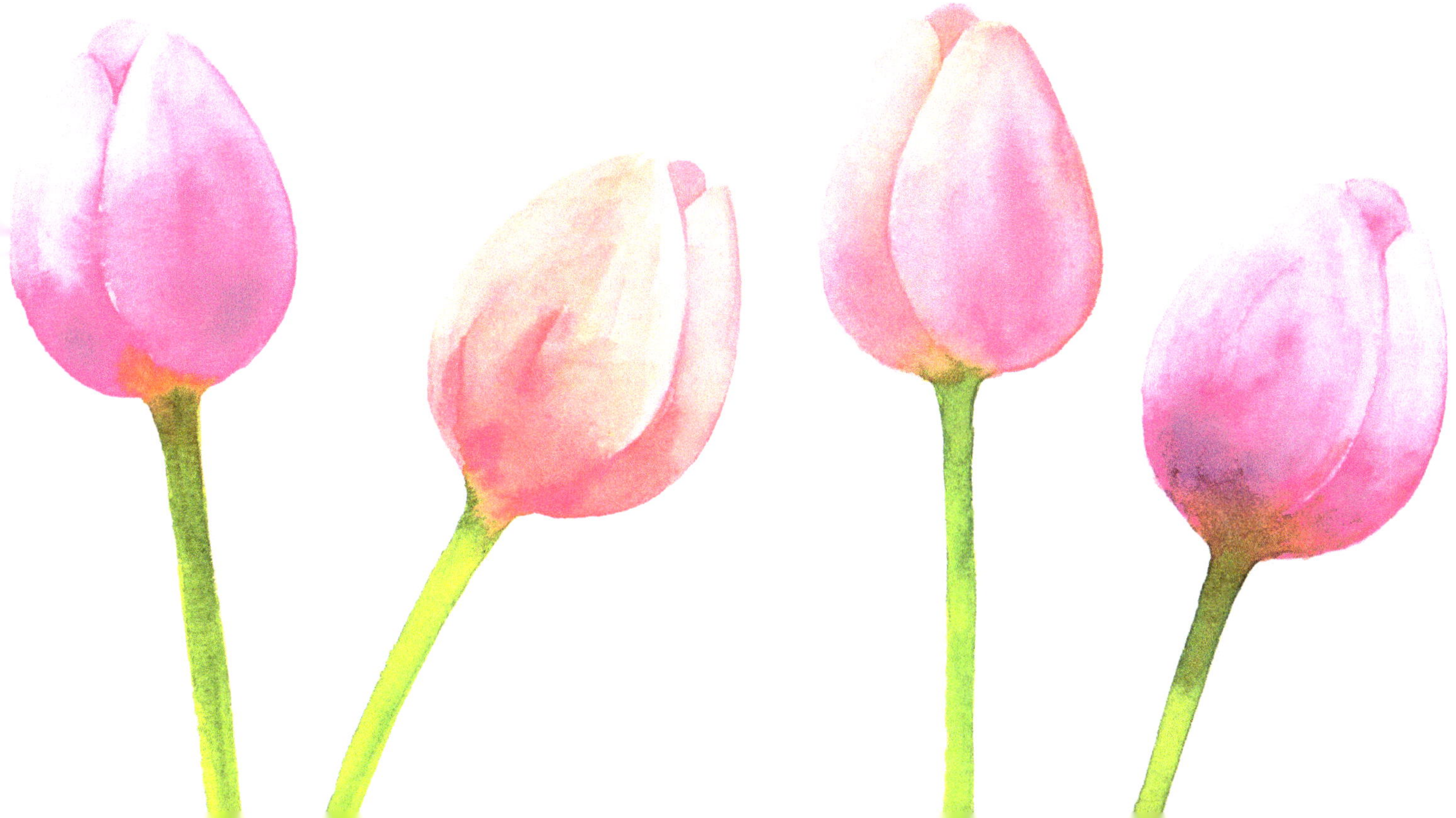

Contents

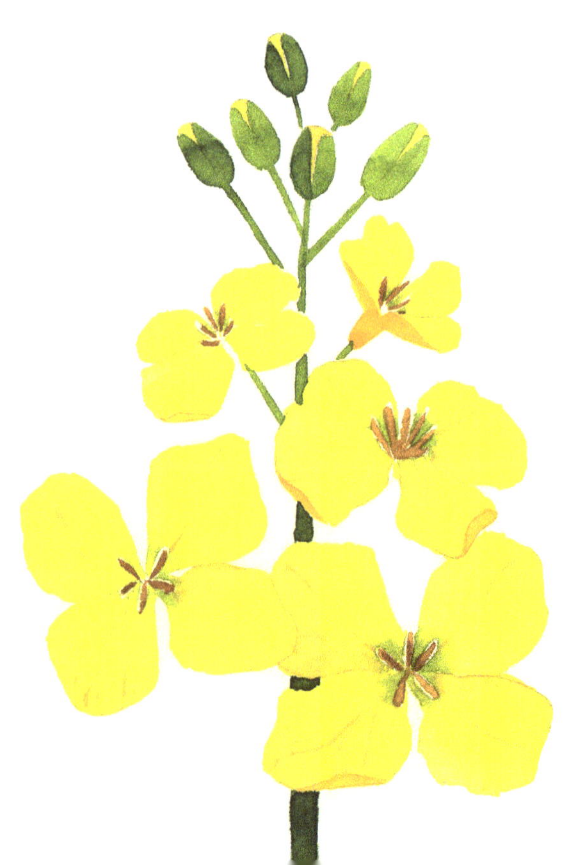

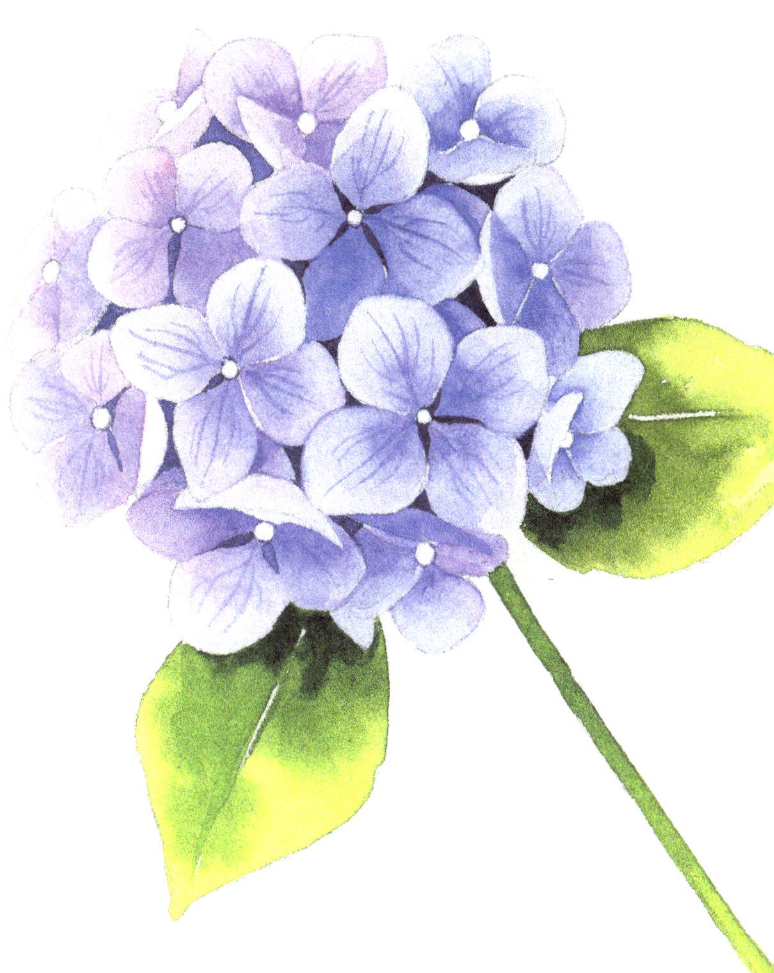

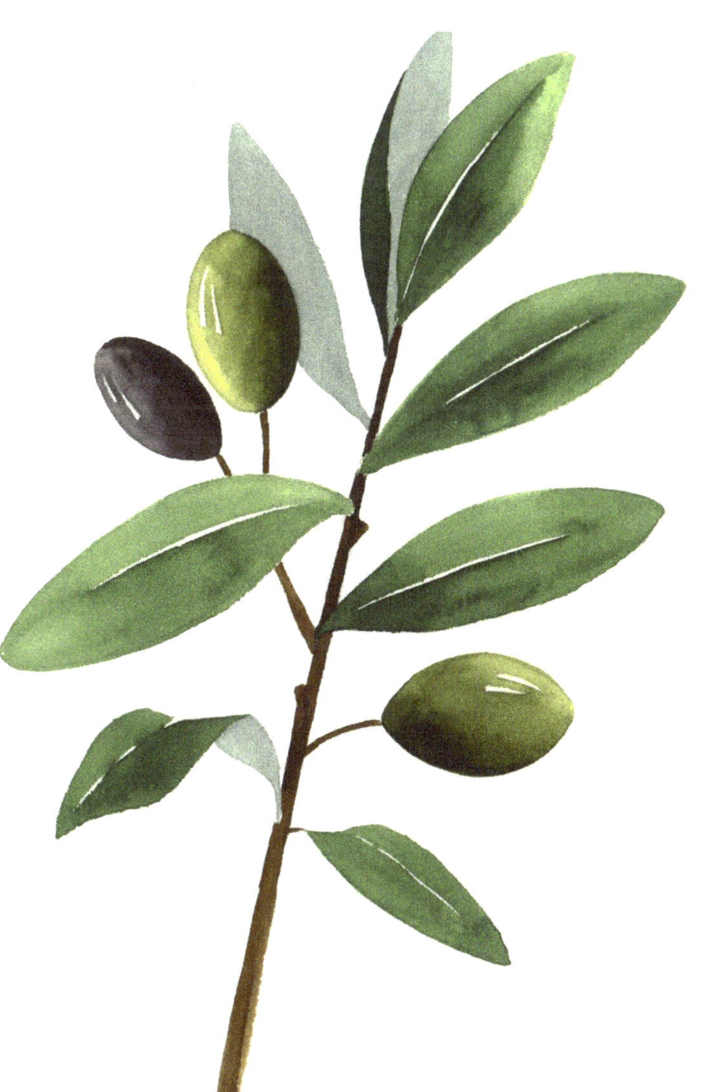

Introduction

In my work as an artist, I encounter many beginners interested in painting flowers in watercolor. I began to ponder what would be the easiest way to sketch and color flower drawings. I wanted to simplify the complex sketching process by developing simple methods for drawing and painting beautiful flowers, even for someone with basic coloring skills. This book guides you through creating your favorite flowers, from sketching to watercolor painting, illustrating the entire process in a simplified way.

These three tips are for beginners who are starting to learn how to draw.

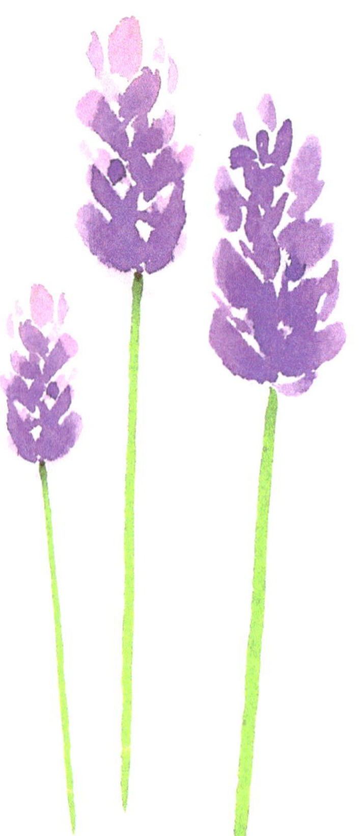

ENJOY THE PROCESS RATHER THAN THE RESULT

As you learn how to draw, you may, understandably, become too focused on creating a magnificent art piece. But no one starts out as a skilled artist. If you can enjoy the process of drawing rather than the result, you will build techniques, and naturally, your skills will improve. There are many ways to enjoy a drawing practice, such as searching for and purchasing materials and tools, observing flowers and plants that you want to draw, or taking a picture of a beautiful flower in the park or on the street. You can prepare a cup of tea or play your favorite song while setting the tools on the table, and you can practice the fundamentals of sketching or coloring, wash the brush and palette after spending the day painting, hang out with friends to draw outdoors, or give your painting as a present. All these experiences are part of the drawing process. So, relax and enjoy your time drawing.

START WITH EASY STEPS

Many types of flowers are around us, both simple and complex. I recommend beginners start drawing and painting simple flowers or large tropical leaves. Flowers with few petals and orderly arrangements that are distinguishable from afar are easier to draw. If you begin with a complex flower without an understanding of the flower's basic shapes, your time spent sketching will take much longer, causing you to feel discouraged. Beginning with simple flowers will help boost your confidence and skills.

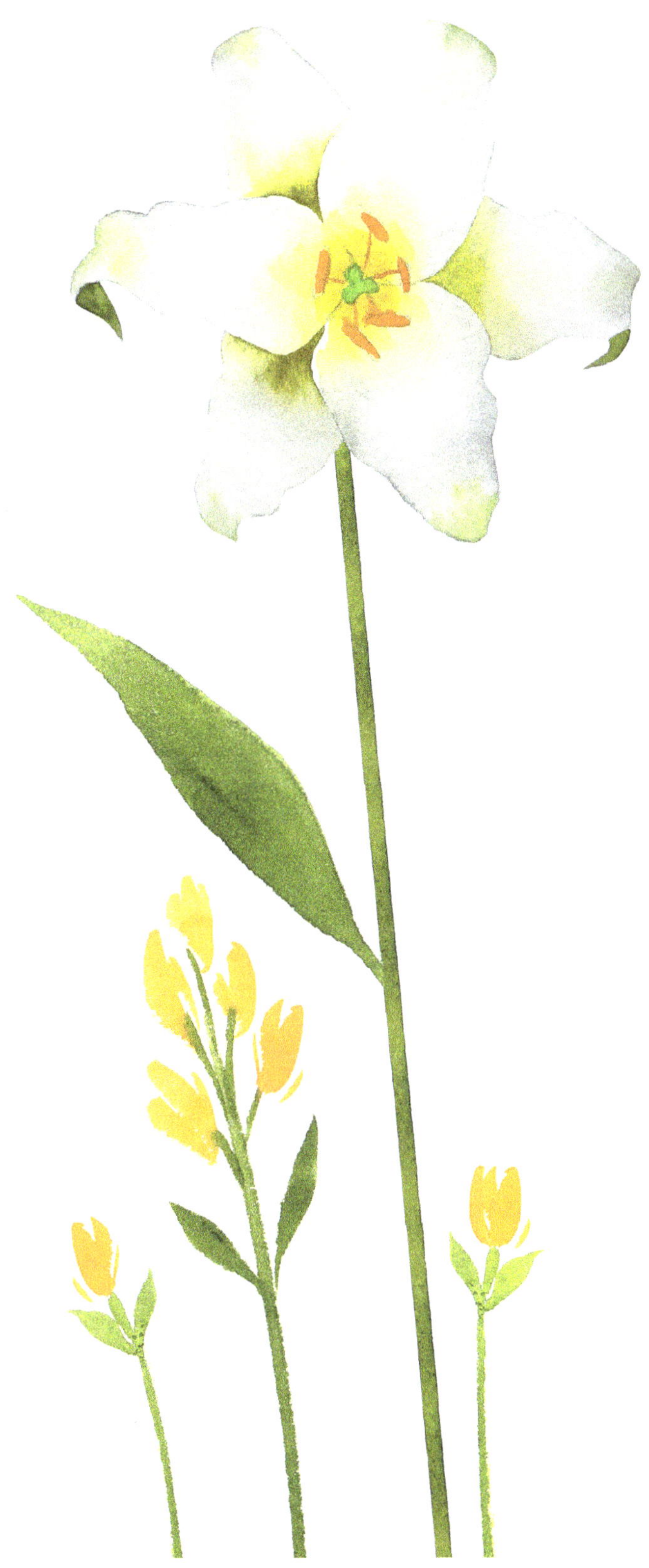

LEARN HOW TO SKETCH

Generally, people only learn to color with watercolors when they're studying watercolor painting. But I recommend you also learn how to sketch as much as possible. I receive a lot of messages from my Instagram followers, and a hefty portion are from those who are at an intermediate level. They say that even though using watercolor was easy because they practiced using a coloring book, they could not color anything else but the designs in the books. Thus, they ended up losing interest in painting. These intermediate-level artists say their interest in painting returned after following my three-step sketching method because they could choose any flowers to work on and create their own sketches. If you study watercolor after learning how to sketch, painting becomes more interesting, and it also helps improve your skills.

The process of drawing and painting gives you as much joy as the artwork itself. Learning and improving your skills one by one with the help of this book will hopefully give you a sense of self-satisfaction and joy. My wish is that this book will aid you in your drawing and painting journey and widen your path.

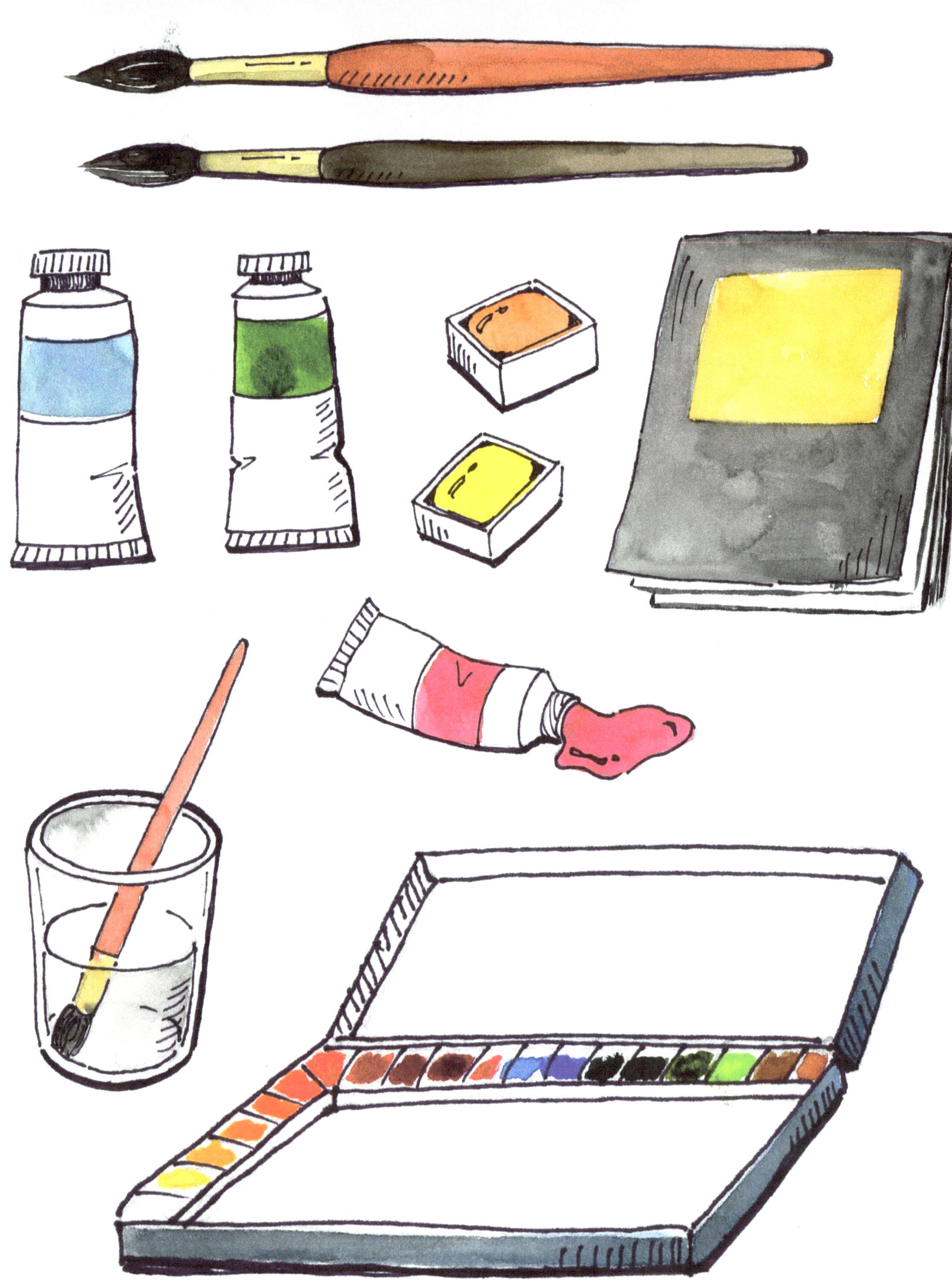

1

Materials

Purchasing materials for a new creative pursuit is definitely fun. The process isn't always easy, however, because so many types of materials are available. Testing all the materials first before purchasing them would be ideal, but that's not easy for beginners, especially if they're not familiar with the supplies and may have trouble judging quality. In this chapter, you'll learn about basic materials for drawing and painting, such as pencils, watercolor paints, and brushes, and how to work with them. You can also refer to the Resources (page 124) for more information on the materials I use.

THE BASICS

Art supply stores are filled with materials, but you only need a few to draw and paint flowers. Basic materials for watercolor painting include watercolors, a palette, paper, a brush, water, paper towels, scrap watercolor paper for testing, and a pencil and an eraser for sketching. Every flower painting in this book was painted using the materials in this photo, which are also my go-to supplies. Let's take a closer look at these basics, focusing on the tools in the photo.

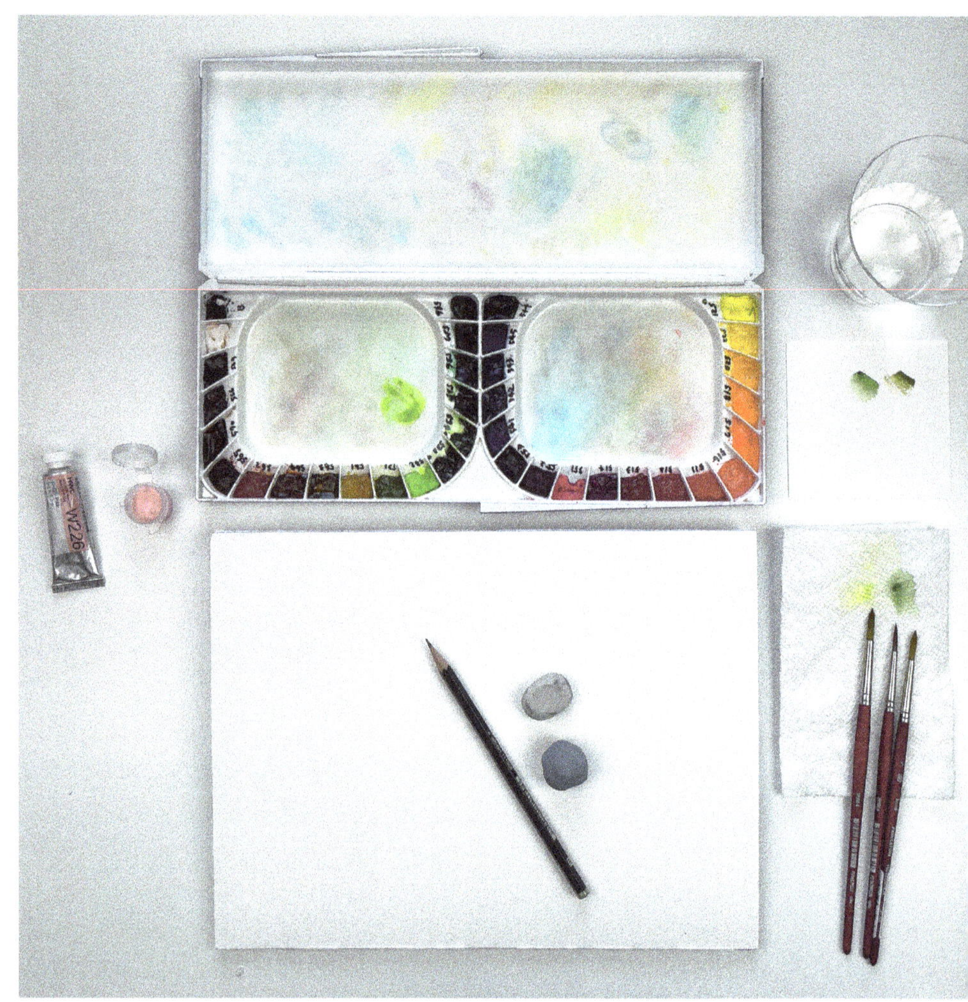

If you're left-handed, place the water, scrap watercolor paper, paper towel, and brushes on your left.

WATERCOLORS

I recommend using reasonably priced professional-grade watercolors for painting flowers, even for beginners. These paints use better-quality pigments compared to student-grade watercolors and offer strong, clear, and vivid colors with longer-lasting lightfastness and higher transparency. However, it doesn't mean all student-grade watercolors are bad. If you're not ready to make such an investment, purchase the best watercolor set you can afford and upgrade when you can.

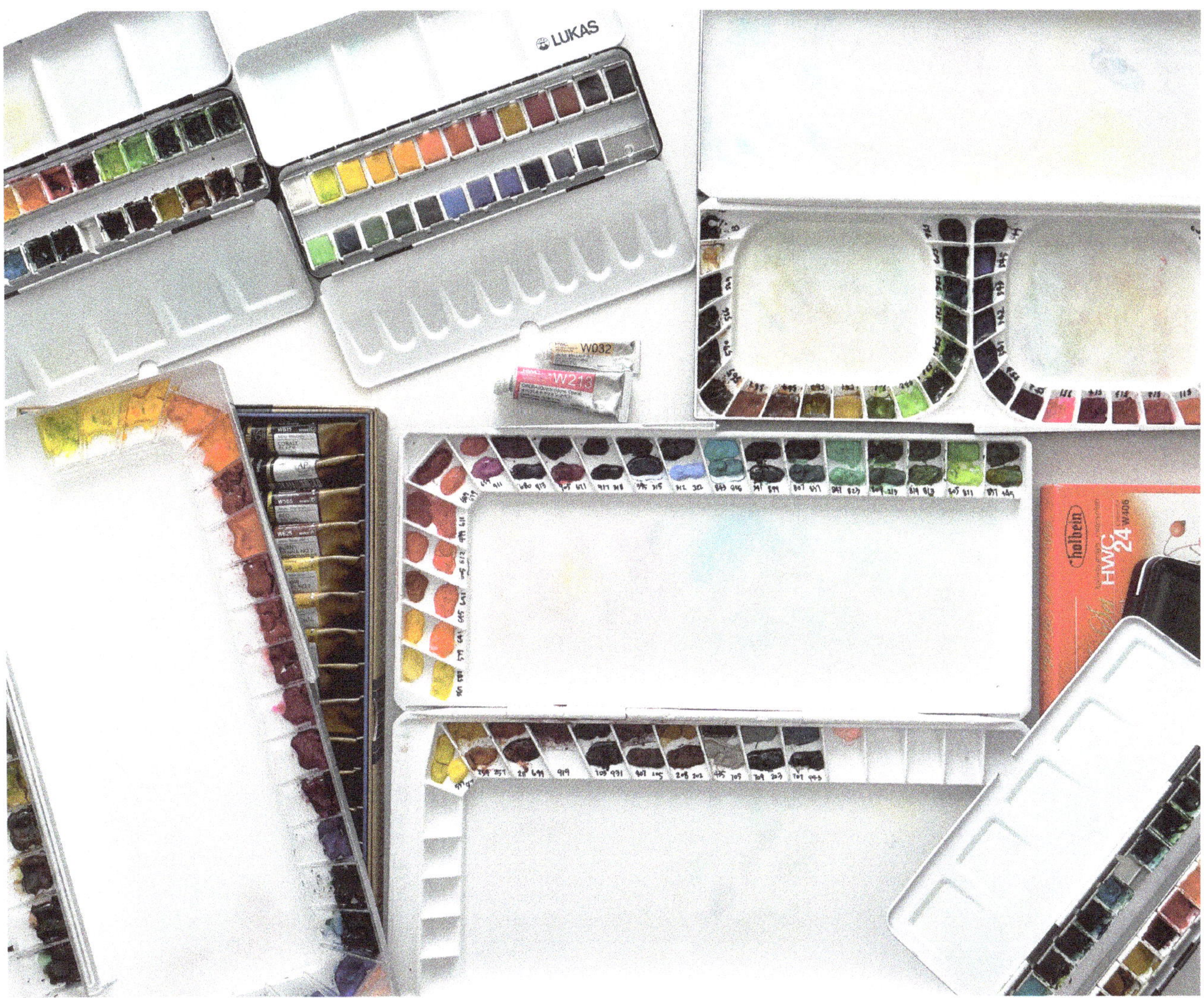

COLORS

Throughout the projects, exercises, and lessons, I use specific paint colors (written in uppercase; generic equivalents are provided where possible). But don't be held down by my choices. Feel free to use whatever colors you have or experiment with mixing colors together to find the shade I used.

Starting with a set that has a range of colors is a good idea. Beginners especially may not be confident yet with mixing colors, and blending colors using just a few shades can be difficult. On the other hand, having too many color choices can cause confusion. Watercolor sets typically include twelve to ninety colors, so a set of about thirty-six is a good place to start. For the lessons and projects in this book, I mainly used professional-grade Mijello Mission Gold 36-color tube watercolors.

Tube and Pan Watercolors

Two primary forms of watercolors are available on the market: pan and tube paints. The former comes as a hardened paint cake in a small, individual pan. This ready-to-use paint doesn't need to be squeezed from a tube, and you can easily change the setup and layout of your palette by moving pans around and exchanging colors. Tube watercolor paints are liquid and can be squeezed directly onto a palette. These offer vibrant colors, and you can blend shades without the contamination you can get by dipping the same brush into multiple pans.

Some artists like to squeeze tube paints into palette wells or individual pans and allow them to harden, making them more portable. Tube paints also allow you to create several different palettes with just one set of paints. For example, I used a set of paints to create two palettes: a large one I use at home, and a small one for traveling. The leftover colors in the tubes can be stored without being contaminated.

When you begin to paint, you may find you need colors that aren't in your paint set, or you may prefer colors from other manufacturers. In most cases, you should achieve good results and have no problem mixing paints from different manufacturers. For example, some paintings in this book used Holbein's Shell Pink. I often use this color by itself to create pink petals, eliminating the need to mix colors every time. Purchasing one or two frequently used pastel-toned paints separately is a good investment, especially for beginners, because they offer consistent colors and increased transparency. Pastel tones can be a little tricky for beginners to mix because blending certain colors and adding white can affect the paint's transparency.

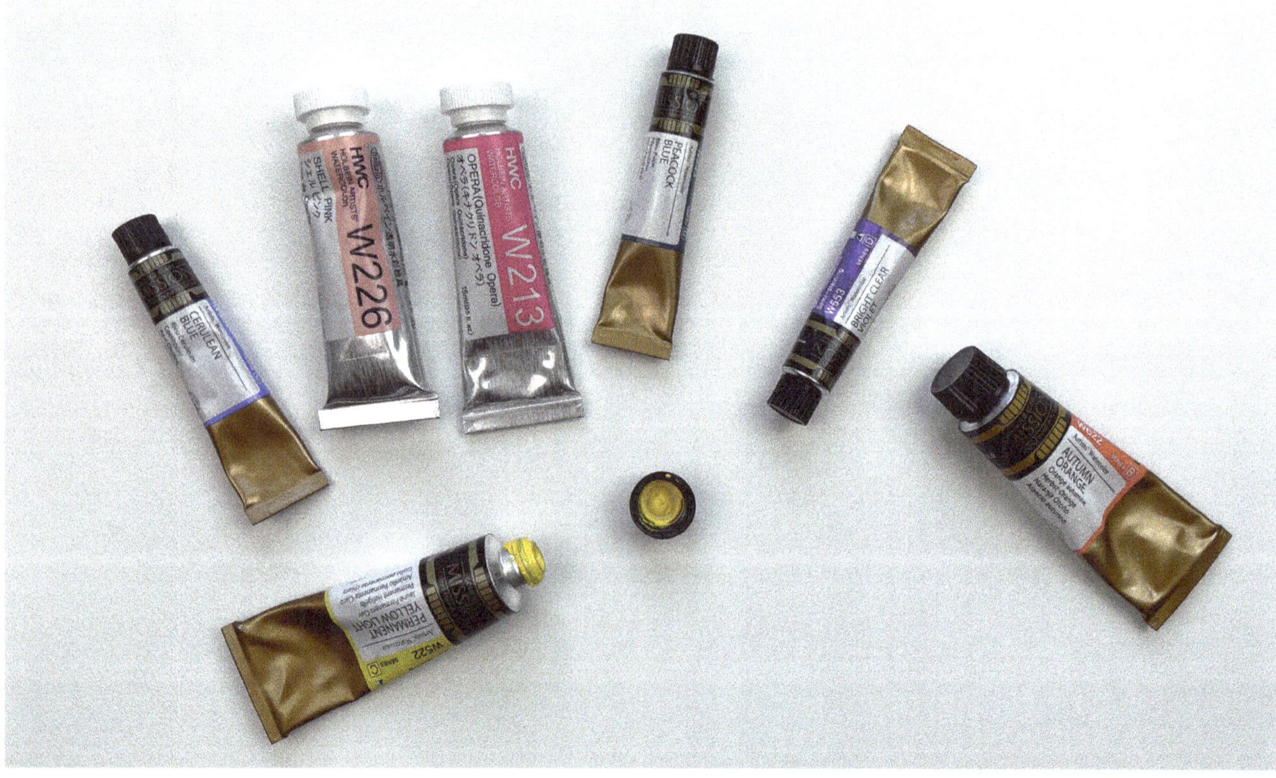

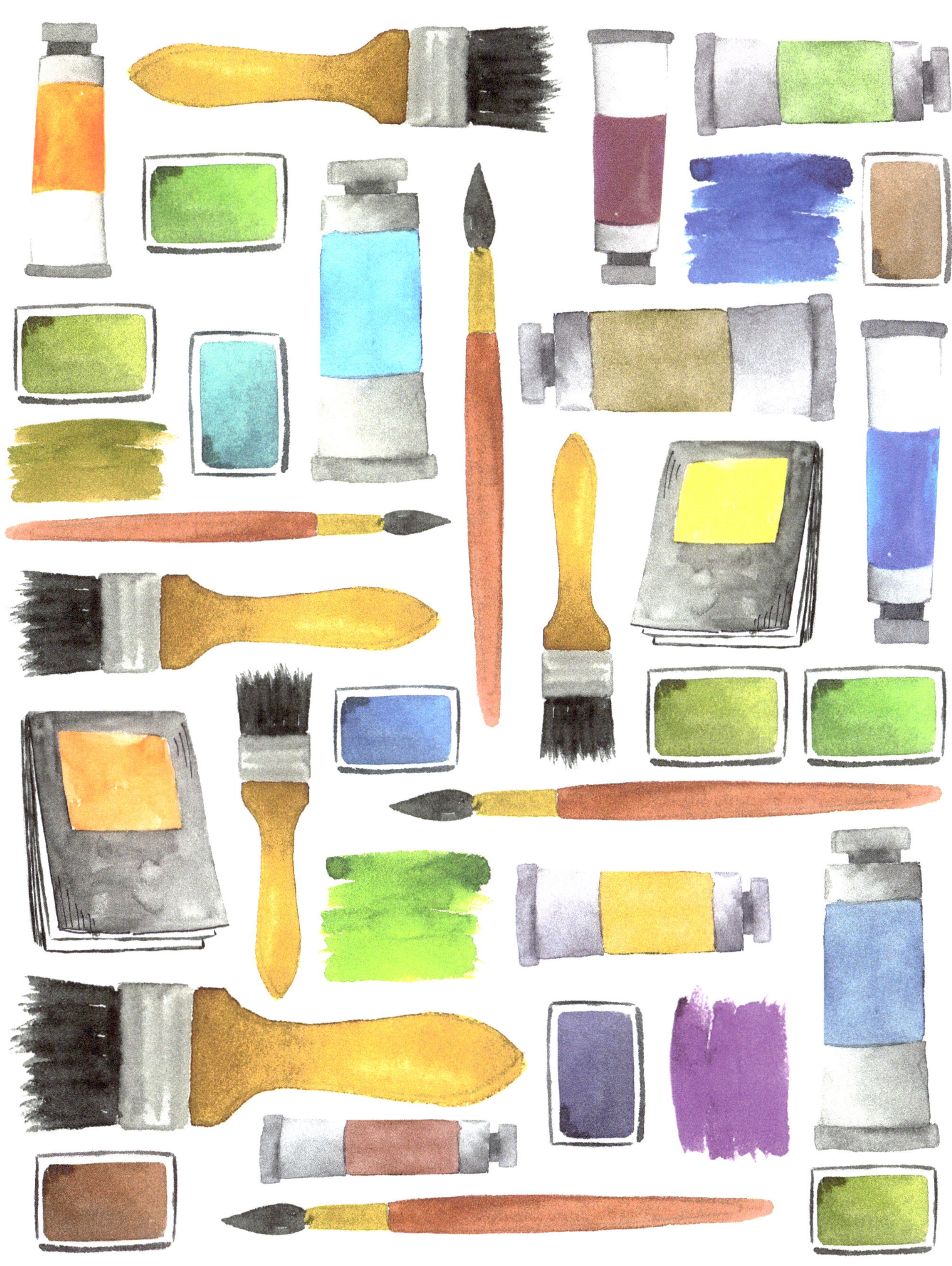

Adding Tube Watercolors to a Palette

To add tube watercolors to a palette, place the top of the tube in a well, as shown. Squeeze out the paint starting in the far end of the well and continue until it is filled. Leave the palette out to dry and, after a week or two, the watercolor will harden. Make sure it's completely dry. Otherwise, you'll use more watercolor than you need when painting.

If you purchase a set of watercolors, you can arrange the colors in the palette as shown on the package, or you can make your own arrangement. I keep the order as is.

To allow the watercolor paints to dry, open the lid of the palette and place it on a flat surface to avoid spilling the paint.

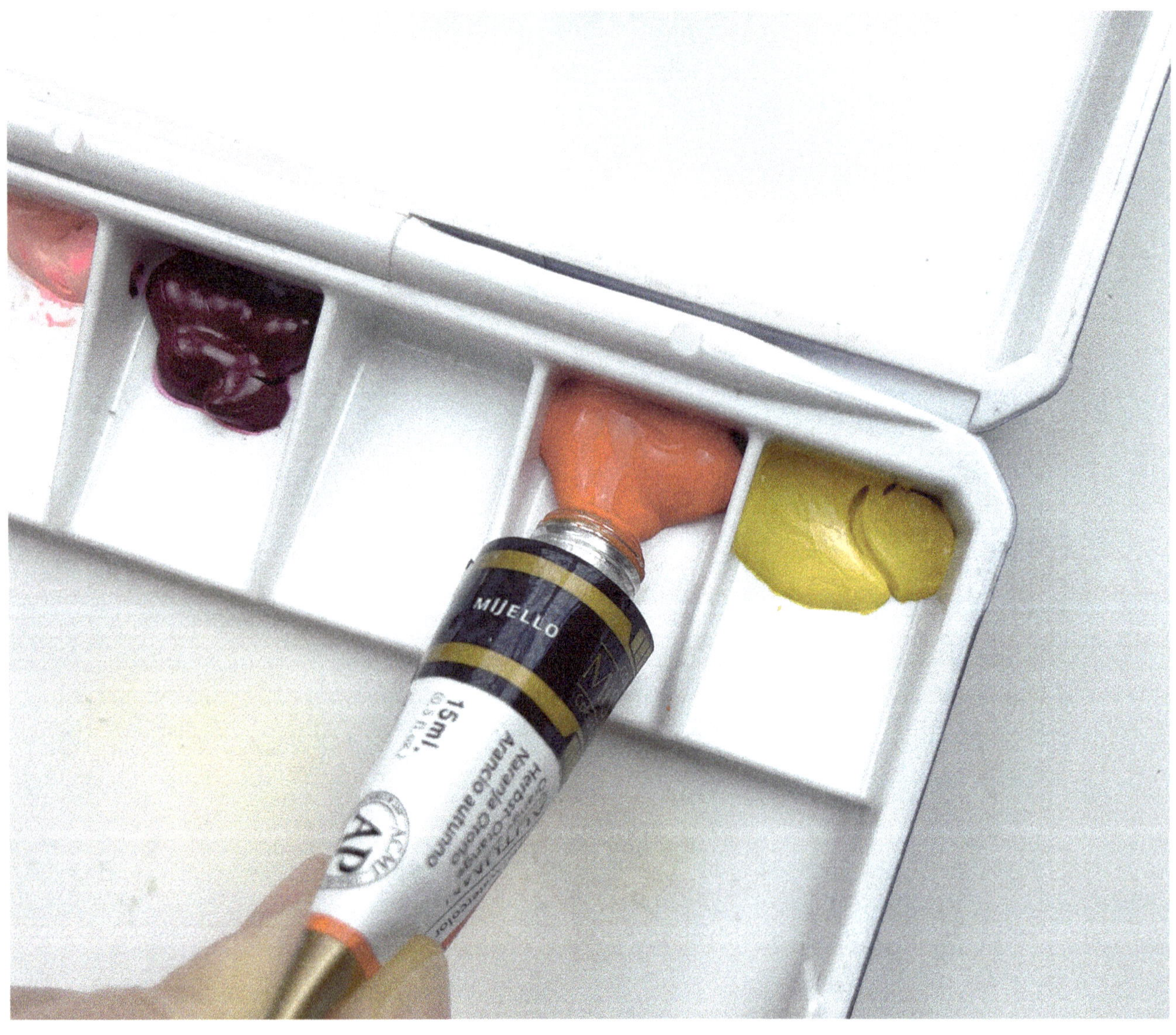

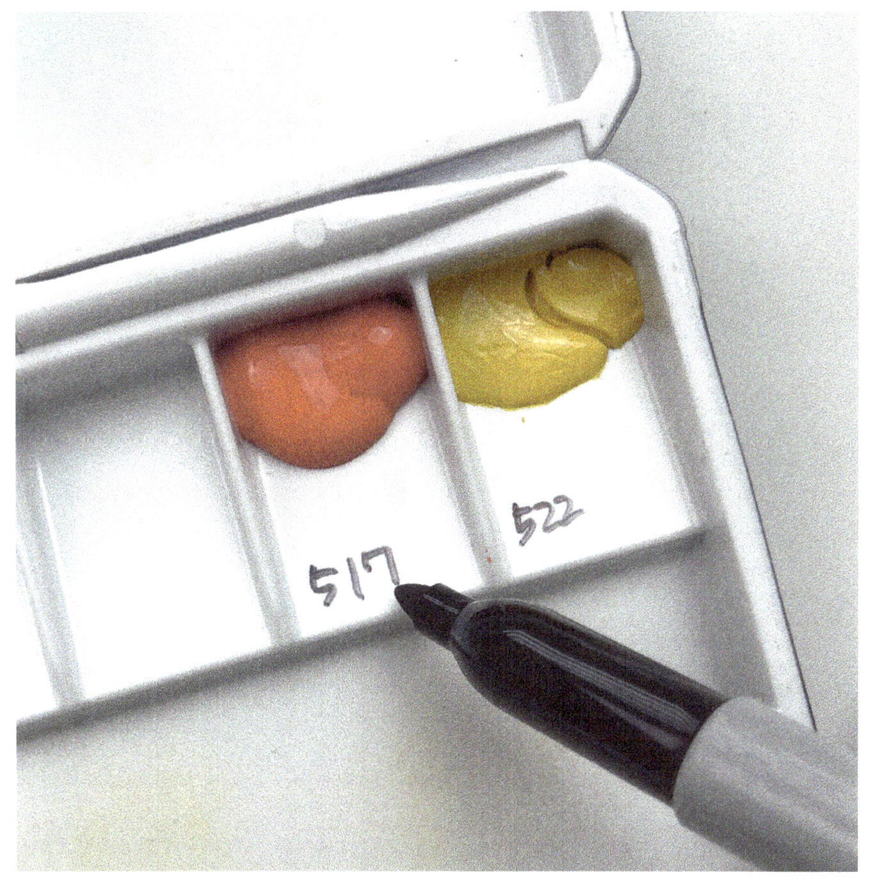

When writing numbers on the palette, be sure to use a permanent marker.

Watercolor paints have names as well as numbers because it's sometimes difficult to identify a color by eye when it's in the package. By marking the paint's number on the palette well and on a color swatch, you can easily refill or find the color you need—just use the color chip.

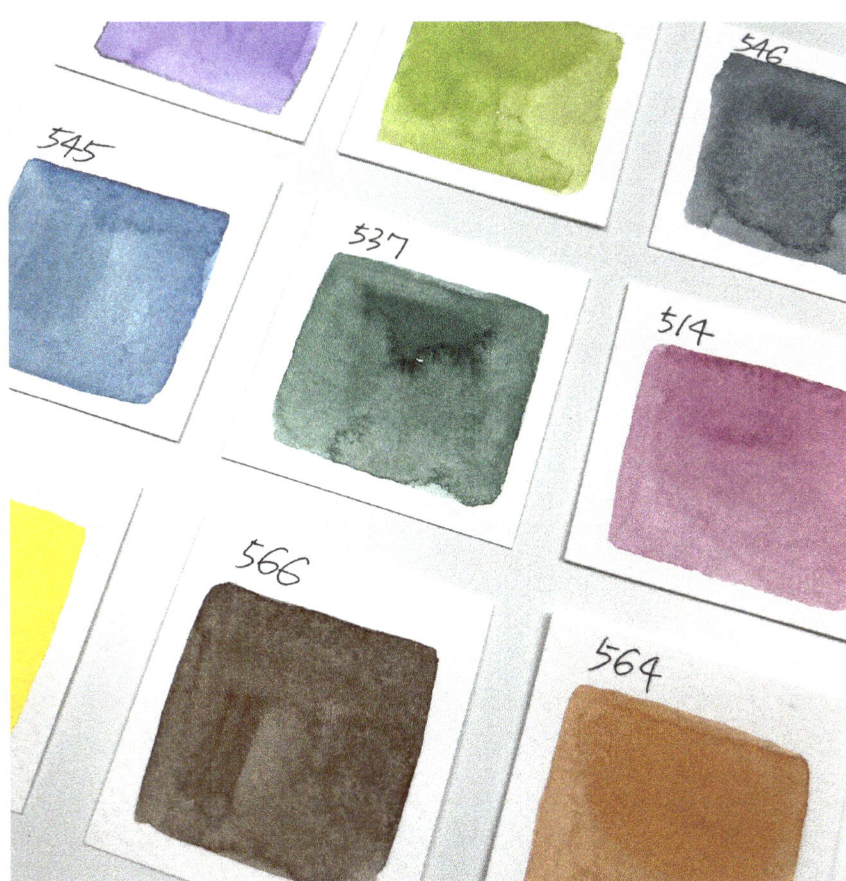

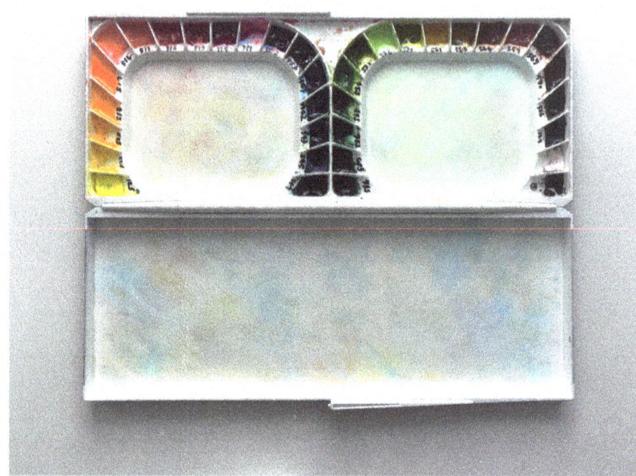

PALETTES

Paint palettes are typically made from steel, plastic, or ceramic. The size of the palette varies depending on the number of wells that hold paint. The palette in the picture is made of plastic and has 36 wells. Sometimes, palettes are included when you buy watercolors such as the Mijello Mission Gold 36-color set; the palette pictured was included with the paints.

BRUSHES

When choosing a paintbrush, remember that the smaller the number, the smaller the bristles, and the larger the number, the larger the bristles. For the techniques and lessons in the book, I used Princeton Velvetouch Series 3950 round brushes in sizes 4, 5, and 6. (For some of the paintbrush techniques, larger round brushes will be used.) These are synthetic brushes that have pointed tips, which is characteristic of round brushes. They allow you to paint thick and thin lines, create details, and produce a variety of brushstrokes.

A QUICK GUIDE TO BRUSHES

Watercolor brushes are made of synthetic or natural hair. One of the differences between the two is the ability to hold water. Here is a quick guide:

* **SYNTHETIC**: These brushes return to their original shape when wet. The tip of the brush is pointed, which is good for making various lines and details. However, it doesn't hold as much water as natural hair brushes.
* **SYNTHETIC/NATURAL BLEND**: These also return to their original shape when wet. The tip is pointed, good for making lines and details. Their ability to hold water is also good.
* **NATURAL**: These brushes are durable and soft and have an excellent ability to hold water. Kolinsky sable brushes are a good natural-hair choice for beginners.

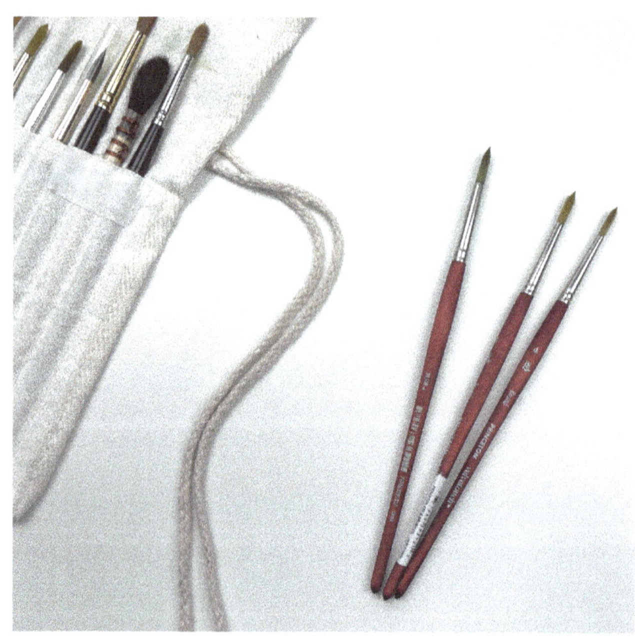

These brushes are reasonably priced and the bristles have good elasticity, meaning they return to their original form when wet, making them suitable for beginners. I don't recommend using brushes that shed or lose bristles. When choosing brushes, purchase the best quality you can afford; better-quality brushes offer better results, and you'll feel less frustrated, especially when starting out. The Resources section on page 124 has more information on brushes, and you can also ask for help from knowledgeable salespeople at an art supply store.

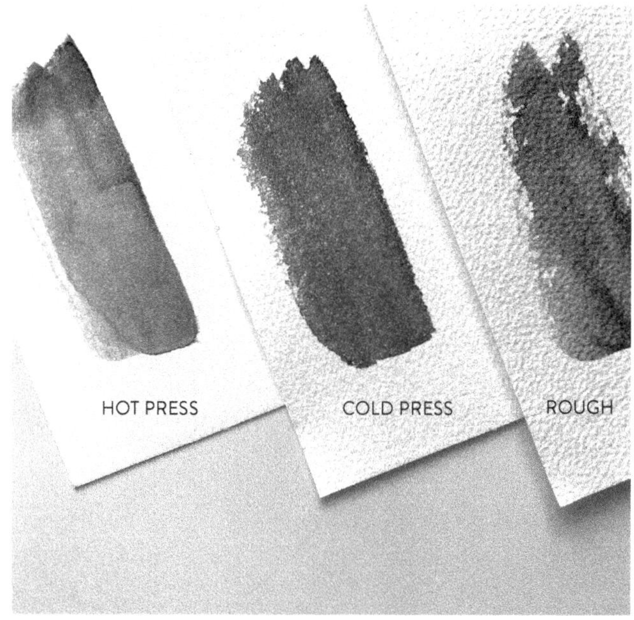

WATERCOLOR PAPER

Watercolor paper comes in three types, each with a different texture: hot press, cold press, and rough.

* **HOT PRESS:** The smooth surface of this paper is suited for detailed work. However, water isn't absorbed into the paper as evenly as with cold press or rough paper, so it can be difficult to control water and paint.

* **COLD PRESS:** This paper has some texture to it but is not as coarse as rough paper. Water and watercolor paints spread evenly, allowing you to incorporate a number of techniques in your work. It's a great paper for beginners and is the most versatile and popular among artists.

* **ROUGH:** As its name implies, this has the roughest texture among the three, and you can easily see and feel the texture. This paper is suitable for large paintings but not recommended for detailed work.

Paper pad covers include all the information about the paper, such as the weight, texture, and contents. For the techniques and projects in this book, I used Fabriano Artistico Extra White 100% Cotton Cold Pressed 300g paper, which is made specifically for watercolor. The name may be long and complex, but it's favored by watercolor artists and should be easy to find. The higher the cotton content in paper, the more evenly the water is absorbed, which allows paint to spread smoothly without creating stains.

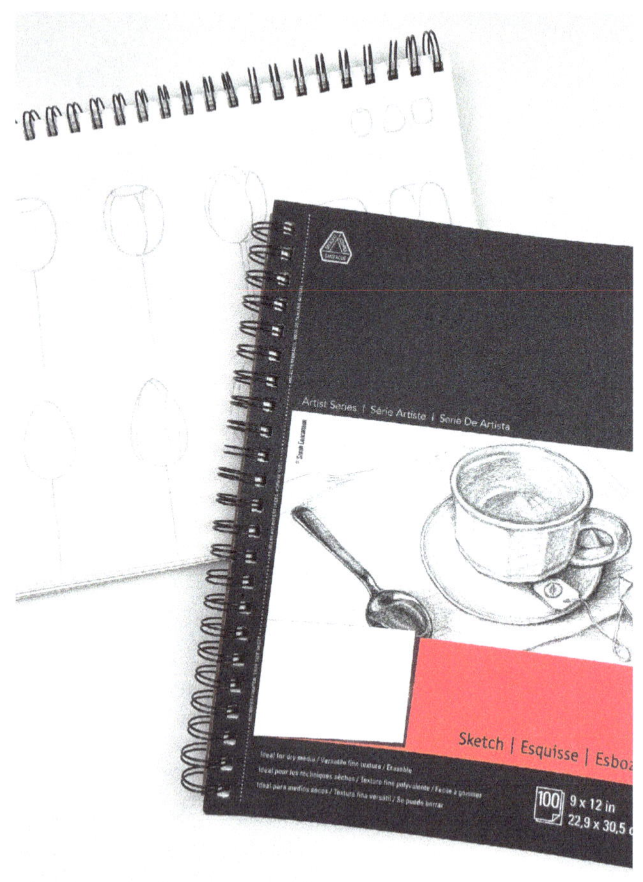

THE BEST PAPER FOR THE JOB

When you first learn how to paint, choosing the right paper to work with can be as tricky as choosing watercolors. Most experts say artists should use high-quality watercolor paper. However, if you're a beginner, you can use inexpensive acid-free watercolor paper to practice before upgrading to better-quality paper. Moderately priced papers that I've used for practice include Bockingford (made by St. Cuthberts Mill), Studio Watercolor (made by Fabriano), and Montval (made by Canson). By trying different types of paper, you'll soon discover the best paper that suits your style.

SKETCHING PAPER

For sketching in pencil, paper size and texture aren't that critical, so use whatever paper you prefer. I use a 9" × 12" (23 × 31 cm) Canson Universal Sketch pad with a spiral binding.

OTHER MATERIALS

PENCILS

Pencils are used for sketching and drawing, but they're the easiest supplies to find. Different types of pencils can be used to achieve different effects, but for the sketches in this book I used an HB pencil, which can be found at any art or craft supply store and online. The "H" stands for hard and the "B" stands for black. H pencils are harder and make lighter lines, and B pencils are softer and make darker lines Both are graded by number, from 2H (darkest) to 9H (lightest) and from 2B (lightest) to 9B (darkest). HB is considered a medium-hard pencil and works well for sketching outlines before coloring.

ERASER

Putty or kneaded erasers may be unfamiliar to some, but they're recommended for drawing since these erasers don't produce eraser shreds or crumbs. To remove a mark, simply press the eraser onto the paper and lift. These erasers also absorb charcoal pencil marks by lightly pressing and lifting.

Soft erasers (used for art) can lighten pencil lines by pressing them onto marks, or by tapping them lightly on the paper. Either type of eraser can be used for drawing.

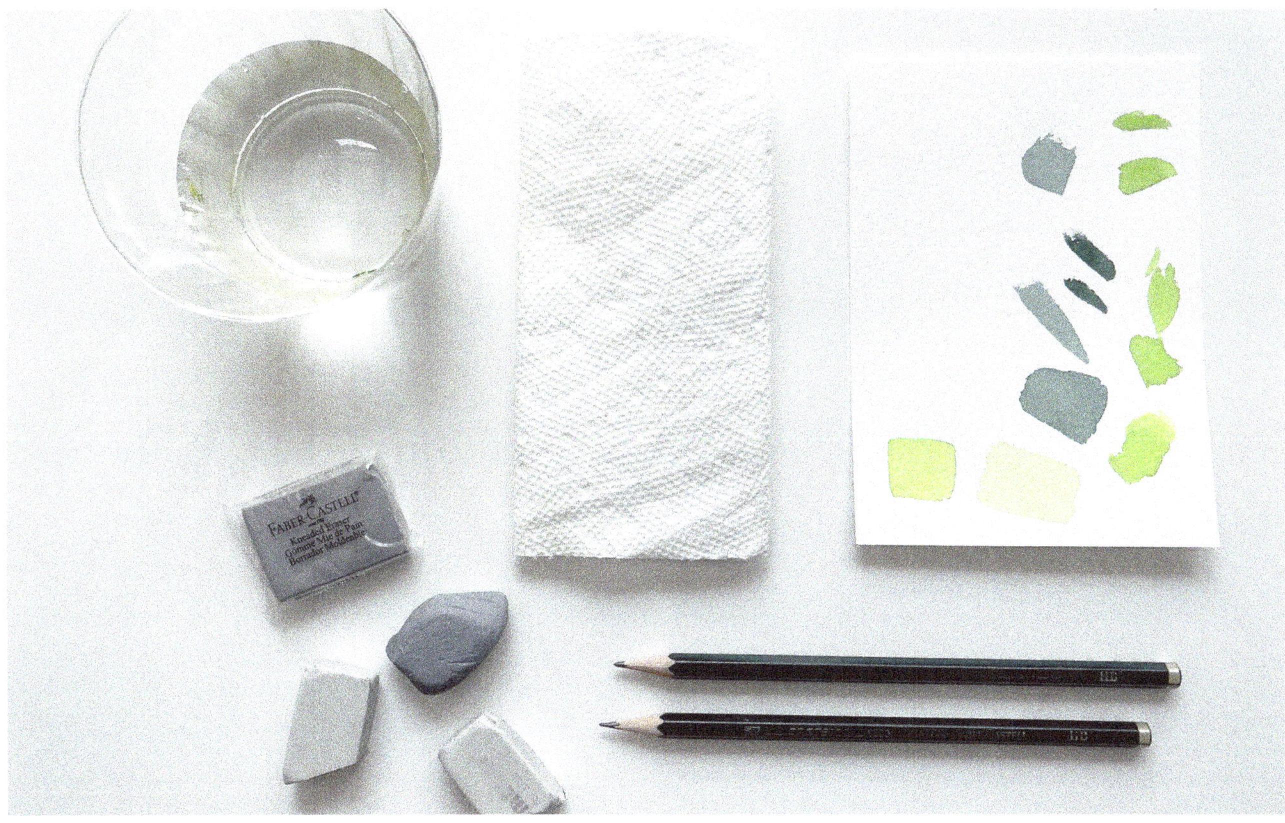

WATER JAR

I recommend a moderately sized water jar. Make sure it's not too deep or wide for your brushes. Never leave your brushes in a water jar for extended periods of time because this can damage both the bristles and the handle.

PAPER TOWELS

Have paper towels or a small cloth towel or rag on hand for wiping water off your brushes after washing. This helps control the amount of water the brush holds.

WATERCOLOR PAPER SCRAPS

Use scraps of watercolor paper to test paint shades, the water-to-paint ratio, and the amount of water in the brush before painting.

MASKING FLUID

Masking fluid creates a barrier on the paper so no paint or water can be absorbed. You can use masking fluid to create white flower petals. When the masking fluid is removed, the petals will remain white, or whatever color the background is. You can also use masking fluid to create small details such as flower stamens or to make large patterns.

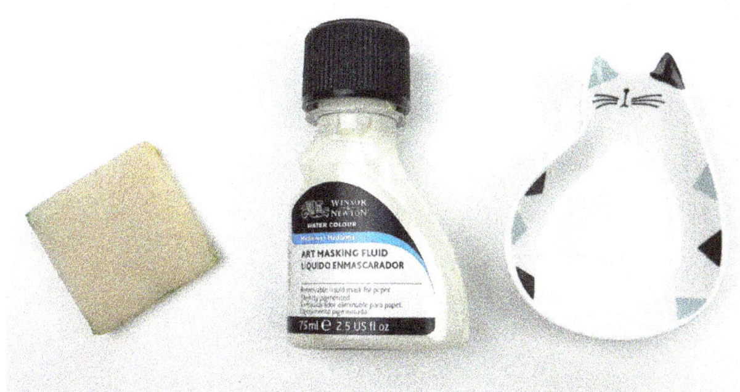

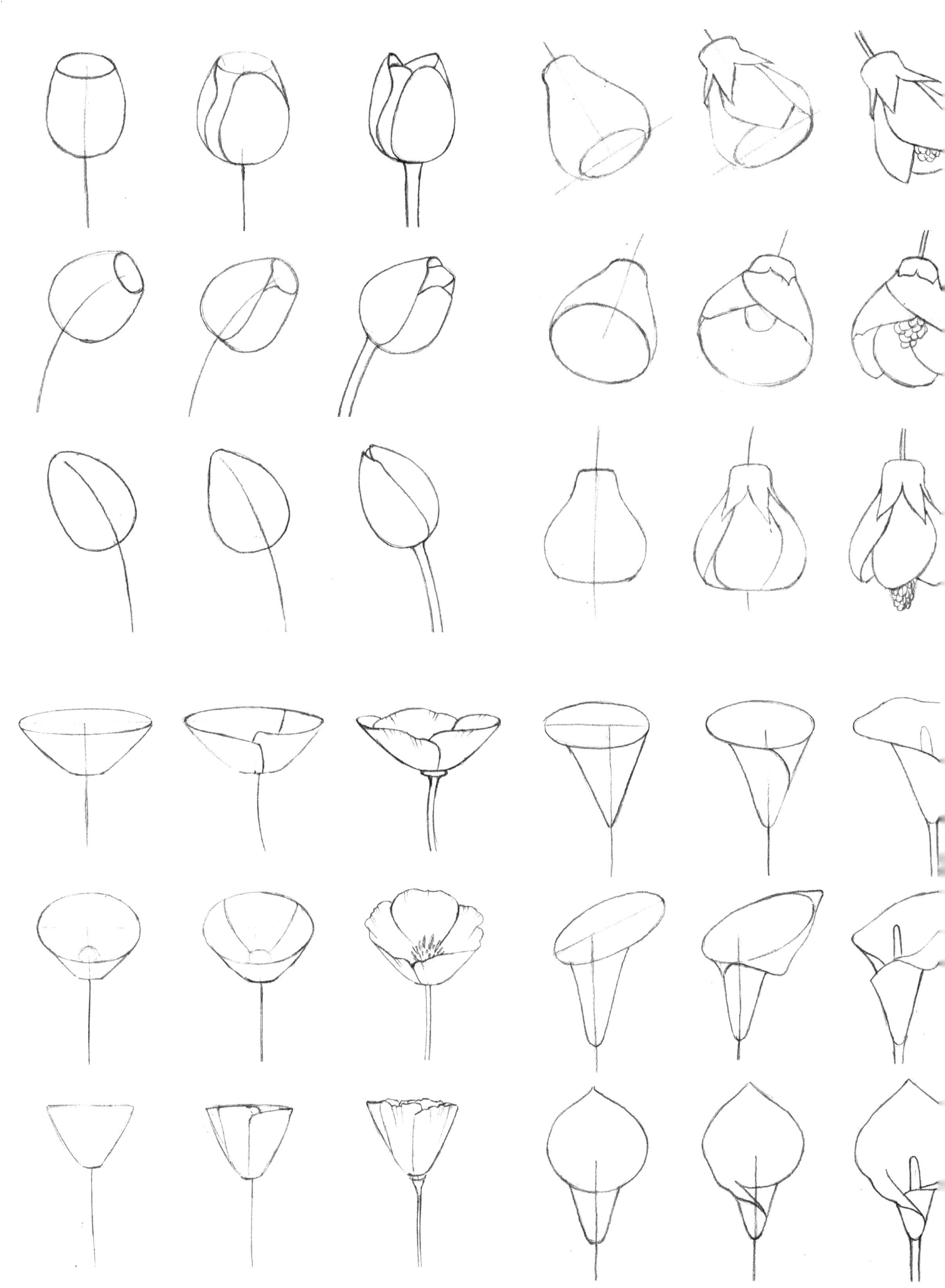

2

How to Sketch Flowers in Three Simple Steps

The first challenge when drawing flowers is copying their exact appearance onto paper. Sketching renders the appearance and characteristics of a subject, and creating an underdrawing is the first step in painting. If you follow the steps and draw with me, no matter how simple or complex the flower, you'll easily overcome the challenges of sketching them. I believe this process can help all beginners gain confidence and courage. You'll say, "I can do it too!"

SKETCHING BASICS

To sketch flower shapes well, we need to analyze the fundamental shapes and polish up our drawing skills. But mastering such skills can require a lot of time and effort. Sometimes beginners find it difficult to become adept at drawing, and they give up. To help overcome that barrier, I split the drawing process into three simplified steps. In the Three-Step Sketch, you'll analyze basic flower shapes, draw those shapes on paper, and then depict the flowers realistically by adding details. While sketching techniques can vary according to purpose and technique, for the lessons in this book you'll create outline sketches that form the underdrawings for paintings.

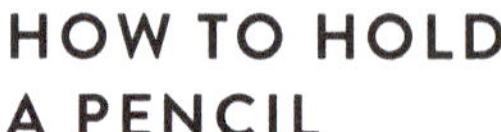

HOW TO HOLD A PENCIL

You can draw a variety of lines by holding the pencil in different ways. Holding the pencil as if you're writing allows you to create short lines and detailed work.

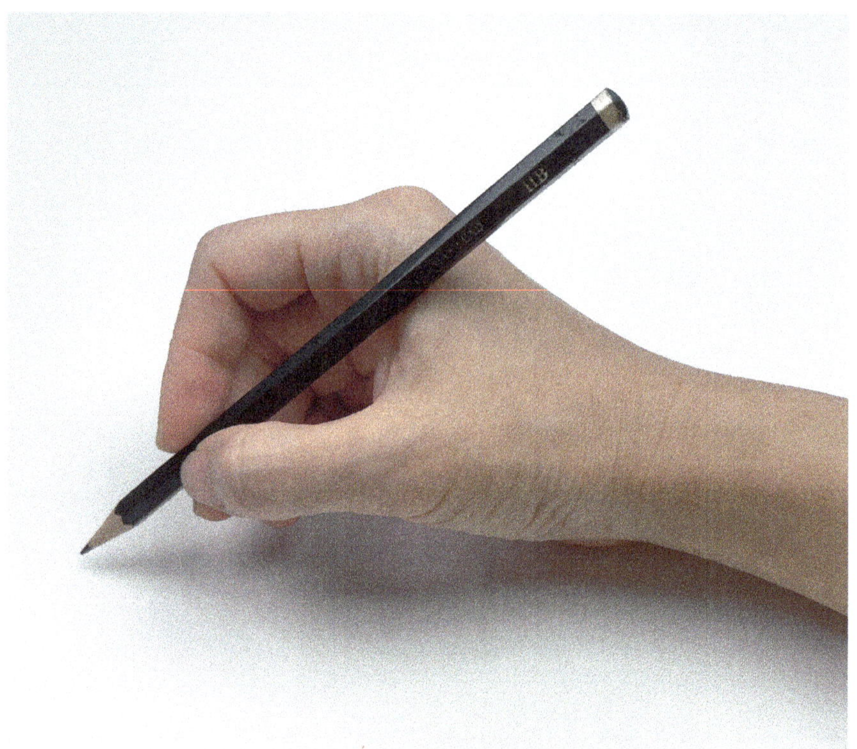

Holding the pencil close to the point is great for creating short lines and detailed marks.

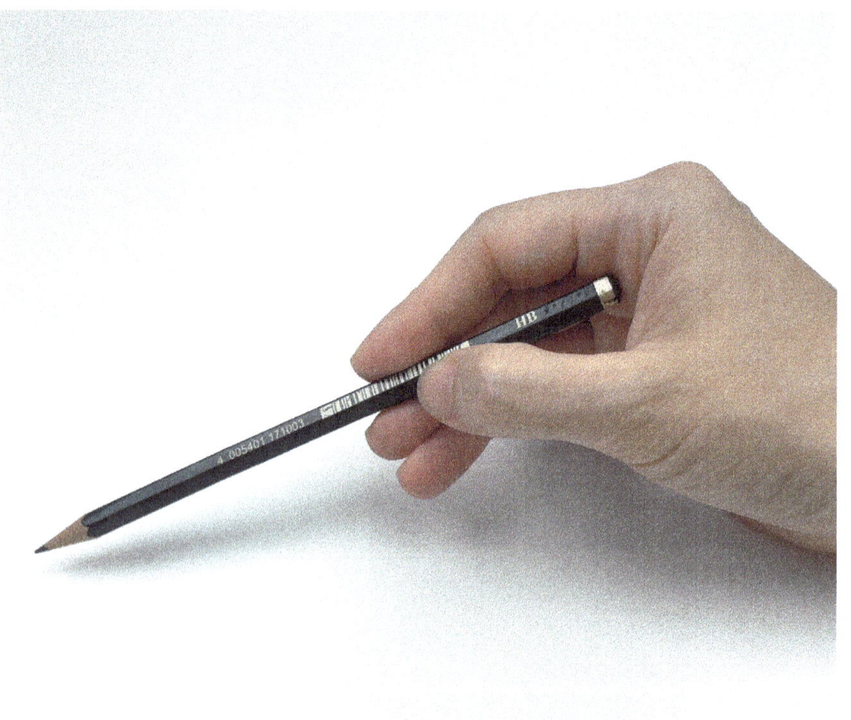

Holding the pencil at the end is ideal for drawing long lines and circles.

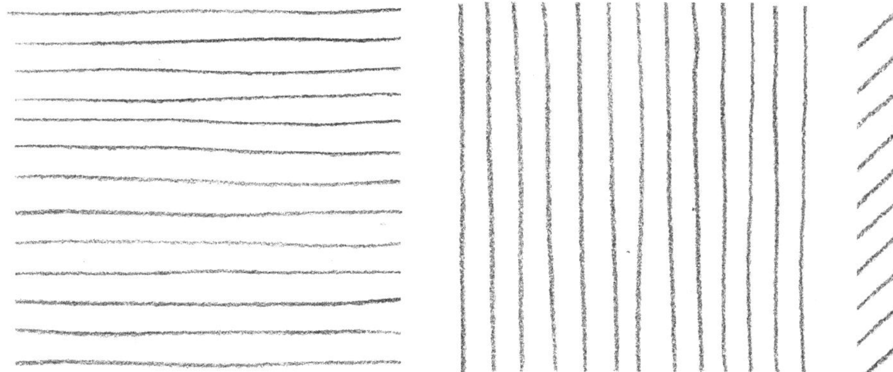

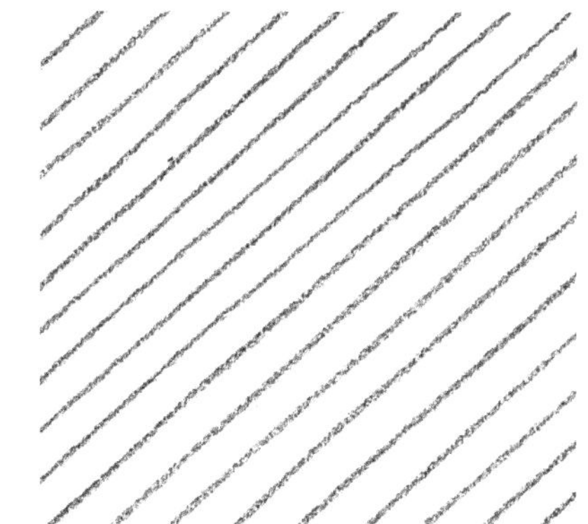

Straight lines are the most fundamental in line-drawing exercises. Draw a series of straight lines horizontally, vertically, and diagonally. Avoid slanting and curving the lines, striving to create clean, straight lines.

DRAWING LINES

When learning how to swim, warm-ups are essential before diving into the pool. Drawing also has a warm-up: drawing lines. If your hand and arm don't move smoothly, drawing lines can be challenging. The following line-drawing exercises are designed to help relax your fingers, wrist, and arm muscles.

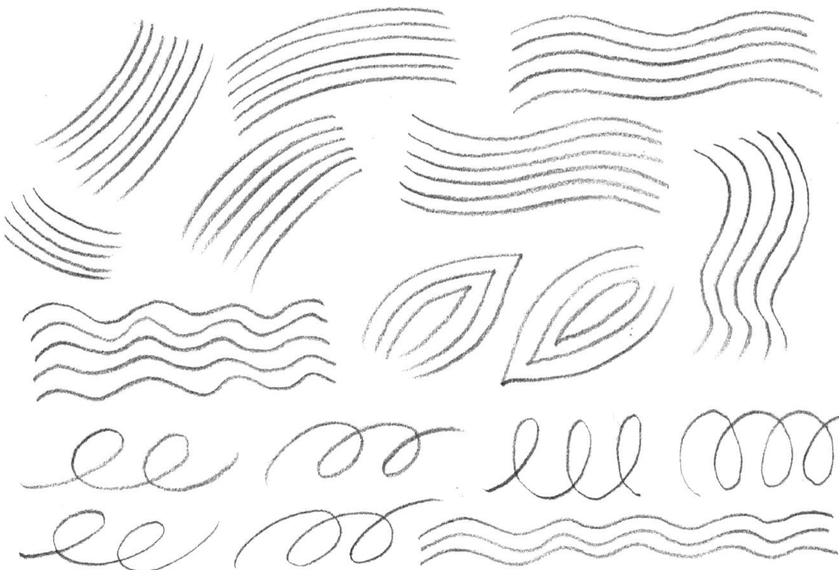

Curved lines are often used in sketching flowers. Practice drawing a series of short and long curved lines, irregular curves, wavy lines, loops, and leaf shapes.

DRAWING SHAPES

Drawing circles may seem easy, but making them precise can be tricky, even for experienced artists. Most of the flower sketches start with creating circles. Following these guidelines will make the process easy for drawing flowers. Practice drawing circles and ovals with the guidelines as shown, trying to make them even and balanced.

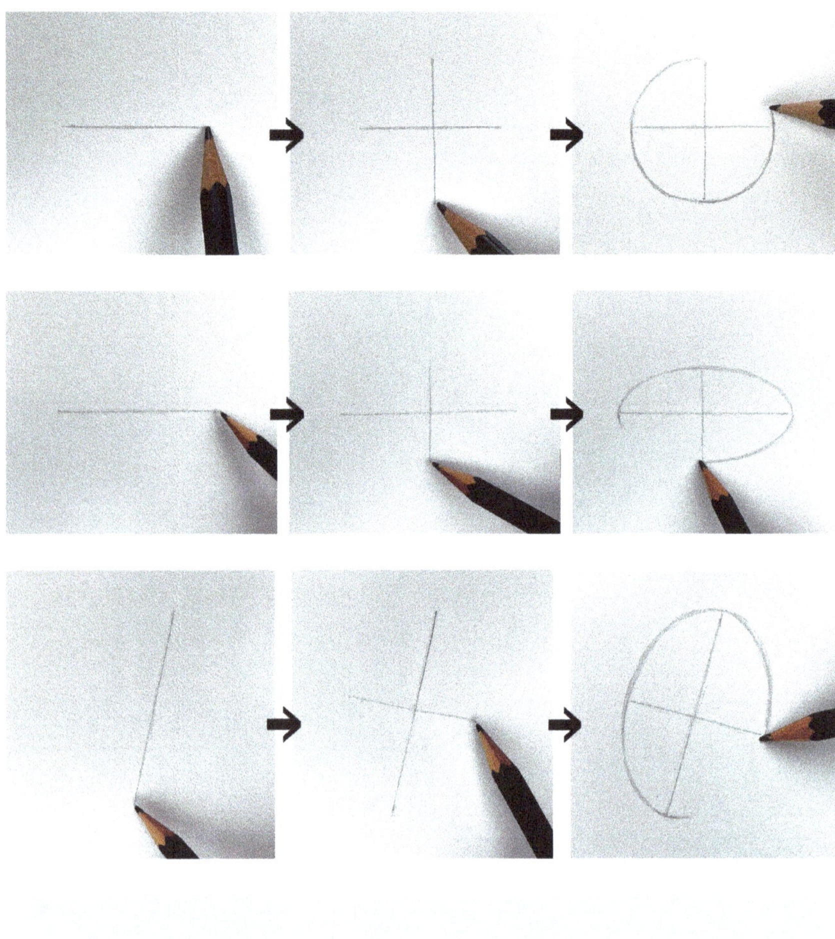

The larger the circle, the more challenging it is to draw, so make several lines. You can erase unnecessary pencil lines in the last step of the sketch, so don't worry about drawing neat lines.

Drawing a circle

1. Create a horizontal line.
2. Cross a vertical line of similar length in the middle of the horizontal line.
3. Connect each vertex with a curved line to draw a circle.

Drawing an oval

1. Create a horizontal line.
2. Cross a vertical line in the middle of the horizontal line. Make sure one of these lines is longer than the other.
3. Connect each vertex with a curved line to draw an oval.

Drawing a slanted ellipse

1. Draw a slanted vertical line.
2. Cross a slanted horizontal line in the middle of the vertical line.
3. Connect each vertex to draw a slanted ellipse.

THE THREE-STEP SKETCH

The three-step sketch refers to the following sequence I developed to help people draw and portray flowers realistically. This is a good starting point for learning how to draw a variety of flowers.

1 Find and quickly draw the basic shapes that make up the flower's form.

2 Subdivide the shape proportionally to determine the placement of the petals.

3 Draw the petals in detail, then draw the other parts of the flower, such as the flower cup, stem, and stamen.

Looking at the example of the sketched roses in three steps will help you understand the process.

THE EFFECTIVENESS OF A THREE-STEP SKETCH

Many beginners sketch each petal in detail when drawing the whole shape of a flower. Sometimes artists focus on partial flower forms when beginning a drawing, only to create a distorted flower shape due to the lack of proportion.

The three-step process first depicts the basic shape of the flower as a whole and then gradually defines it in partial form, minimizing the problems previously mentioned and reducing the time it takes to complete the sketch. This process may seem quite simple, but its purpose is fundamental to the shape sketches and helps solve basic flower-sketching problems.

Starting with this chapter, you'll learn more about sketching in three steps with examples. Try this simple exercise to better understand the three-step process.

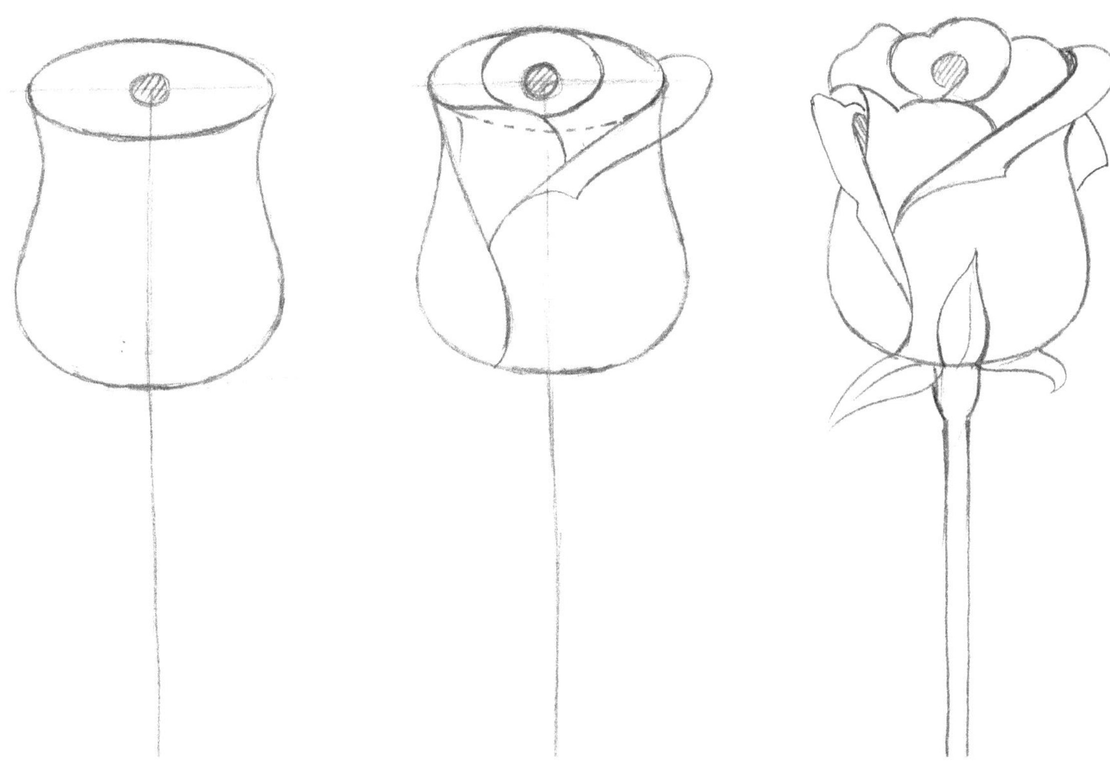

EXERCISE: DRAW A DAFFODIL

Drawing a daffodil is a good place to start because its shape is symmetrical and a combination of an oval and a cone. In this exercise, you'll draw a slightly tilted daffodil from the side. Draw the basic form by observing the shape of the flower first. Many people look at details such as the appearance or the number of petals, the color, wrinkles in the petals, and the features of the stamens. But in this case, observation means noticing and identifying the overall shape of the flower and in which direction the flower is facing.

Draw an imaginary line through the center of the flower and you'll see that it's angling downward a bit. Notice that there are two types of petals with different shapes and locations. Observe the petals on the outside and you'll see the circular formation of six petals stretching out in all directions. If you simplify the overall shape of the outer petals, you could draw them with a round plate. The inner portion of the flower has a cylindrical shape. Both the plate and the cylinder look oval from this perspective because they're viewed from the side.

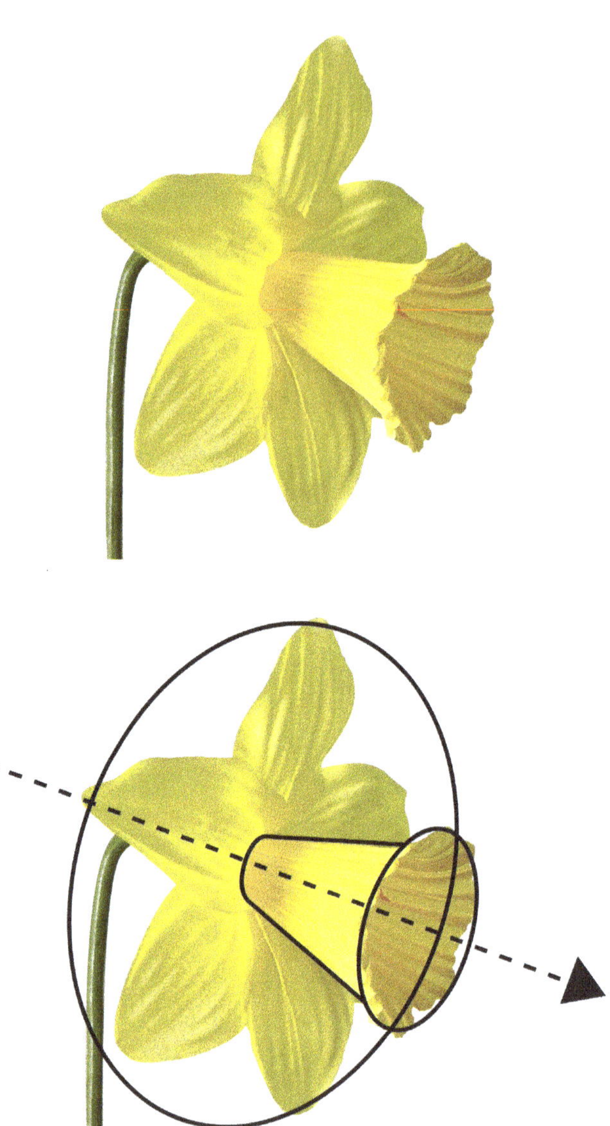

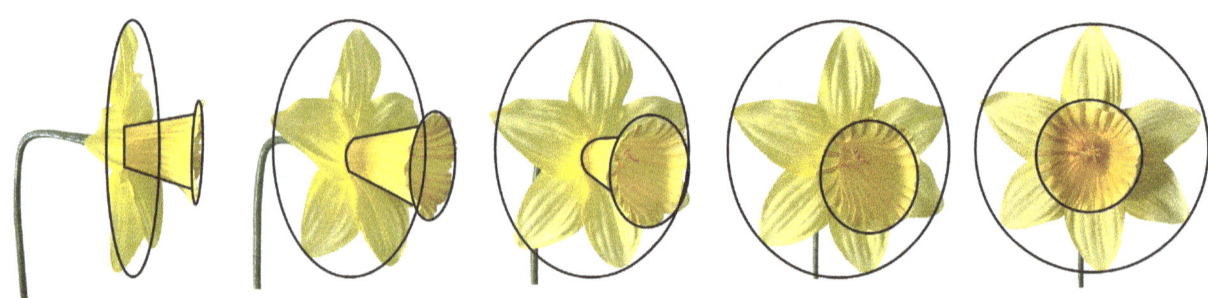

I created simple outlines to show the basic shapes of the daffodil from different angles. You can clearly see the direction and key shapes of the daffodil as it goes from a profile view to a straight-on angle.

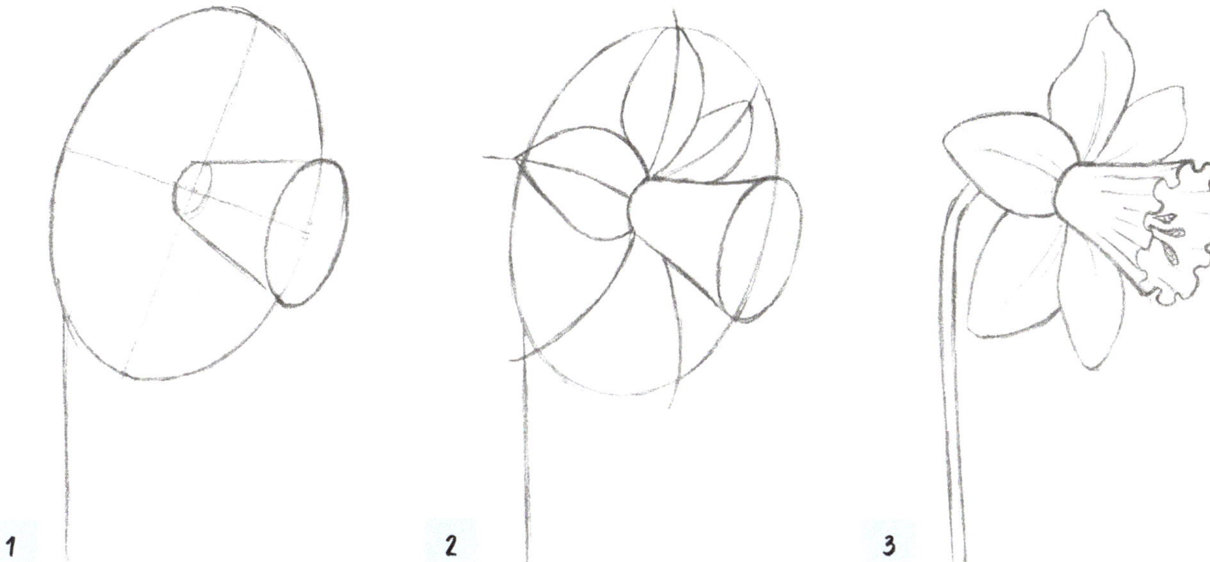

1 Draw a slanted vertical line and a slanted horizontal line that intersects in the middle of the vertical guideline. Create an oval by connecting each vertex. Add a cone in the middle of the oval to outline the basic shape of the daffodil (see "Drawing Shapes," page 24). Horizontal and vertical lines are not only guides to drawing an oval, but they are also guides to the location and angle of the cone. Add a line for the stem. Completing this first step means you've finished 70 percent of the sketch—that's how essential this step is. When building a house, raising sturdy frames is important. Likewise, the basic shape is critical for sketching flowers. Without a good first-step sketch, the overall shape will be disproportionate no matter how well you draw the second and third steps.

2 Place the guidelines according to the number of petals and then draw each petal with an almond shape, making sure to space them evenly. Note the curve of the guidelines; this will help create the curve of the petal. Note that in this drawing, you can't see the guidelines from step 1; they were erased to show the step 2 guidelines more clearly. However, you can leave the original guidelines in while drawing the flower.

3 If you look at the outer edges of the petals, you'll see that some have a wavy line while others have a simple curve. Some petals end in sharp points, while others are rounded. Add these details to create a realistic sketch. Add curved lines to the petals to indicate creases and wrinkles. Draw a wavy outline on the outer edge of the cone to create a ruffled edge and add wrinkles and creases to the cone. Draw stamens inside the cone. Thicken the stem to finalize the daffodil.

The sketch lines shown in the book are dark so you can see shapes and details. When sketching for watercolor painting, keep pencil lines light.

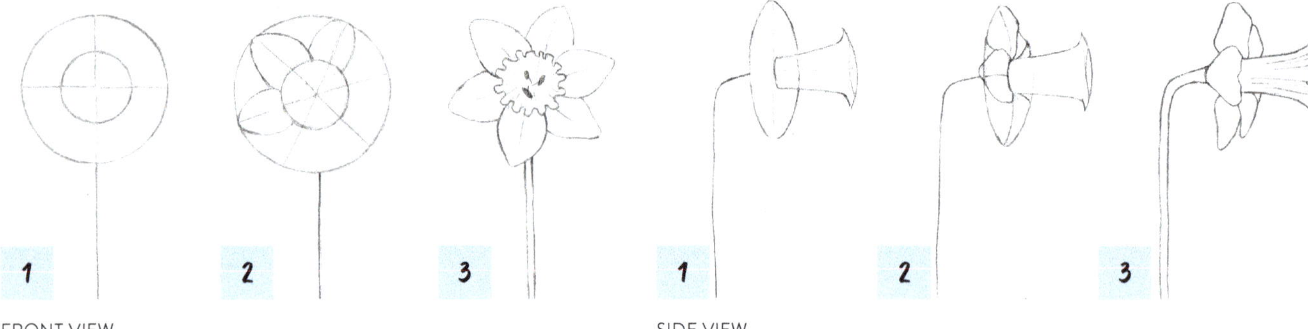

FRONT VIEW

SIDE VIEW

To draw a daffodil from front view, follow the same three-step process.

1 Draw a vertical line and cross a horizontal guideline in the middle of it. Create a circle by connecting each vertex. Create a small circle in the center of the large circle. Add a line for the stem.

2 Place the guidelines according to the number of petals and then draw each petal, making sure to space them evenly.

3 Draw a wavy outline on the outer edge of the small circle to create a ruffled edge and add wrinkles. Draw stamens inside the small circle. Thicken the stem to finalize the daffodil.

To draw a daffodil from a side view, follow the same three-step process.

1 Draw a vertical line and intersect it in the middle with a short horizontal guideline. Create a narrow ellipse by connecting each vertex. Draw a cone in the center of the ellipse. Add a line for the stem.

2 Place the guidelines according to the number of petals and then draw each petal.

3 Draw a wavy outline on the outer edge of the cone to create a ruffled edge and add wrinkles. Thicken the stem to finalize the daffodil.

When drawing daffodils at different angles in one frame, it is recommended to create an overall composition by starting a sketch with guidelines. Mark the size, position, and angle of each flower, stem, and leaf with a simple line. Arranging and organizing subjects with simple lines in this early stage makes it easier for you to create a picture of the desired composition at the end. Complete your sketch by adding details such as petals, stems, and leaves based on the guidelines after you complete the arrangement of daffodils with simple lines.

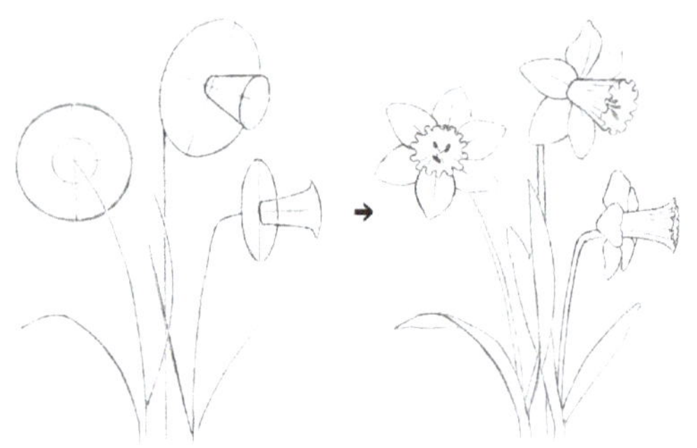

You can get a better perspective of your drawings by looking at them from a distance. When sketching shapes, place the paper far away from you and study the forms. You'll easily catch what needs to be fixed.

BASIC FLOWER FORMS

Because many flowers are circular and symmetrical, we can find several three-dimensional basic forms through observation, such as a bell, bowl, cone, or cup, with circular cross-sections. Although some flowers may have a combination of basic forms (such as the daffodil's circular and cylindrical shapes), once you master observing the overall shape of a flower, you can quickly find a basic form hidden in that flower no matter how complicated it is.

At some point, you may want to draw asymmetrical or uniquely shaped flowers, or flowers placed at different angles. If you keep practicing the process of observing and finding basic shapes in simple flowers, you'll soon be able to draw complex flowers easily, and you'll be able to freely choose the flowers you want to draw.

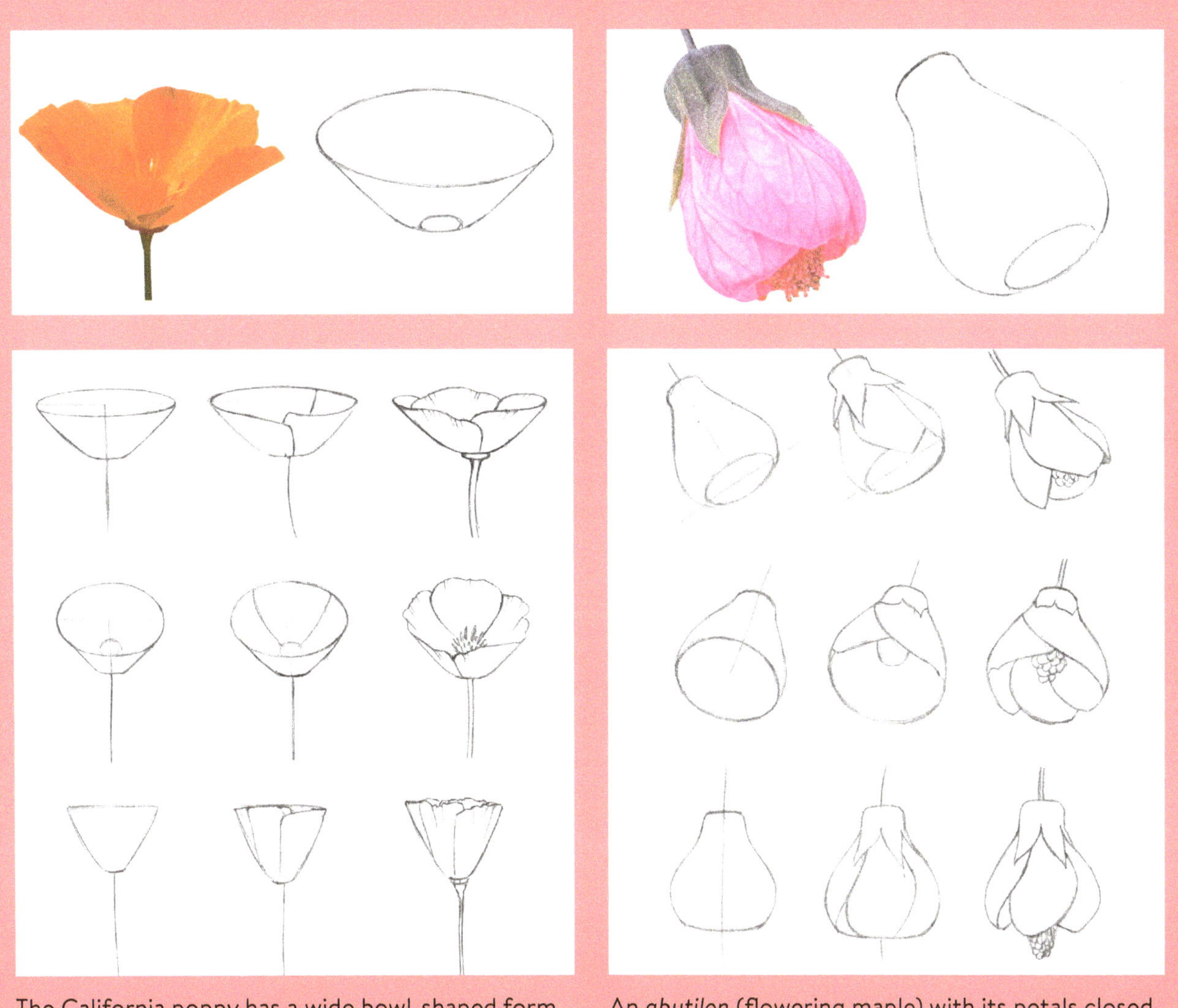

The California poppy has a wide bowl-shaped form.

An *abutilon* (flowering maple) with its petals closed has a bell-shaped form.

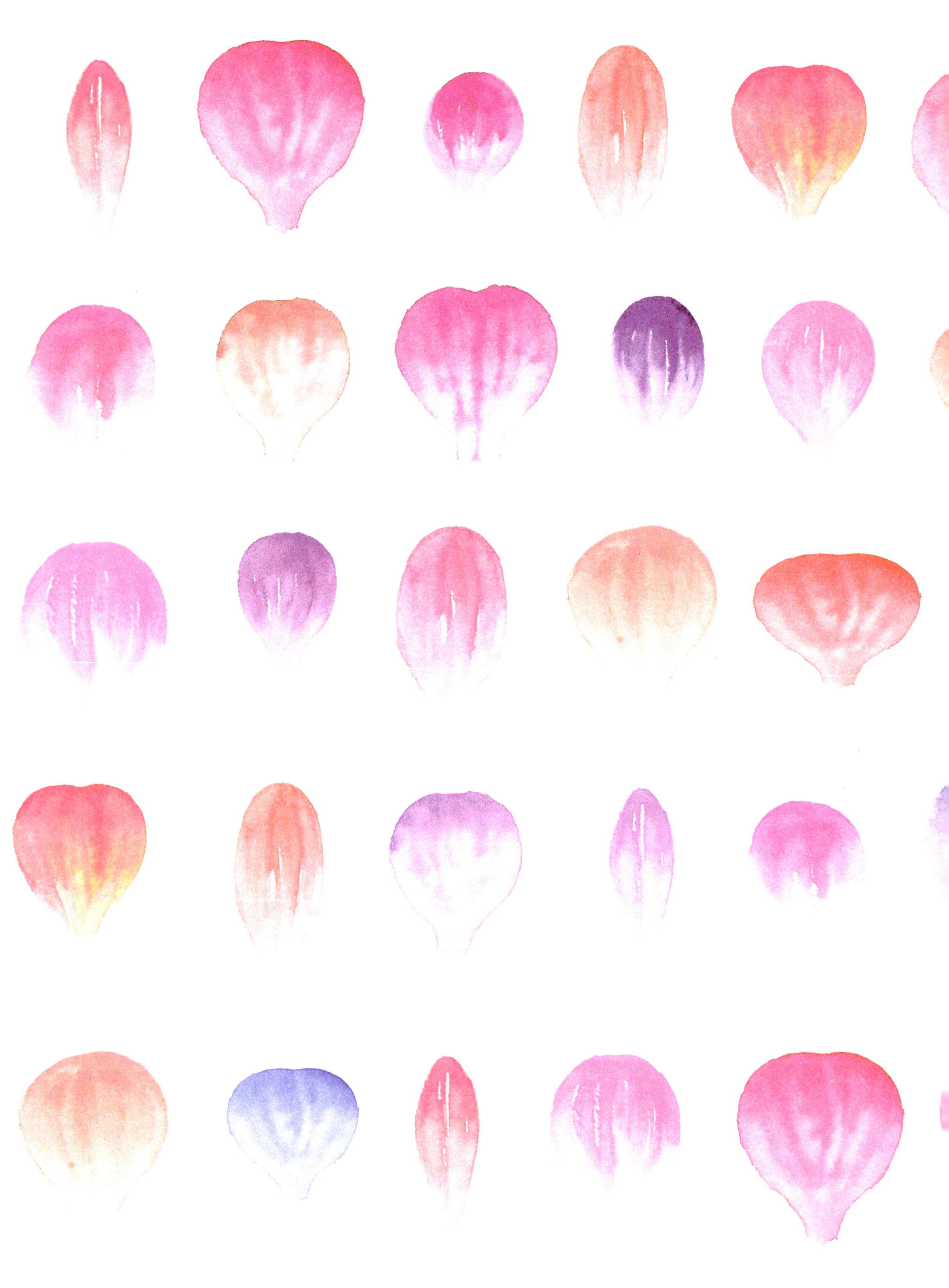

3

Basic Watercolor Techniques

Once you experience the dramatic transformations that happen when you mix water with watercolor paint, you'll find watercolor more attractive than any other medium. In this chapter, you'll learn brush techniques, watercolor painting techniques, and how to use color effectively. Combining these methods will help your flower paintings come to life.

WATERCOLOR DENSITY LEVELS

Before diving into brush techniques in earnest, let's talk about the term "density level," which will be used frequently in this book. Watercolor is just pigment mixed with water. The density level represents the amount of water mixed with watercolor paint in five levels. The Level 5 density refers to a thick and vivid color with very little water mixed with the paint, whereas the Level 1 density means a very light color with a lot of water mixed in. The image below shows density scales created by adjusting the amount of water mixed with each color in five levels.

Because you can adjust the brightness and darkness of colors with the amount of water in watercolor, practicing this density scale will be very helpful in developing your ability to produce a desired color. The density level of the darker colors can be more subdivided because they have a greater range of color changes according to the amount of water. However, for your convenience, the density level of all colors in this book will be divided into only five levels. As you learn how to paint, not only will you have to learn how to adjust the water quantity, but you'll also learn some brush-handling techniques.

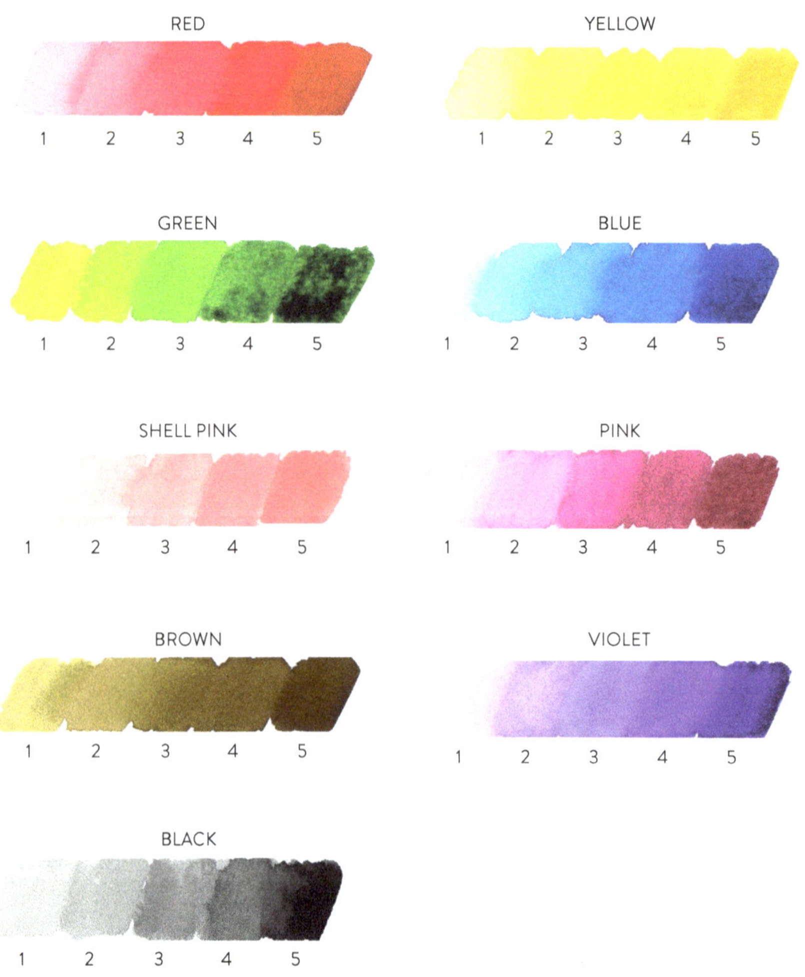

BRUSH TECHNIQUES

As I mentioned in chapter 1, the watercolor painting lessons in this book feature round brushes in sizes 4, 5, and 6. They're similar to the size of a pencil, so even if this is your first time working with paintbrushes, you should find them comfortable to use.

THE ANATOMY OF A PAINTBRUSH

Becoming familiar with the various parts of a paintbrush will help you learn brush techniques.

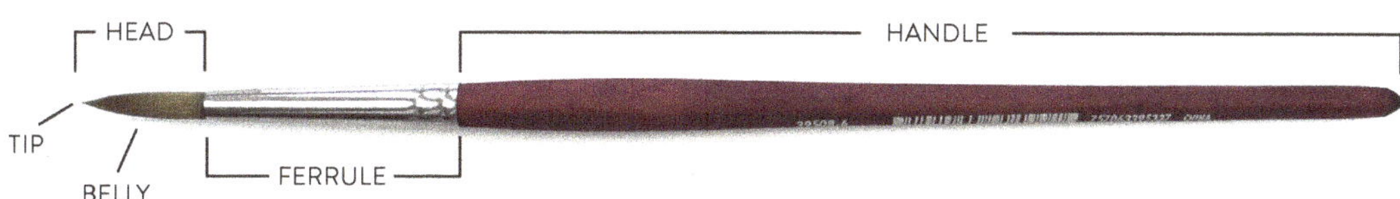

HOLDING THE BRUSH

Hold the brush as if you're holding a pencil for writing. Place your wrist on top of the paper and make sure you're relaxed—don't tense up or hold the brush too tightly. As you go through the exercises, the thickness of your lines may differ depending on where you hold the brush. Likewise, the shapes of the strokes may change depending on the pressure and direction of the brush.

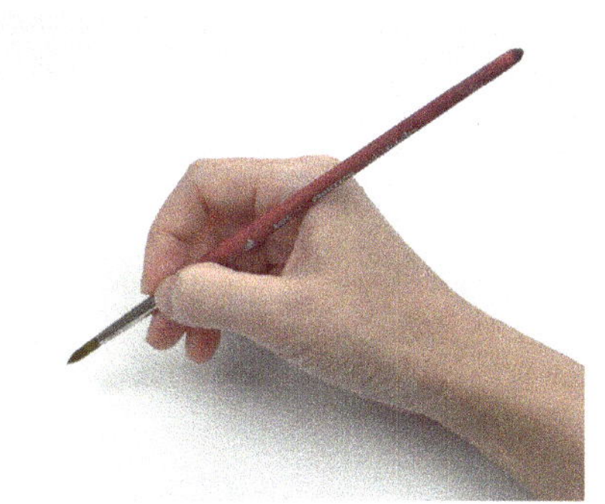

Holding a brush nearer to the head is helpful for coloring small areas and thin lines, as it gives you more control over the marks you make.

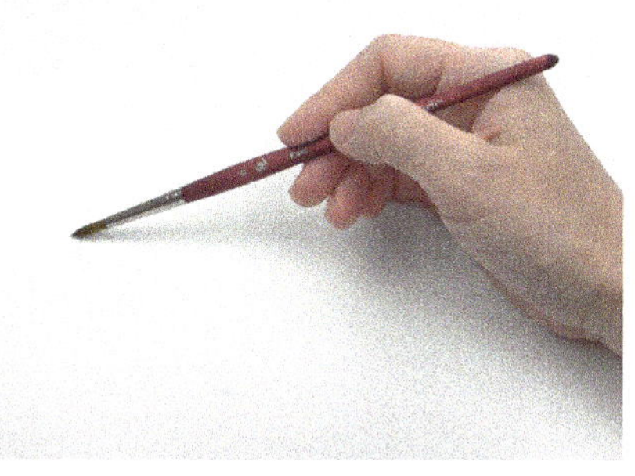

Holding a brush in the middle is useful for coloring wide areas or thick lines because it allows you to easily make broad, bold strokes.

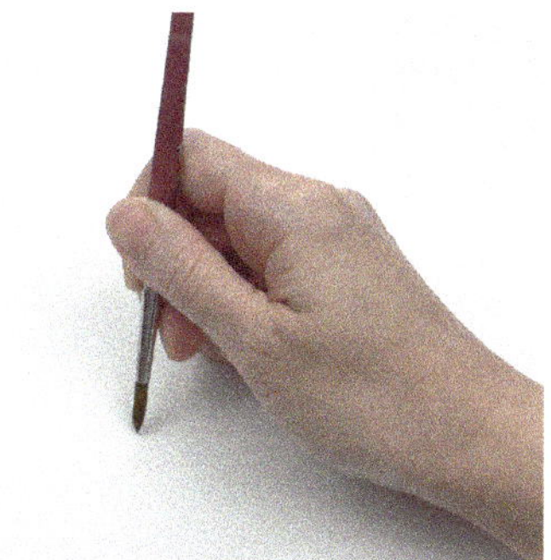

Holding the brush close to the head at an angle makes it easier to create dots, short strokes, and detailed work.

BRUSH CONTROL

Now, let's use the brush and watercolor together.

If this is your first time creating a watercolor painting, your wrist might feel tense. If so, I recommend starting with the line-drawing exercises first. This will ease the muscles surrounding your wrist and you'll learn to control the pressure of your hand, which will help stabilize your brushstrokes.

For these exercises you'll need a jar of clean water, watercolor paper (see page 17), paintbrushes (see page 16), and paper towels. Use round brushes size 6 and larger as they're more suited for stroke exercises.

1 Wet the brush head. Load the moist brush with any color of paint **(A)**. Blend the pigment and water in the mixing area of the palette **(B)**. You've made a color! You should have an adequate amount of color to paint several lines.

2 Hold the brush lightly near the head and paint a short straight line and a long straight line using the tip of the brush. Then, hold the brush in the middle and paint thick and thin short lines. Try painting vertical lines too.

While you can paint short lines by moving just your wrist, it's better to move your wrist and lower arm when painting long lines. This helps prevent the brush from shaking so your lines are clean and neat.

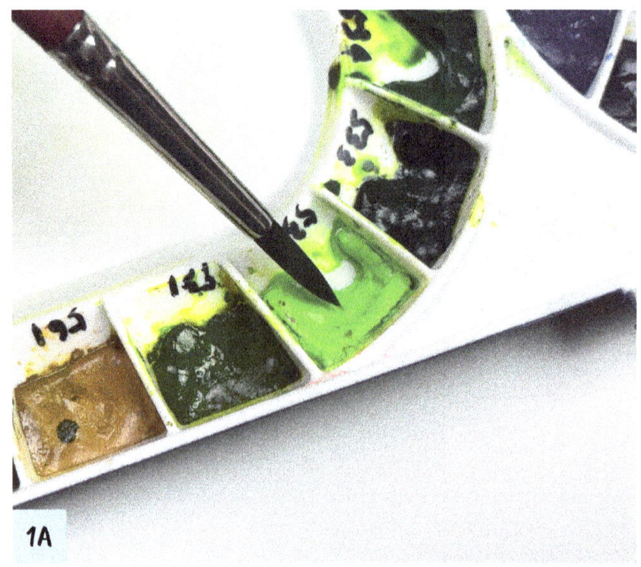
1A

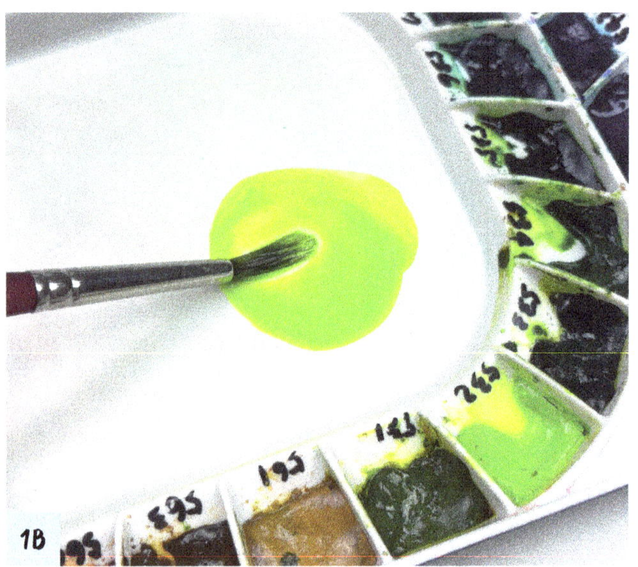
1B

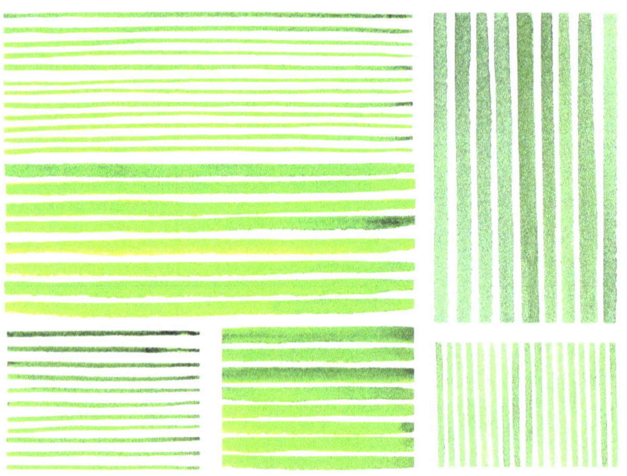
2

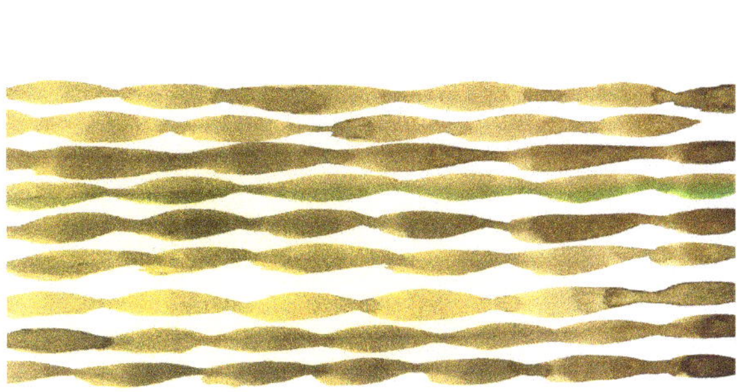

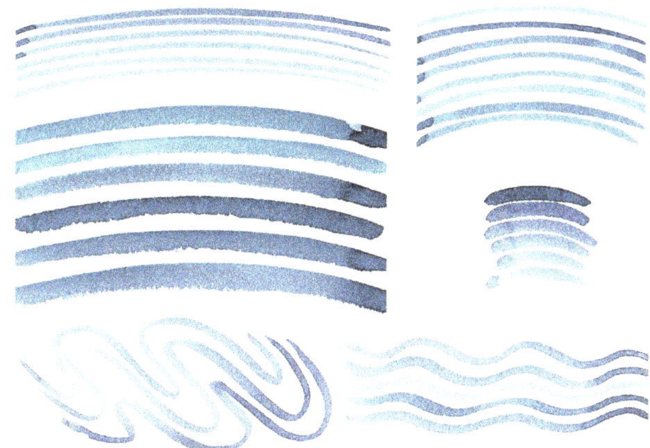

3 Here, you'll see how your strokes can change depending on how much pressure you exert or release on the brush. Load the brush with paint and place the tip on the watercolor paper. Pull the handle of the brush to create lines. As you're pulling the brush, exert enough pressure to allow the belly of the brush to touch the paper. The belly will spread and make thicker strokes. Pull the brush again and lift it to make thinner strokes, using just the tip. Repeat this process.

4 Lightly hold the brush near the head as you did in step 2 and paint short and long curved lines. Hold the brush handle in the middle and paint thick curved lines. Paint curved lines in various directions. This exercise is good practice for drawing stems, and painting short and thin curved lines will help with creating petal patterns.

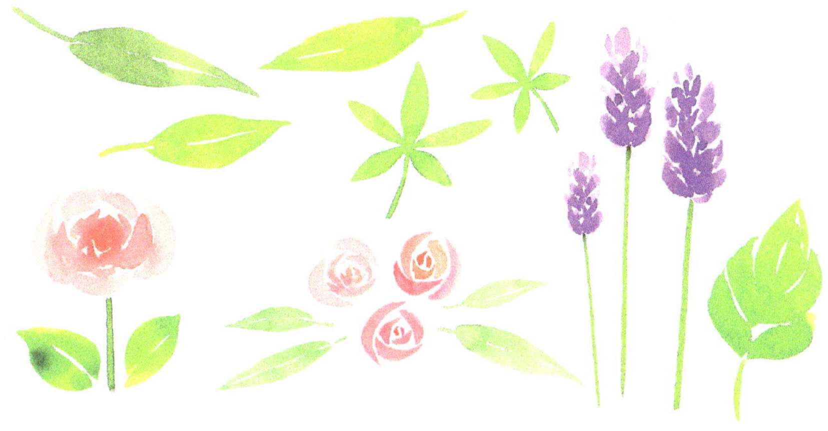

Painting flowers without making an under drawing is called loose watercolor. You can create leaves and petals by exerting and releasing pressure on the brush as you did in the thick and thin line painting exercise. This practice results in varied strokes that change depending on the pressure and direction of your hand.

WATERCOLOR PAINTING TECHNIQUES

Standard watercolor painting techniques include wet-on-wet, wet-on-dry, and gradient. Depending on the type of painting or the artist's style, a painting may employ one or multiple techniques to convey a diverse ambience.

Adding a color over another color creates new shades. Here, you can see new colors created when analogous and complementary colors bleed into each other.

WET-ON-WET

Wet-on-wet refers to the technique of applying wet paint onto a wet paper surface. To prepare the wet surface for this technique, add clean water with a clean brush to the area you want to paint. You can also use this technique on previously painted areas that are still wet.

In the wet-on-wet technique, the water absorbed by the paper and the pigment interact to create a variety of blends and washes. This technique also creates blurred and blended borders, which are called soft edges.

When you brush clean water onto paper and add one or two drops of pigment, you'll see the pigment spread. The way it spreads will be different depending on the amount of water absorbed by the paper. Wait until the paper absorbs enough water; this will help the pigment spread well. If you apply pigment too soon or too late and the paper starts to dry up, the pigment will spread less.

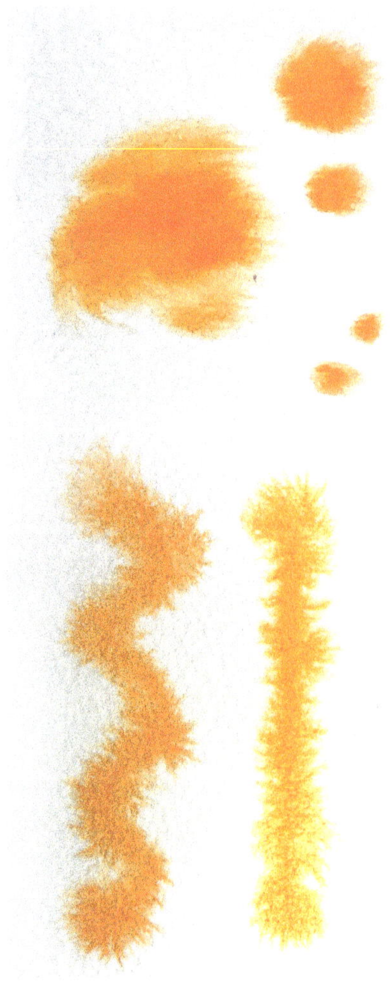

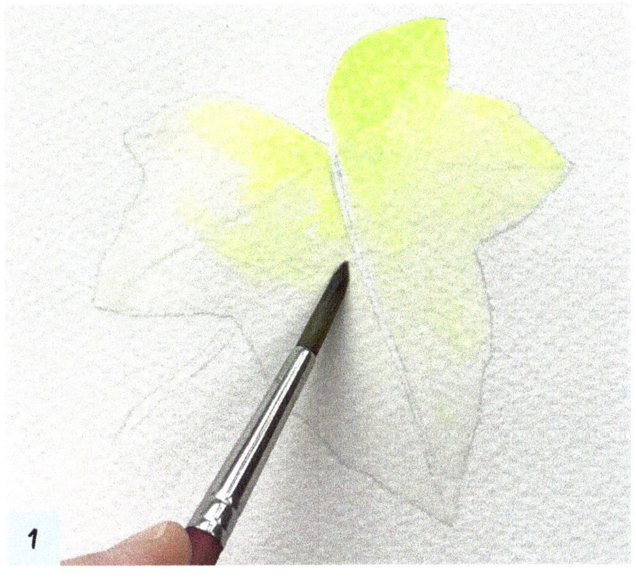
1

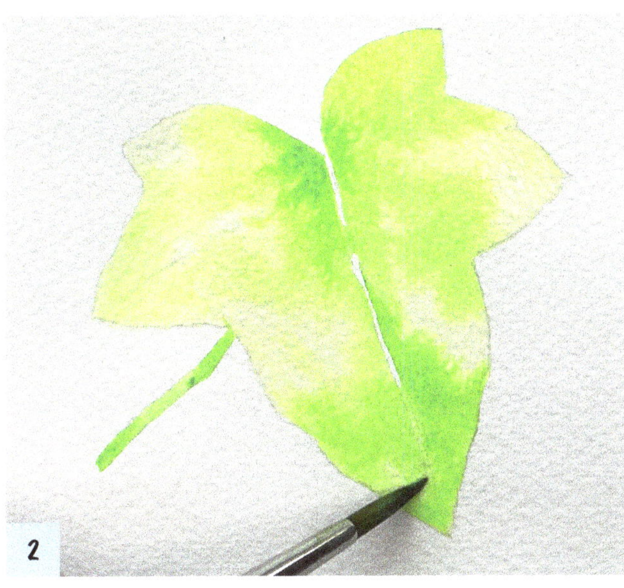
2

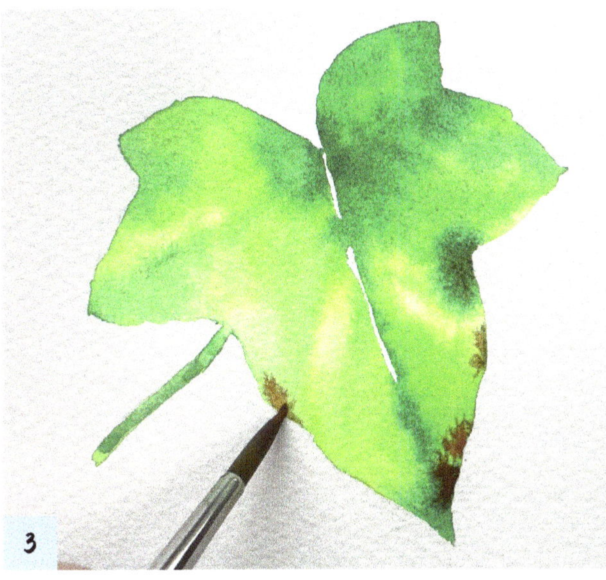
3

EXERCISE: WET-ON-WET LEAVES

In this exercise, you'll use the wet-on-wet technique to color leaves. The paper should stay wet until you finish painting so the color can spread effectively, so try to work quickly.

1 Draw a light outline of an ivy leaf and stem on watercolor paper, adding a few veins within the leaf. Wet the paper inside the lines with clear water, using a round brush. You don't have to apply a lot of water; if it starts to roll off, you've used too much. Blot the excess with a towel or rag. Apply Level 2 density (see page 32) yellow-green paint on the upper part of the leaf. Once you touch the paint-filled brush to the paper, you'll see the color spread toward the bottom of the leaf.

2 Before the paint dries, color the bottom of the leaf with Level 3 density Hooker's Green. Place the brush in the top center of the leaf and apply the paint carefully. The two shades of green will blend naturally to create another medium-value color.

3 Accent the upper right and bottom parts of the leaf with Level 3 Viridian, creating a strong color contrast to the lighter shades. Lightly tap the outer line of the leaf with Light Red. Since green and red are complementary colors, when blended they'll create a neutral brown. This helps produce the look of a natural ivy leaf.

WET-ON-DRY

The wet-on-dry technique involves applying paint to dry paper. You can apply watercolor to the paper and then add clean water. You can also add a new color on top of a dry color. Wet-on-dry painting is distinguished by its defined edges. You can intensify the tone by layering the same color or a new color on top of the base color. The wet-on-dry technique works well for creating details.

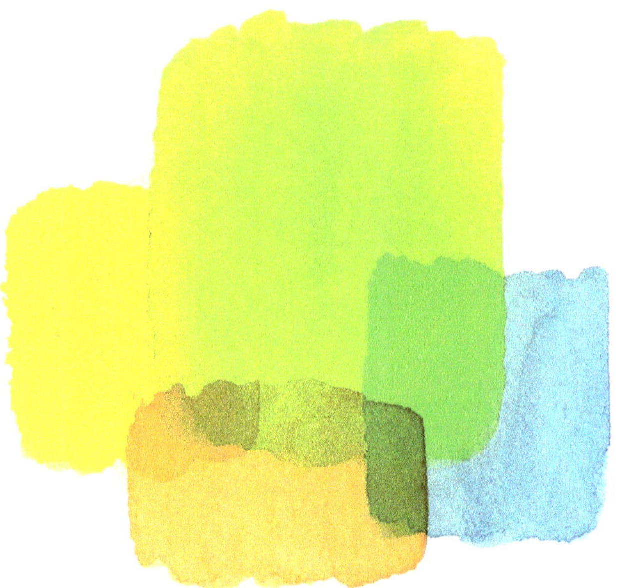

When applying a color on top of another dry color, the result will be a mid-tone shade in the intersection of the two colors. Notice that there's a clear or hard edge between the strokes.

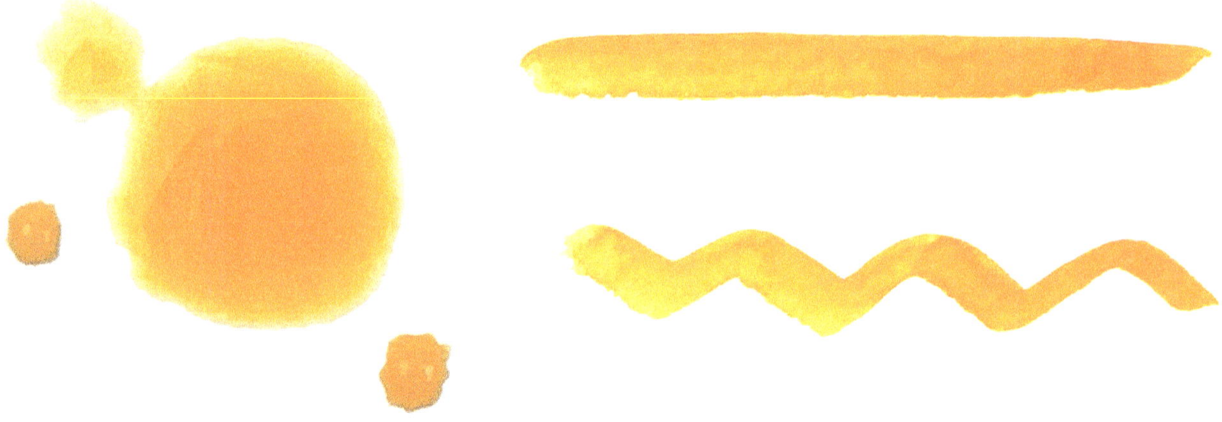

When paint is applied to dry paper, it doesn't spread or blend, but stays intact.

EXERCISE: WET-ON-DRY FLOWER

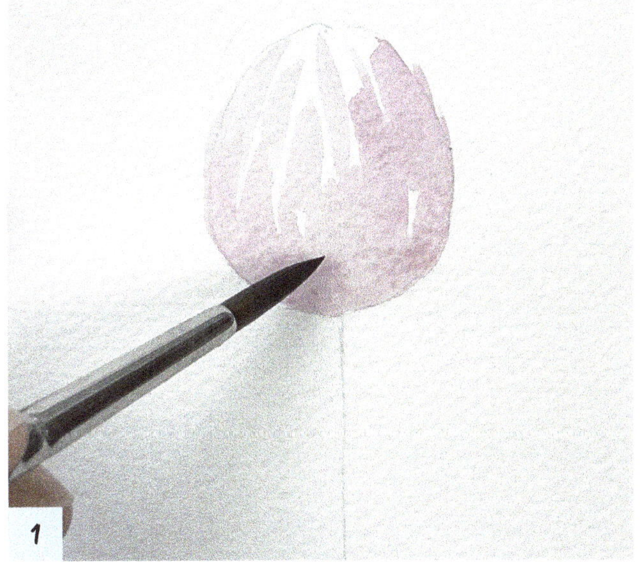

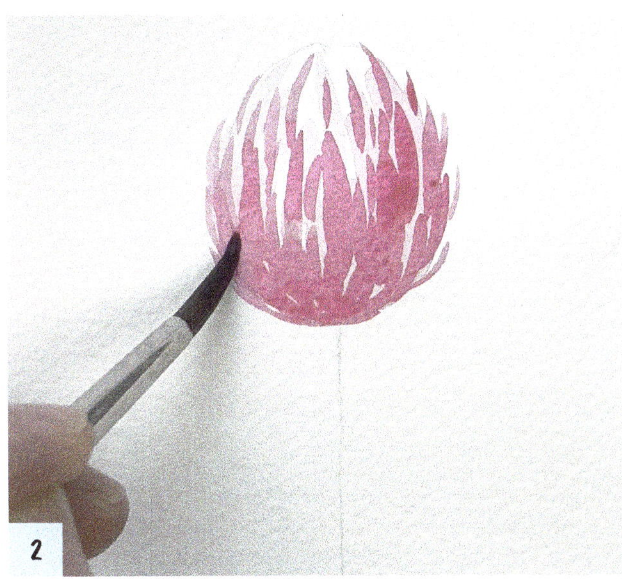

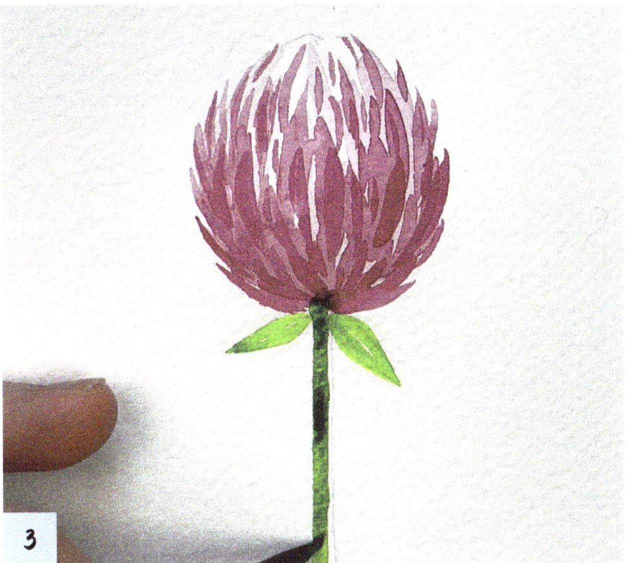

1. Draw a light outline of a globe amaranth on watercolor paper. Paint the bloom with Level 1 density red-violet, making sure to leave some white of the paper showing. Remember that you are painting on dry paper, meaning clean water isn't applied to the paper. Allow this layer to dry.

2. Use Level 3 density red-violet to fill the top of the blossom, using thin curved strokes following the shape of the blossom. Create wide gaps between the strokes. Use thicker strokes to fill in the middle of the blossom with little gaps between the strokes. Use thicker strokes to fill in the bottom of the blossom without gaps. The clear edge of the stroke should be evident.

3. Use Level 5 density red-violet to fill the top of the blossom with thin strokes. Use thicker strokes to fill the bottom of the flower. The strokes should not cross each other, but they should be irregular to make the petals look full. Paint the stem and sepals using Hooker's Green.

FLAT WASH

This technique is used to get a smooth and even finish in one density level without changing color. If you don't have enough paint to cover the area you're painting, you'll have to make more paint, so make sure you have enough at the beginning. Recreating the same color and value is difficult, and there will be a difference between the color you initially applied and the color you applied later. While the lessons in this book don't focus on flat washes, this exercise will help you control your painting speed and the amount of watercolor you use.

If you find you have excess watercolor at the end of a brushstroke, use the brush to spread it out. Another way to remove excess watercolor is by cleaning the brush with water and blotting it dry with a paper towel, then using it to soak up the surplus watercolor. Or you can touch the surplus watercolor with the edge of a paper towel, which will absorb the extra paint.

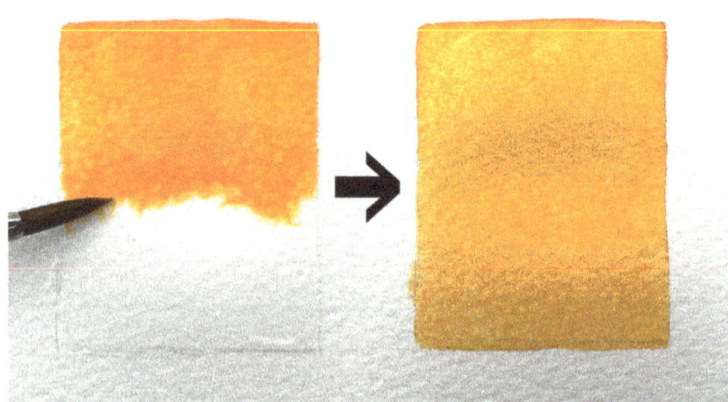

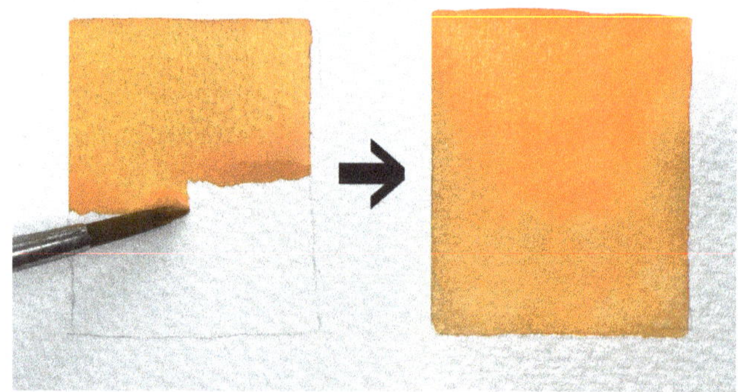

Wet-on-Wet Flat Wash

Lightly mark out an area with pencil on paper and wet the area with clean water and a brush. Apply paint to the area. When the paper is wet, the watercolor will spread out. The paint can usually be applied evenly by blending the watercolor well using a brush.

Wet-on-Dry Flat Wash

Dry paper absorbs water very quickly, which means that the brush loses watercolor quickly. In order to successfully create a flat wash on dry paper, it's essential to make an ample amount of watercolor on the palette and paint continuously.

GRADIENT TECHNIQUES

Painting a shape with even color can be difficult because there's a tendency to focus on painting the edges first, which may result in staining as the colors dry. However, practicing flat washes on a variety of sketched shapes will help you paint evenly without creating stains or beads.

Gradient techniques, or graded washes, allow you to create a seamless transition from a light color to a dark one. A variegated wash incorporates two colors, with one blending into another. I'll refer to both as gradient techniques because many of the floral painting lessons use both techniques to create gradients. Gradients are very useful for painting flowers as petals and leaves often contain different values of the same color or a mix of colors.

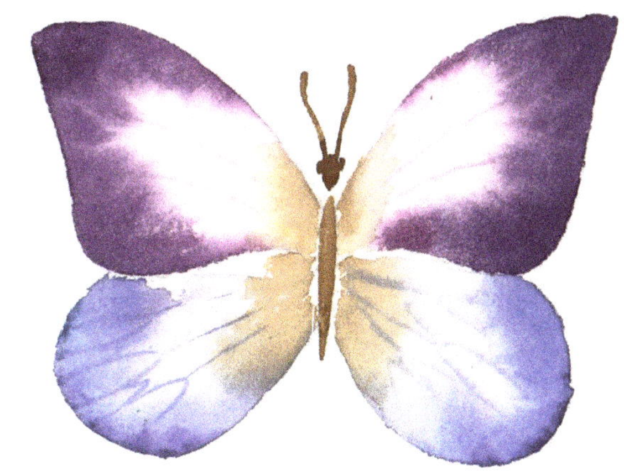

Here is an example of the wet-on-wet gradient. Different colors naturally spread and mix with each other, creating a wonderful blending effect.

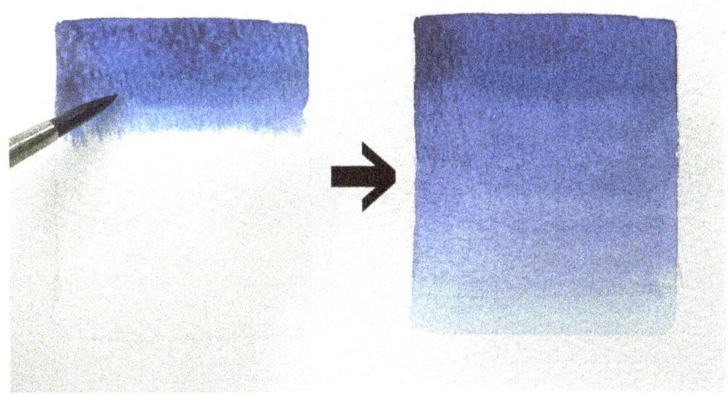

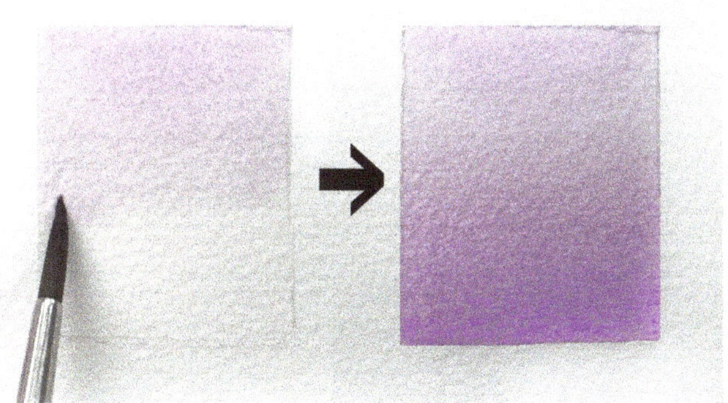

Wet-on-Wet Gradient

Sketch a shape on watercolor paper and apply clean water to the area. Paint the shape with dark blue, starting at the top. Make back-and-forth horizontal brushstrokes. Repeat the strokes, slowly moving down within the area. As the brush moves down, the color will become lighter, slowly fading out.

A gradient can also work in reverse, going from lighter to darker by adding more paint.

EXERCISE: WET-ON-WET PETALS

1 Draw petal shapes on watercolor paper. Working wet-on-wet, apply Level 5 density pink at the upper part of the petal.

2 Rinse the brush with water and lightly blot it with a paper towel. Then drag the color down to fade it.

3 Before the paint dries, paint a random thin vertical line with Level 5 density pink. On a gradient underpainting, the vertical lines spread naturally to form a pattern on the petals.

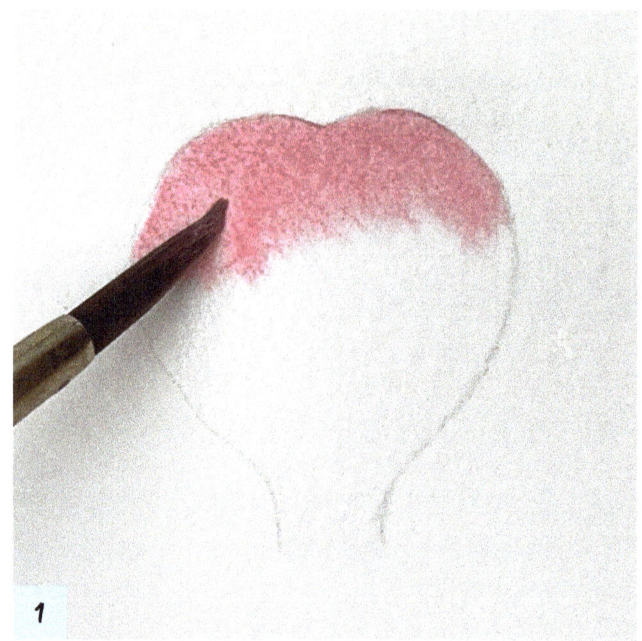

1

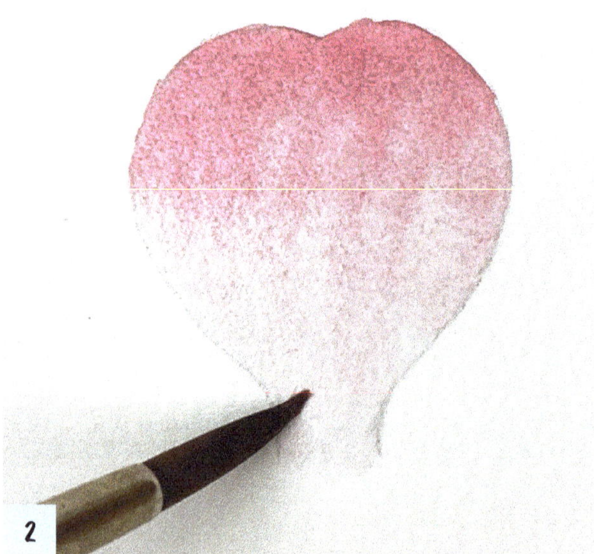

2

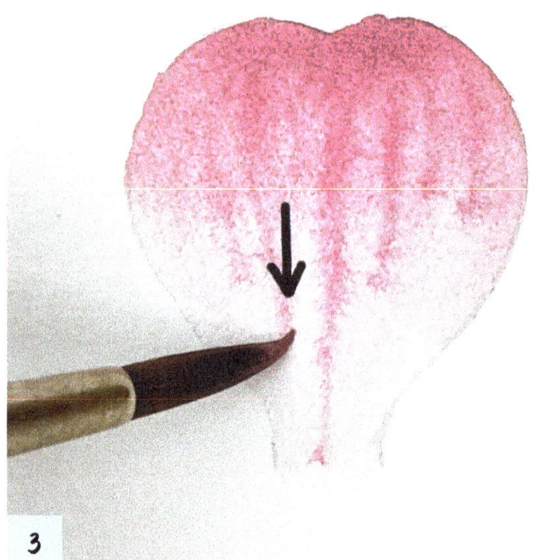

3

Wet-on-Dry Gradient

To create a color-fading effect with the wet-on-dry gradient technique (**A**), continue to dilute the paint with clear water as you add brushstrokes to create the gradient. Apply an ample amount of dense blue color to dry paper where the gradation begins. To continue making the gradation, soak the brush slightly in clean water to dilute the blue a little, then remove some water from the brush using a paper towel. If the brush contains too much water, the diluted paint will run backward and may ruin the gradation. Continue to dilute blue paint with clear water, remove some water in the same way, and then paint with the gradually lighter colors from the bottom edge of the previously painted area.

Wet-on-Wet Variegated Wash

The wet-on-wet technique (**B**) can be used to create a soft gradient with two or more colors. Sketch a shape on watercolor paper and apply clean water to the area. Paint the upper half of the shape with light blue and apply orange on the bottom half of the shape. You can see that the two colors spread naturally and blend together to create a gradient.

Wet-on-Dry Variegated Wash

To create a gradient of two colors using the wet-on-dry technique (**C**), make a wet-on-dry gradient twice with each color. Sketch a shape on watercolor paper. Paint the top third of the shape with light blue and drag the color to the center of the shape. Then, create a wet-on-dry gradient with orange in the opposite direction. You can see two colors blend together to create a gradient.

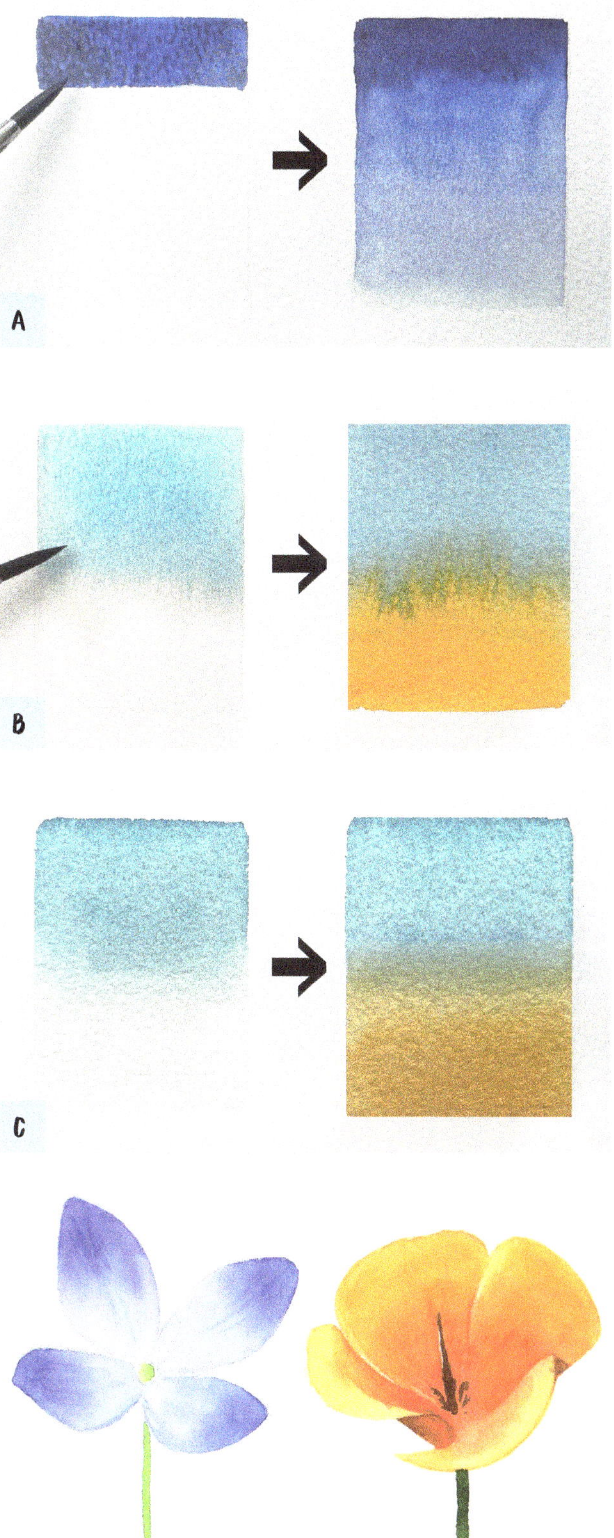

Here are some examples of the wet-on-dry gradient. A wet-on-dry gradient can create a more controlled blending effect.

EXERCISE: WET-ON-DRY PETALS

1 Draw petal shapes on watercolor paper. Working wet-on-dry, apply Level 5 density pink at the upper part of the petal.

2 Draw random vertical lines with different thicknesses.

3 Rinse the brush with water and lightly blot it with a paper towel. Then drag the color down to fade it. Move the brush from top to bottom, not horizontally, to maintain the vertical gradient. Leave some areas white.

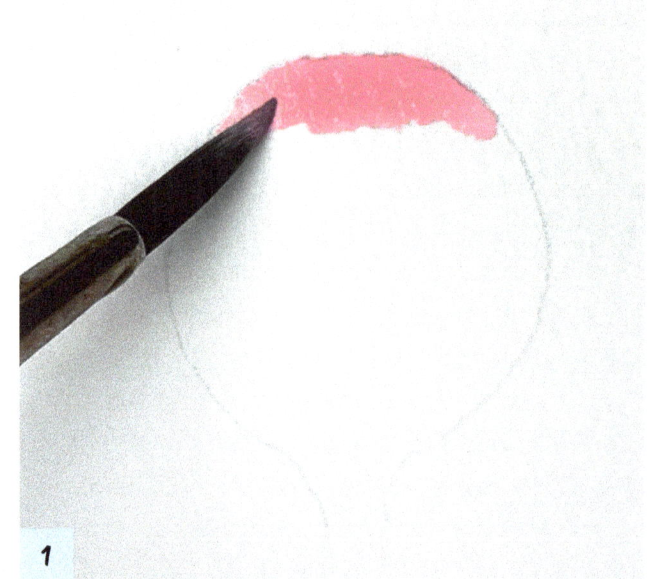

1

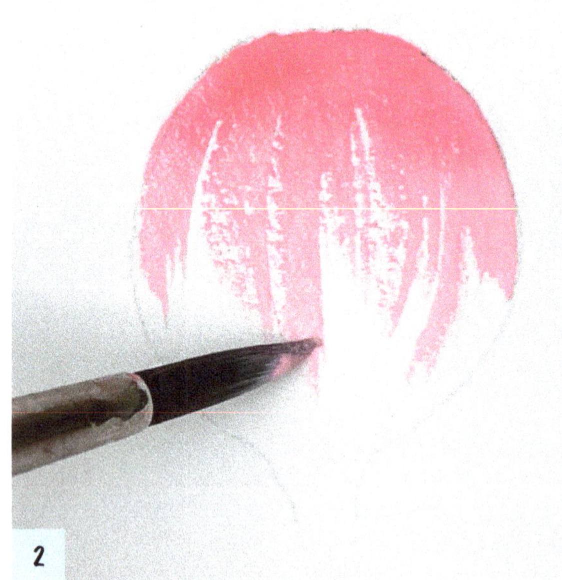

2

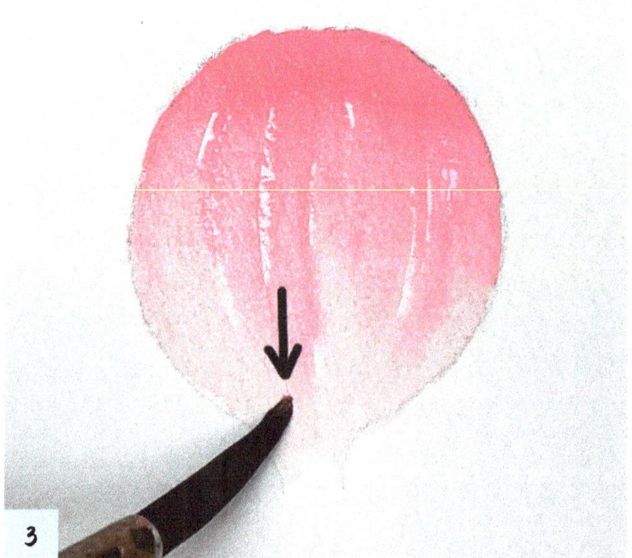

3

The glazing technique can create defined lines in the glazed areas. To remove them, wash the brush with clean water, then lightly blot it with a paper towel. Fade the lines by blending the area with the original color. Repeat the process if more lines are created. Be careful not to remove the original color with the wet brush.

GLAZING TECHNIQUE

The glazing technique modifies the appearance of color by adding a thin layer of color over a previous color after the previous color is completely dry. This method is used as often as the gradient technique in watercolor painting. It can be used to create shading by layering a stronger or complementary color or to enrich overall color expressions by adding different hues over original colors. You can also unify the overall color tone of a painting by adding a thin layer of the same color to the entire painting. Be aware that this last technique makes colors slightly darker and murkier, and a painting may lose its original color and look dull if this type of glazing is used excessively.

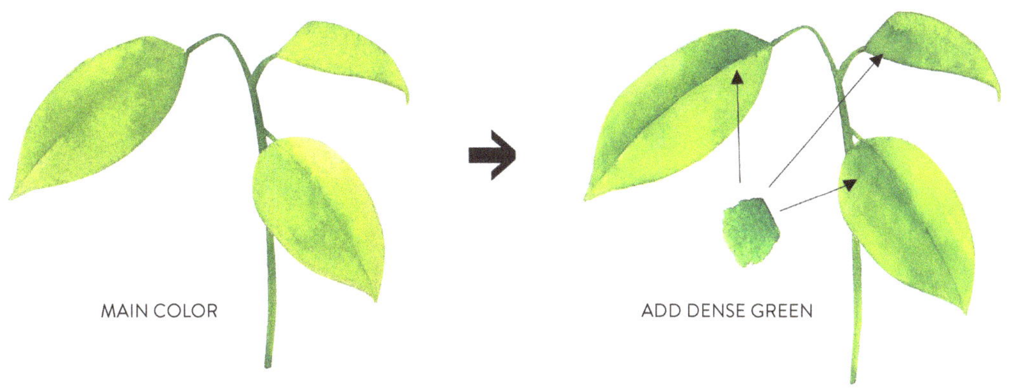

After painting with a main color and allowing it to dry thoroughly, add depth to the leaves by creating layers of colors using the glazing technique.

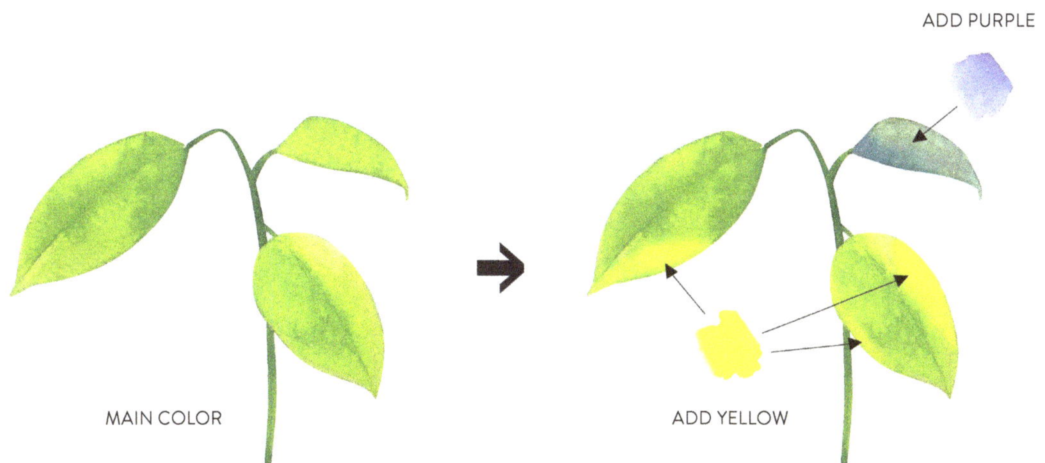

Sometimes, artists use similar colors throughout a painting. Looking at the finished piece, you may notice it's monotonous and flat. To make the painting more lively and rich, add layers of different colors with a glazing technique after the first layers are completely dry. In this example, the colors of the painting became much richer by adding a vivid yellow to the bright part of the leaf using a glazing technique and also by adding yellow's complement, purple, instead of a similar dark green to the backside of the leaf.

MASKING FLUID TECHNIQUE

The masking technique blocks the paper from absorbing water or watercolor. Use it to paint white flowers on a colored background, to create scattered shapes, or to paint small details such as flower stamens.

EXERCISE: PAINTING A WHITE FLOWER

For this exercise, you'll need masking fluid, a rubber cement eraser, a kneaded eraser, a small dish or plate (not used for food), watercolor paper, a paintbrush, and watercolor paint. I recommend using an inexpensive synthetic brush to apply the masking fluid because it can damage the bristles if left on too long.

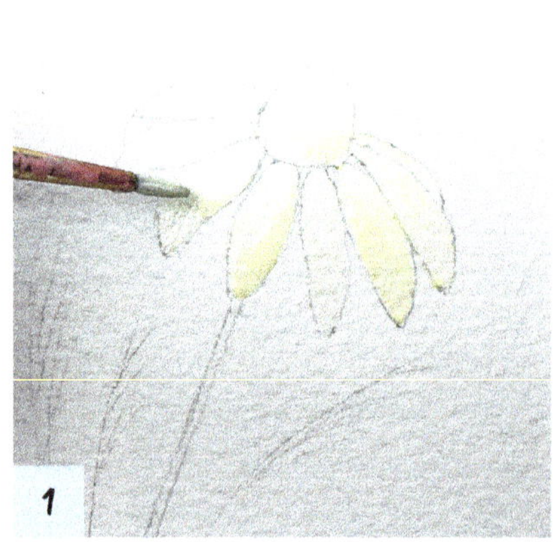

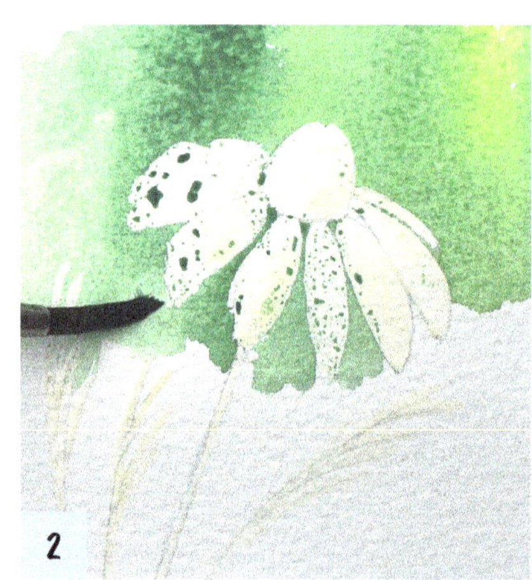

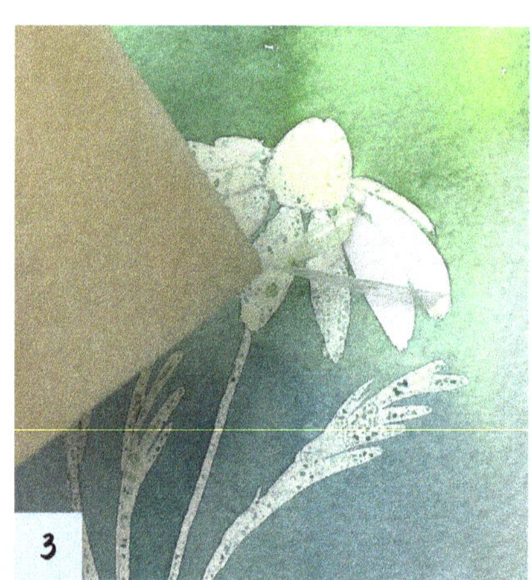

1 Lightly sketch a flower on paper; I drew a coneflower, or echinacea. Apply masking fluid to any areas of the flower you want to stay white (I painted the entire flower with masking fluid for a silhouette effect). Allow the fluid to dry completely.

2 Paint the background around the flower using a wash technique (see page 40).

3 Carefully remove the masking fluid with the rubber cement eraser.

4 Remove the pencil lines with the kneaded eraser.

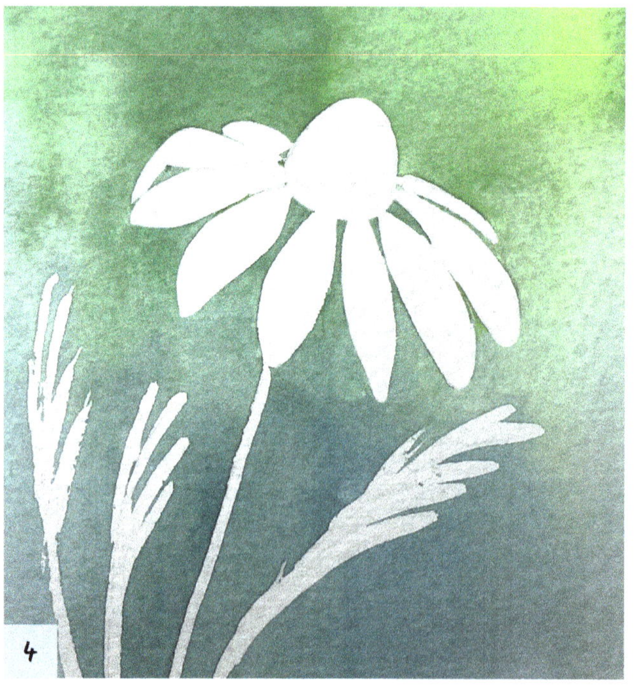

COLOR

Color is used for more than re-creating the hues of a subject—it's an element that expresses and delivers the emotions and message of the artist. Color can suggest temperature, and temperature can suggest a drawing's mood. Vivid colors create a focal point that emphasizes the main theme. Bright colors can also be used as eye candy to catch the viewer's attention. Complementary colors, those opposite each other on the color wheel, illustrate energy and tension. Analogous colors, those next to each other on the color wheel, convey stability and balance.

To help you understand color theory, I'll explain the basic components of colors: hue, value, and saturation.

* **HUE:** Hue is another term for individual colors, such as red, yellow, blue, etc.
* **VALUE:** Value refers to the lightness or darkness of a color. With watercolor, colors can be made lighter by adding more water to the paint. Practicing making value scales for each color will help you to get a sense of how much water should be added to control values for each color. Colors can be made darker by adding less water to increase density or by mixing in a darker color.
* **SATURATION:** Saturation is the intensity of a color. Higher saturation offers more vivid and intense colors, and lower saturation results in duller colors. Colors with high saturation look lively and bright, and colors with low saturation appear calm and muted. To maintain a high saturation, it's best to use a pure, unmixed color. If you need to mix colors, I recommend blending no more than two or three. To decrease the saturation of a color, blend it with gray or a complementary color.

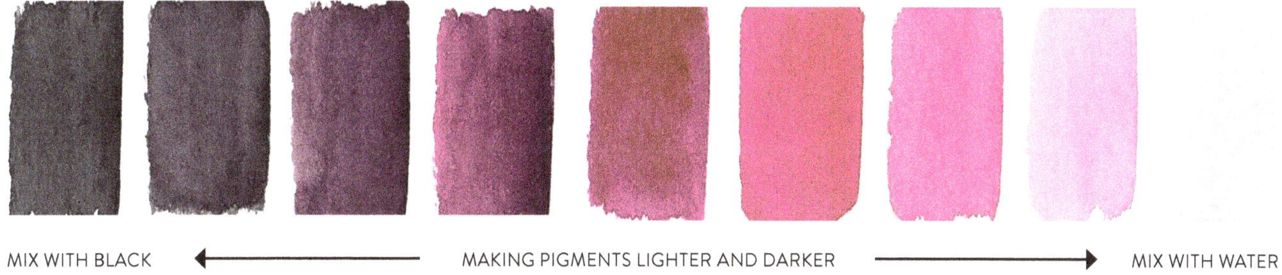

Colors become brighter or lighter when pigments are mixed with water. To make pigments darker, mix them with black.

THE COLOR WHEEL

The color wheel is a guide that shows the relationships of colors. Colors are divided into warm and cool tones, and you can see the impact of colors that are close together on the wheel (analogous) and those that are opposite each other (complementary). Colors are also divided into three categories: primary, secondary, and tertiary.

- **PRIMARY COLORS** include red, yellow, and blue. They're referred to as primaries because they cannot be mixed from any other colors.
- **SECONDARY COLORS** are the result of mixing two primary colors, such as red and yellow to make orange, yellow and blue to make green, and red and blue to make purple.
- **TERTIARY COLORS** are the result of mixing a primary and secondary color, such as yellow and green to make yellow-green, or red and orange to make red-orange.

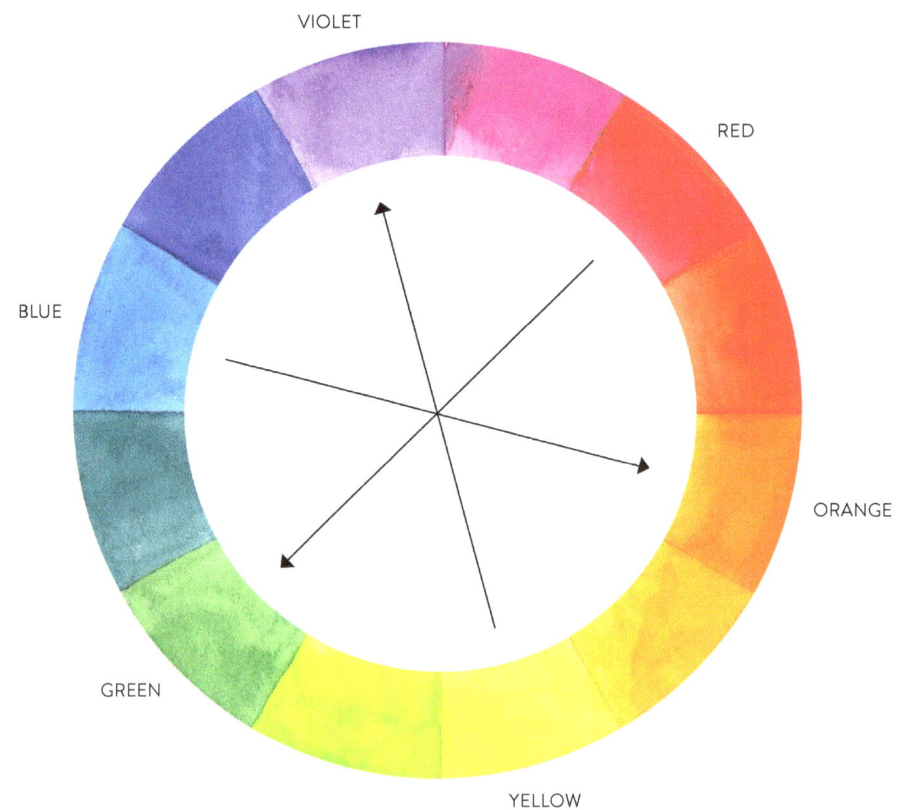

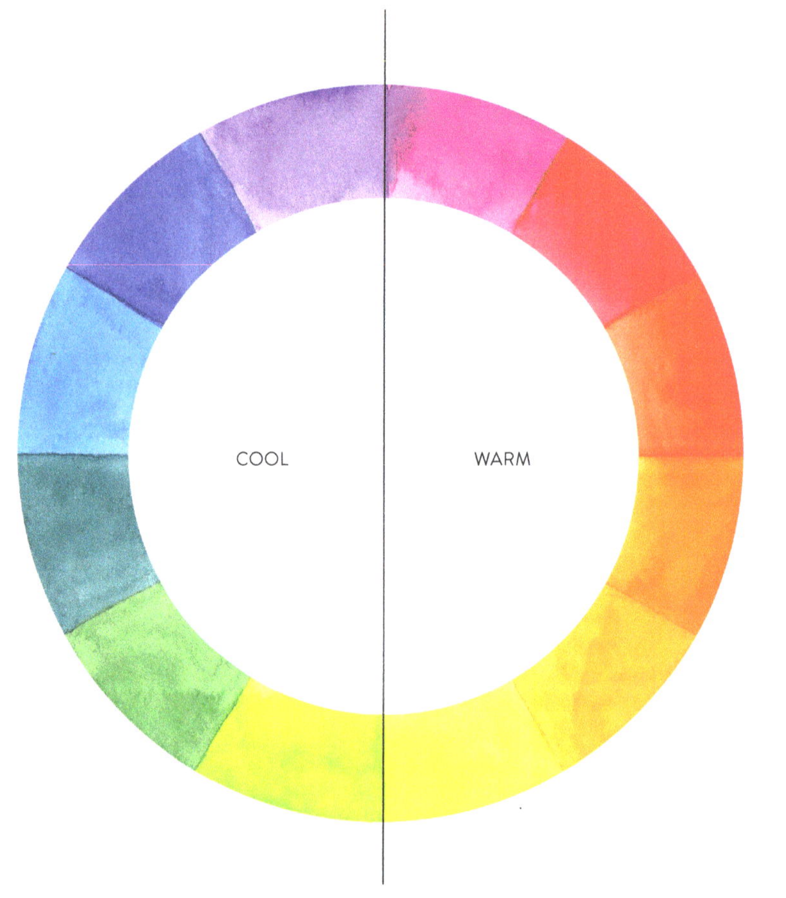

EXERCISES: MIXING COLORS

1. Making Secondary Colors

This exercise helps you understand the colors that result from mixing primary colors. Even though watercolor sets include secondary colors, learning the process will help you understand how secondary colors are created.

Mixing red and yellow creates orange.

Mixing blue and yellow creates green.

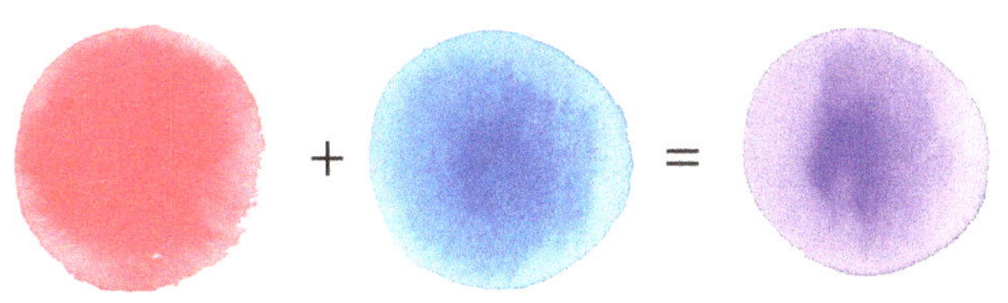

Mixing red and blue creates purple.

2. Making Dark Colors

Mixing bright colors, such as yellow, with black results in a darker, more muted version.

Another way to create dark colors is by mixing a bright color with a more muted secondary color. Here, yellow, a primary, is mixed with brown.

Mixing a color with its complement is yet another way to create a deeper hue. Blending yellow with blue results in a medium brown.

3. Mixing Warm Colors and Cool Colors

Colors are divided into warm and cool tones on the color wheel. When we look at a color, we feel the emotional temperature expressed by the color. Colors that have a yellow base express warmth. Colors with a blue base express coolness. You can create warm colors and cool colors by mixing various hues. By understanding color and temperature, you can imbue a painting with a rich color appearance, which is a key factor in creating a mood.

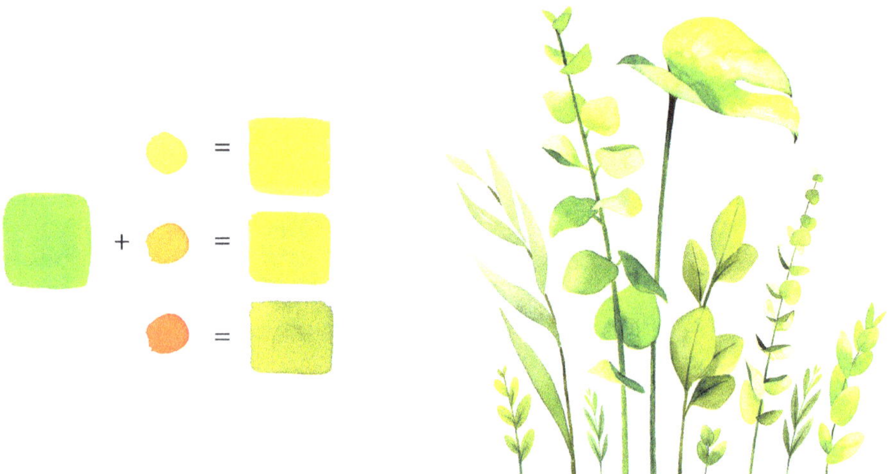

As we see in the color wheel on page 48, yellow and orange belong to the warm color family. To make a warm green, I usually mix green with yellow, golden yellow, and orange. Each warm green made that way is reminiscent of spring.

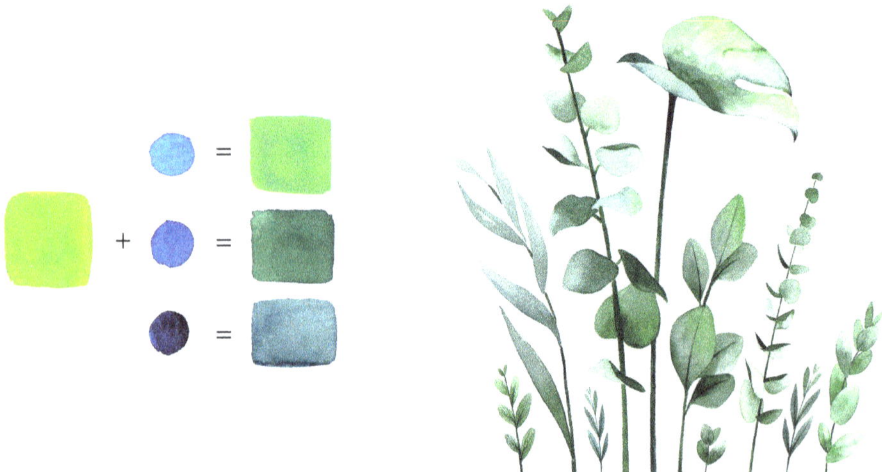

On the color wheel, the blue series belongs to the cool family. To make a cool green, I typically mix green with light blue, medium blue, and navy. Each cool blue made in that way can be used to represent summer.

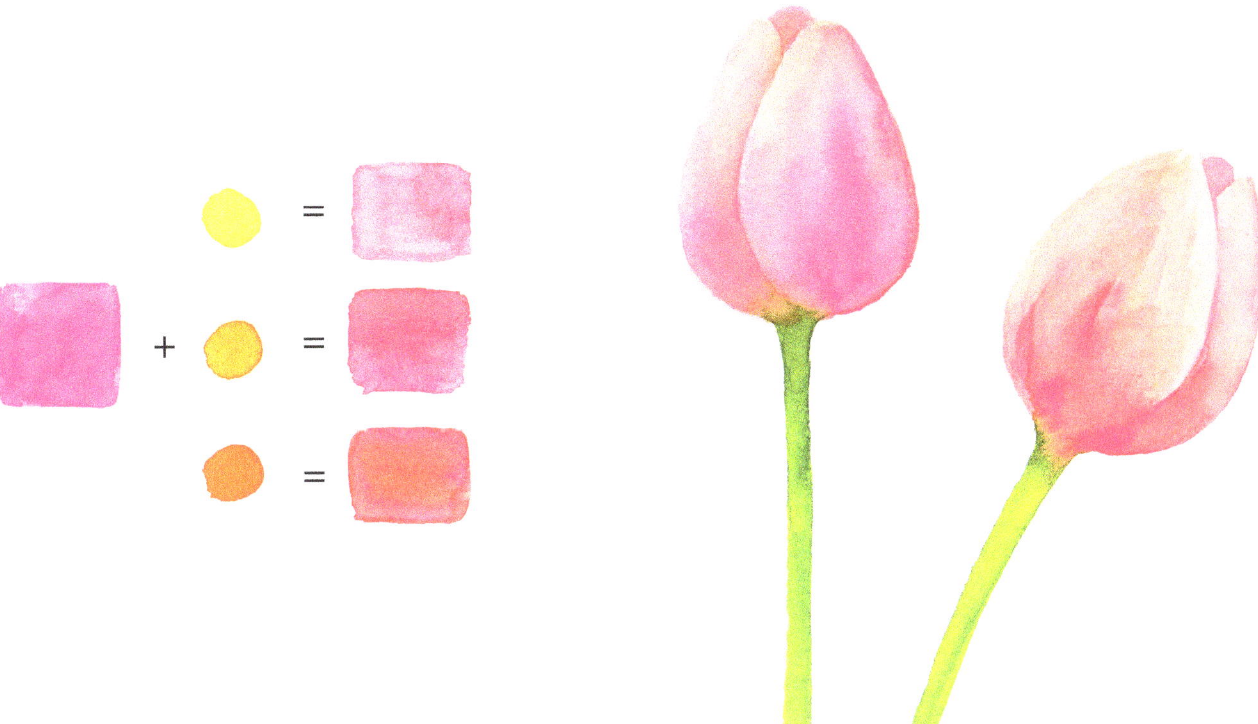

To make a warm pink, I'll mix pink with small amounts of yellow, golden yellow, and orange. This shade of pink is perfect for painting a warm tulip.

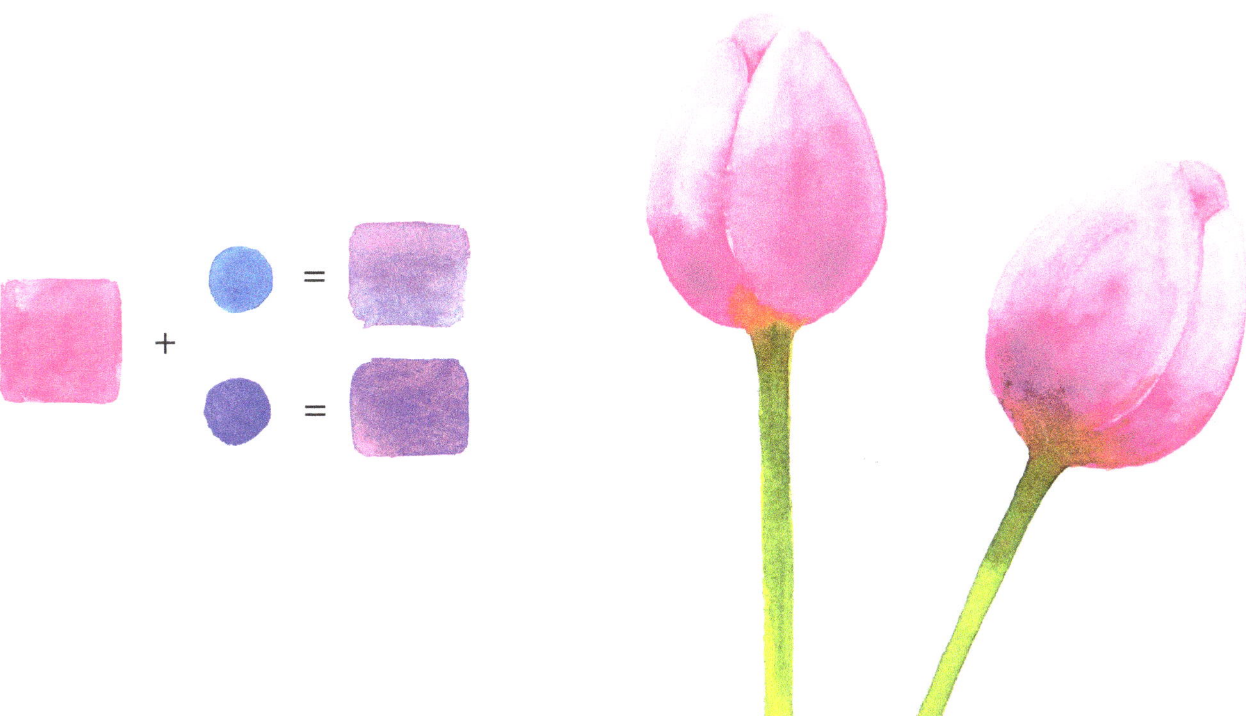

To make a cool pink, I'll mix pink with small amounts of blue or violet. This creates a cool tulip.

4. Mixing Neutral Colors

Beginners often have difficulty painting white flowers. To paint white flowers, gray is often used. You can create a variety of shades of gray, depending on what colors are added to it. Mixing tones such as brown or beige results in warm grays. Mixing them with blue or purple produces cool shades. Using assorted shades of gray, both warm and cool, makes a painting look more interesting.

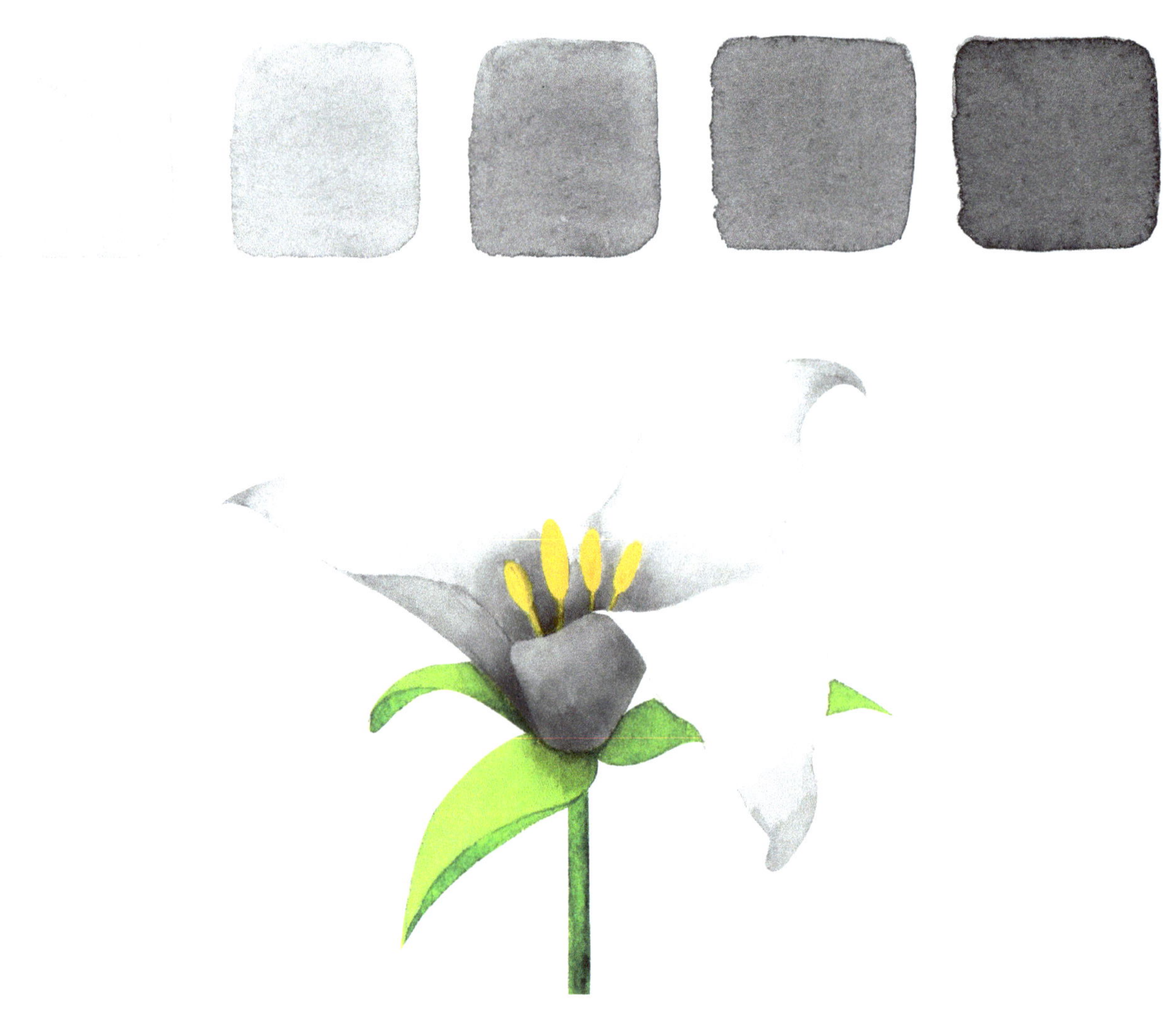

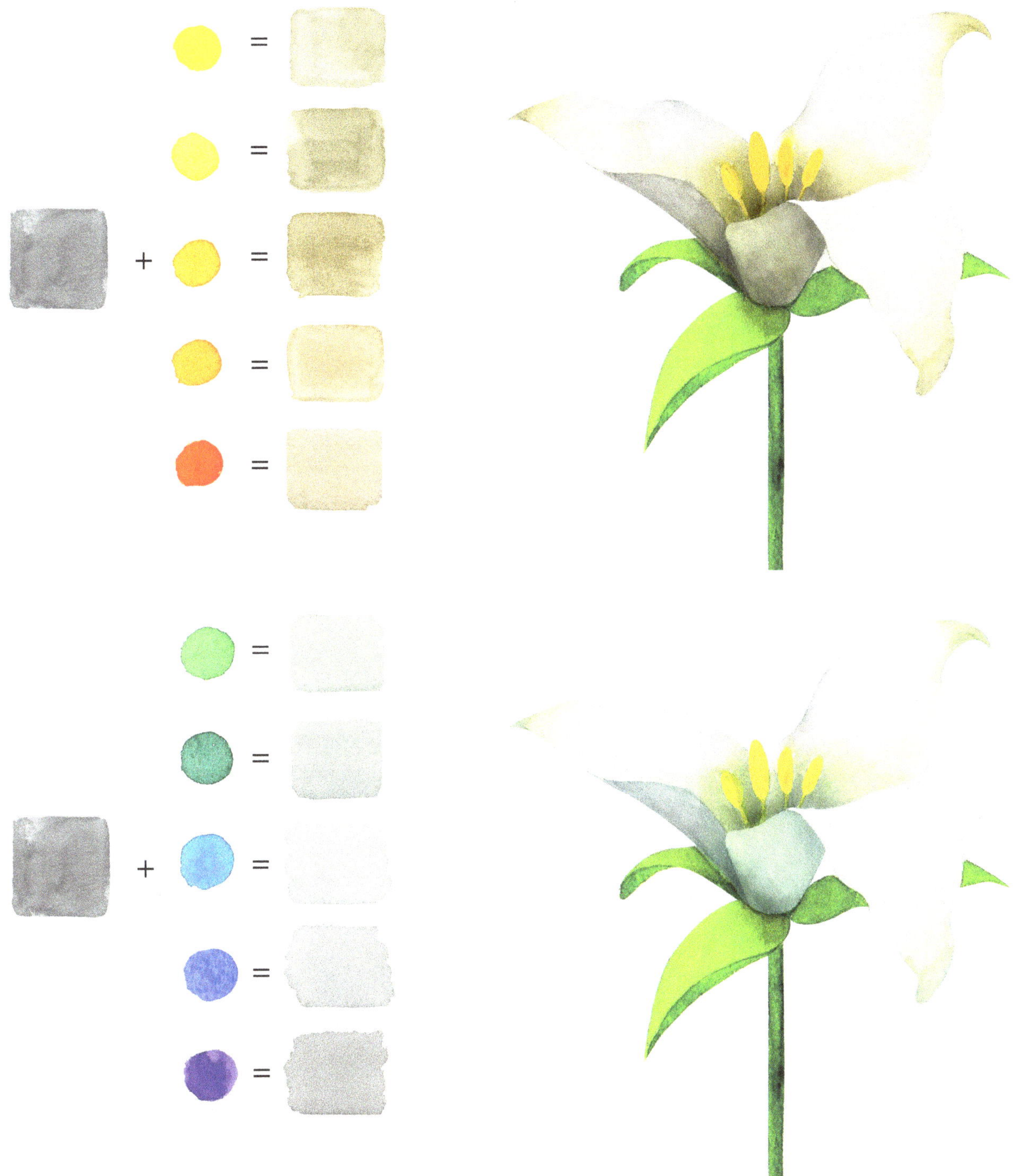

Compare the flowers shaded with gray made from pure black (left) to those shaded with warm (top) and cool tones of gray (bottom). Notice the variation in the tones and colors. One is not better or worse than the others, but each evokes a unique feeling and appeal.

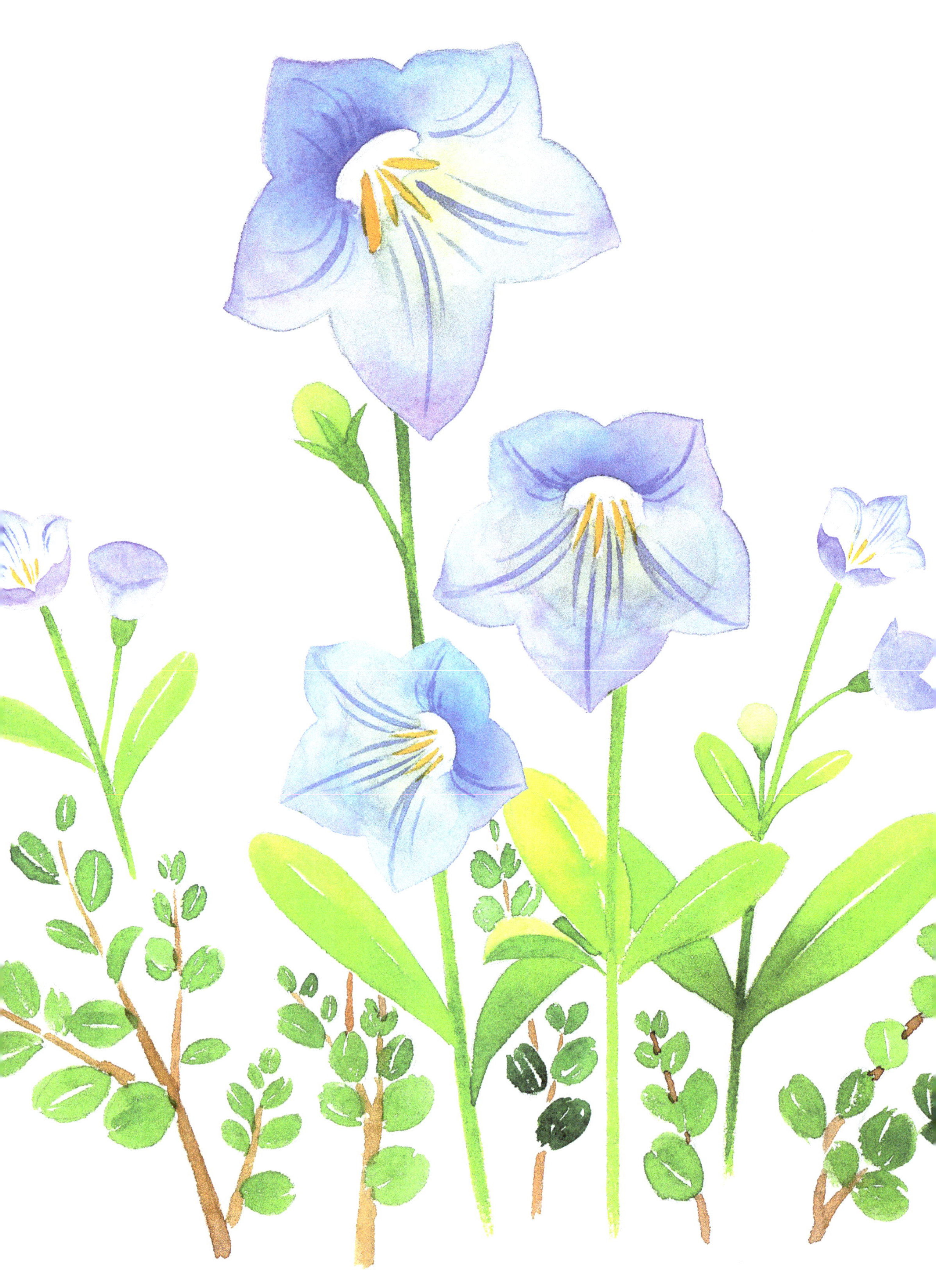

4

Simple Flowers

You're probably excited about drawing and painting flowers with your new sketching and watercolor skills. In this chapter, we'll start with simple flowers with basic forms: cosmos, lily, balloon flower, and hibiscus. You'll learn how flowers are expressed differently depending on the angle, how to color them, and what kind of moods flowers can create when they're in different groupings and perspectives.

Cosmos

The cosmos has a simple shape, but the number of petals makes it look complicated. However, the flower's balanced form makes it easy for beginners to draw and paint.

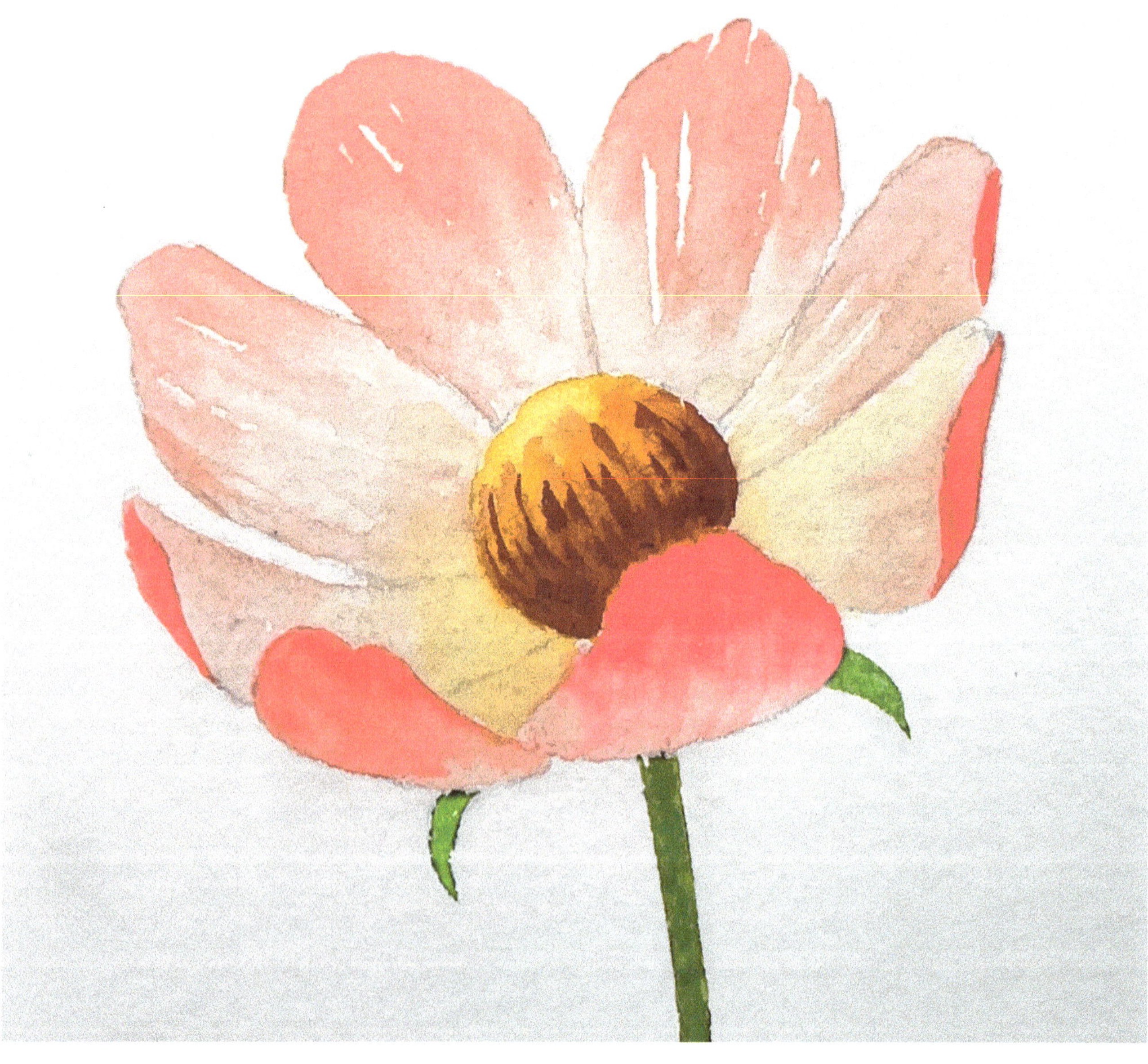

SKETCH THE FLOWERS

You'll learn how to sketch a cosmos in four different angles using the three-step method.

Angle A

1. Draw a long, horizontal oval and draw a guideline through the center. Draw a small circle just below the guideline of the larger oval. Draw the stem, creating a line slightly slanting to the right.

2. Draw eight guidelines radiating from the center circle to mark the positions of the flower petals. Use the guidelines to draw each flower petal. Notice that some petals are curved, and some curve so much that the reverse side of the petal shows.

3. Draw a detailed outline of petals, creating some with folded tips that show the reverse side. Add some thickness to the stem and draw a sepal to make a complete cosmos. Erase the guidelines.

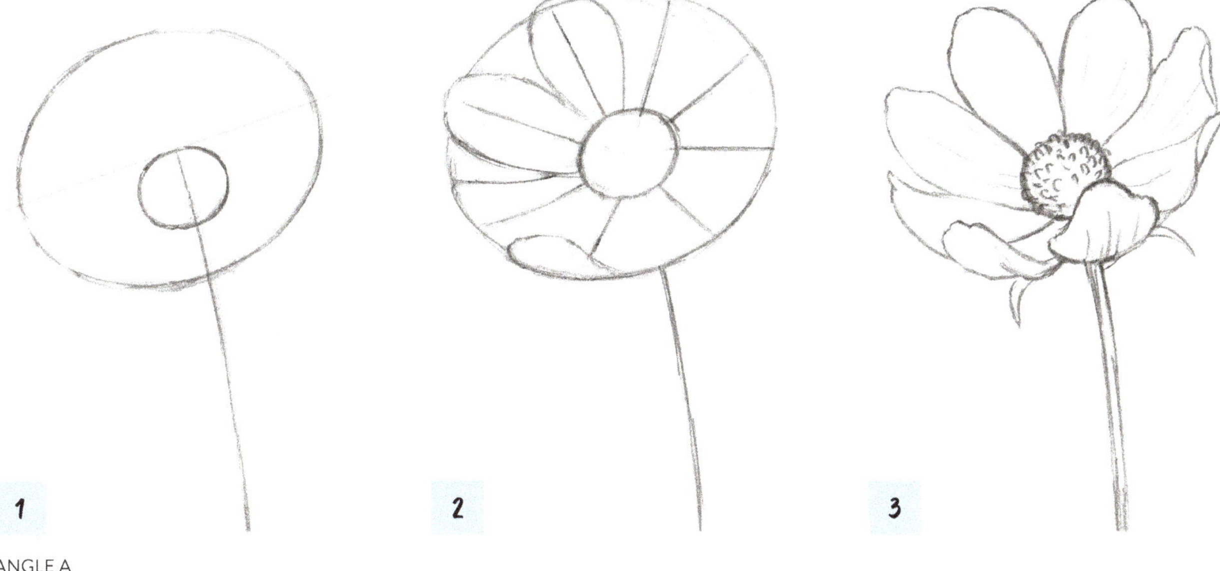

ANGLE A

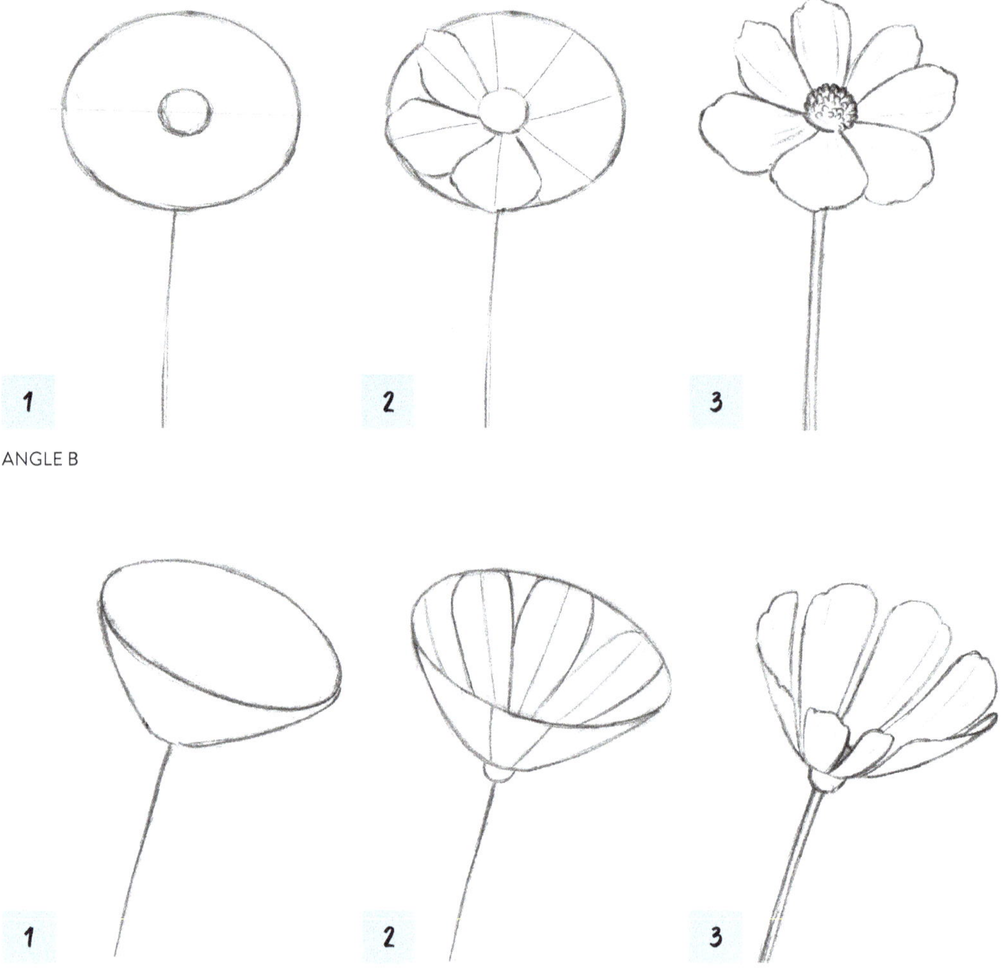

Angle B

Draw the flower using the three-step method following Angle A, steps 1 to 3. For this flower, draw seven petals. While these petals are flat, notice that some overlap.

Angle C

1 Draw a horizontal oval and add a cone. Draw a stem slightly slanted toward the left.

2 Following the shape of the cone, draw six guidelines to mark the positions of flower petals. Use each guideline to draw the flower petals. Draw a sepal at the bottom of the cone.

3 Add details to the shape of the flower petals. Make the tops of the petals a little uneven, and add lines to denote creases and emphasize the petals' curves. Add thickness to the stem. Erase the guidelines.

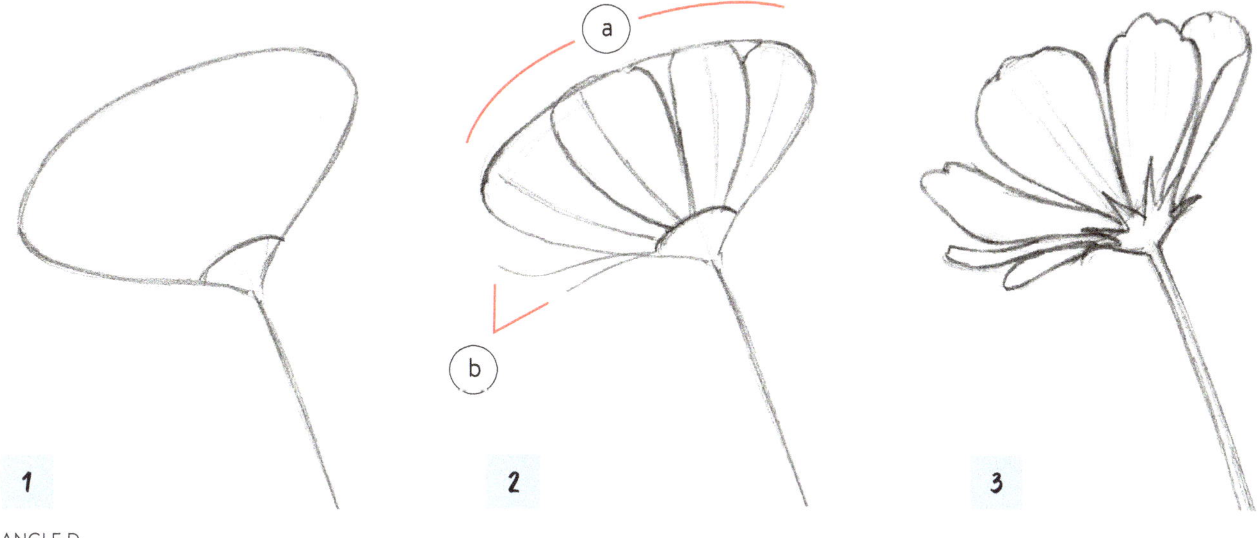

ANGLE D

Angle D

1 Draw a curved cone shape. Unlike the cone in Angle C, which is three-dimensional, this one is flat. Draw a line slanted to the right for the stem.

2 Draw four guidelines for the center flower petals (a). Draw two more guidelines for petals that will be outside the cone shape (b).

3 Add details to the flower petals, again making the tips of the petals uneven and adding crease lines. Create a spiky sepal at the bottom of the cone. Add thickness to the stem and erase the guidelines.

PAINT THE FLOWERS

Angle A

Using different colors on the front and back sides of petals gives flowers dimension and makes them come to life. In this section, you'll learn how to use color effectively to differentiate the front and back sides of flower petals.

1 Sketch the Angle A flower lightly on watercolor paper. Working wet-on-dry (see page 38), apply Level 4 density Shell Pink on the top portion of the flower petals. Instead of coloring the whole area, create streaked brush lines, leaving some portions of the petal uncolored (see "Gradient Techniques," page 41).

2 Thoroughly wash the brush and absorb any surplus water with a paper towel. Don't remove too much water, or the brush will be too dry; a gradient effect requires the brush to be somewhat wet. To create a gradient, drag the color down, moving the brush vertically. You should see the natural fading of the color. Leave some areas white.

3 Continue to use this gradient technique for all petals facing upward.

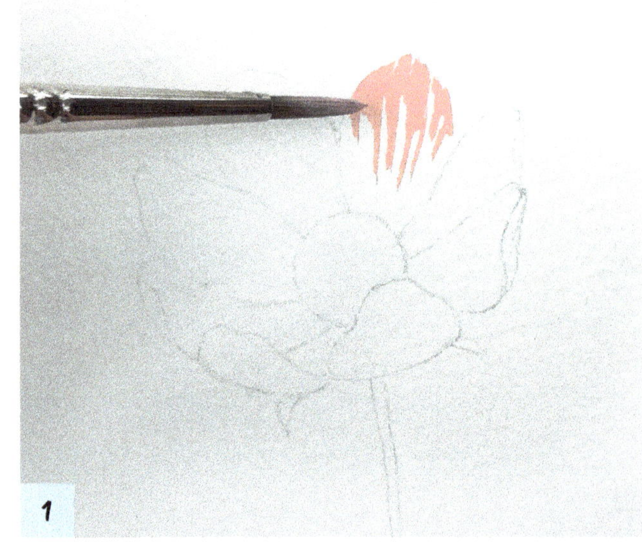
1

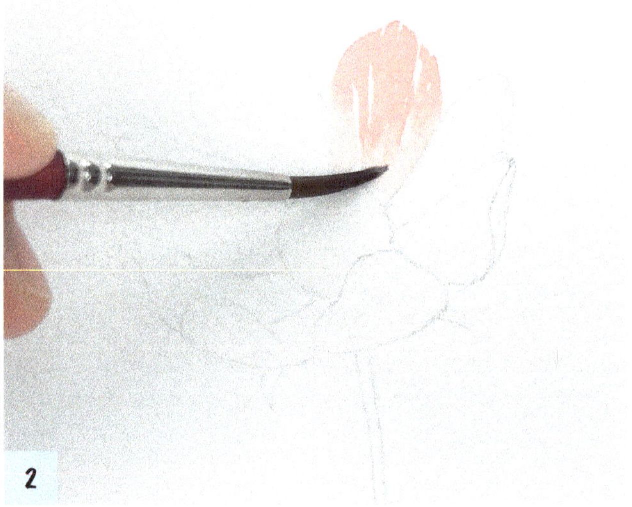
2

Before coloring, check the amount and color of the paint on the brush on a scrap of watercolor paper.

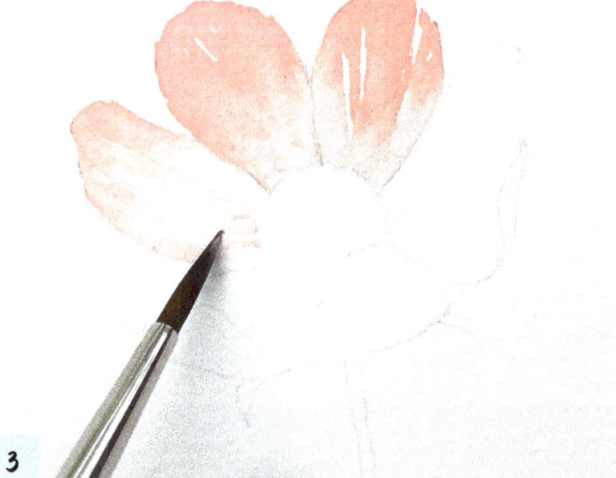
3

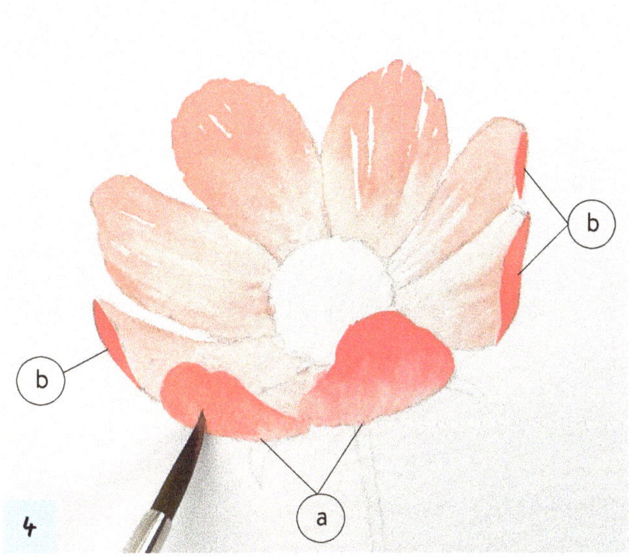

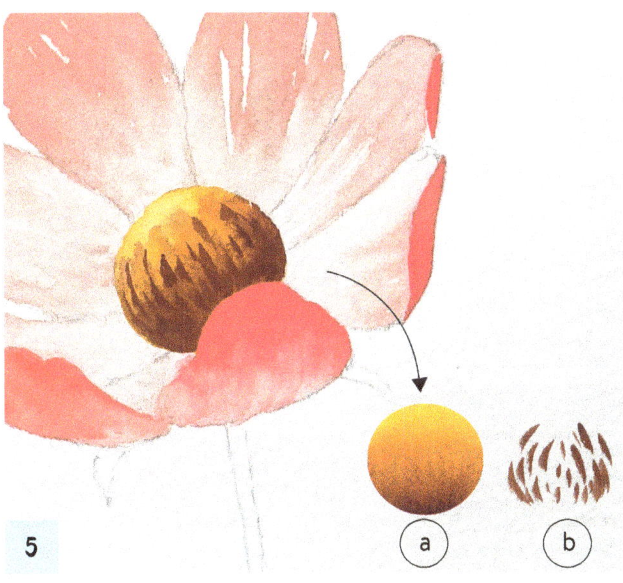

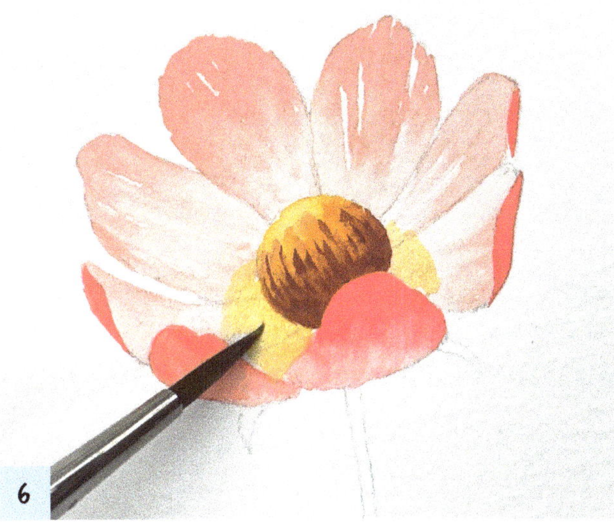

4 For the back side of the flower petals, use a darker pink to distinguish them from the front side. Create a dark pink color by mixing these shades: Opera Pink (vivid, medium pink), Shell Pink (light peach-pink), and orange, in a 4:3:2 ratio. Using Level 5 density color, create a gradient for the largest reversed flower petals (a). Apply the color at the top of the petals, moving it down so it gradually becomes lighter toward the bottom. Apply Level 5 density dark pink on the other reversed petals (b) without creating a gradient.

5 Apply Level 5 density Permanent Yellow Light in the upper half of the circle and apply Level 3 density Light Red to the other half of the circle to make a gradient (see page 41). Before the color dries, add Level 5 density Light Red on the bottom edge of the circle (a). When the main color of the stamen is completely dry, use Level 5 density Light Red to fill the stamen, using short, random brushstrokes (b).

6 Glaze the area around the stamen using Level 1 density Permanent Yellow Light (see "Glazing Technique," page 45). Use the brush to blend the color out so there's no definitive edge. Adding yellow to this area creates a warm mood.

7 Use Level 4 density Hooker's Green on the stem and sepals to complete the flower (see the finished image, page 65).

Angle B

Sketch the Angle B flower lightly on watercolor paper. For the Angle B flower, the petals are flat and only show the front side. Here, you'll learn how to shade two petals that overlap.

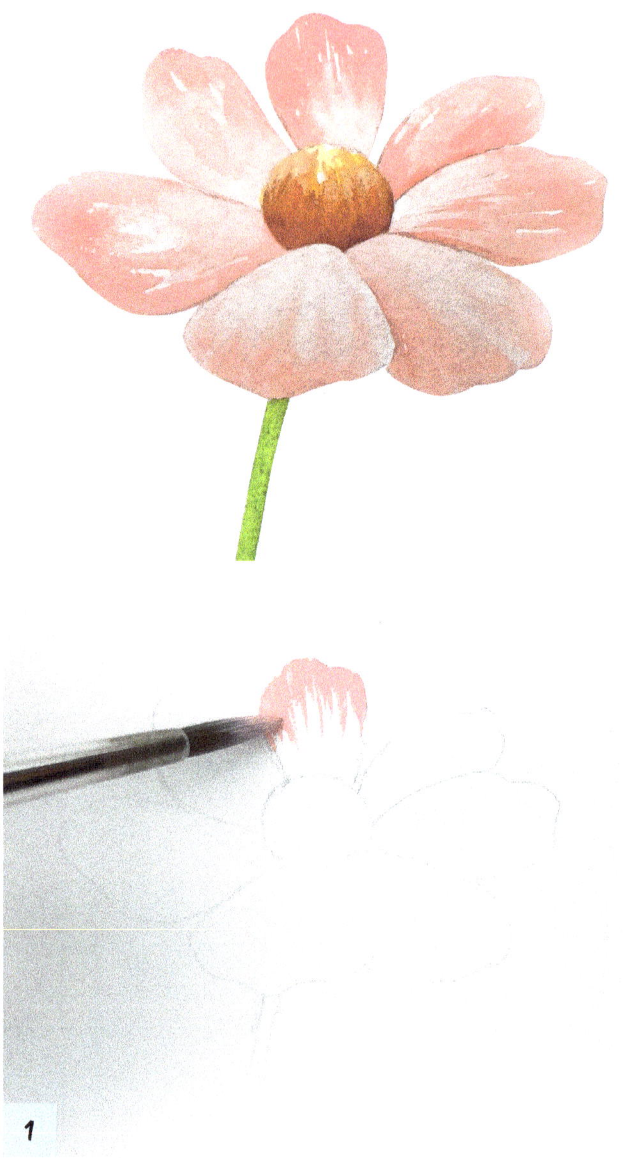

1 The technique for coloring these petals is similar to the one used for creating the gradient for the Angle A flower. Working wet-on-dry, apply Level 4 density Shell Pink on the top half of petal. Create the same streaked effect as before, leaving some parts of the petal uncolored.

2 Thoroughly wash the brush and absorb any excess water using a paper towel. As before, don't remove too much water. Drag the color down by moving the brush vertically, fading the color toward the bottom.

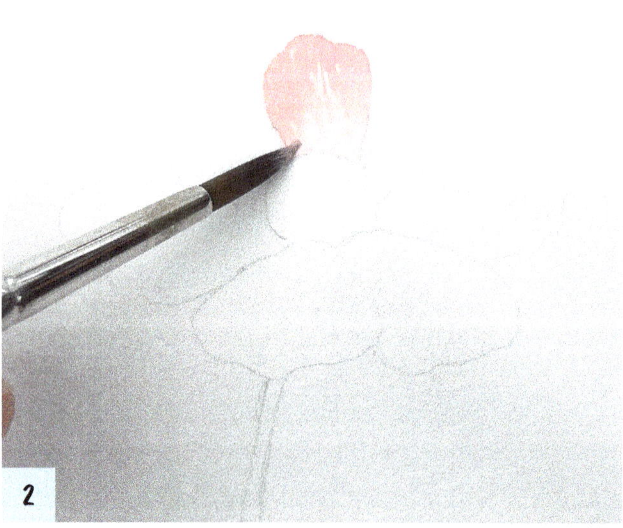

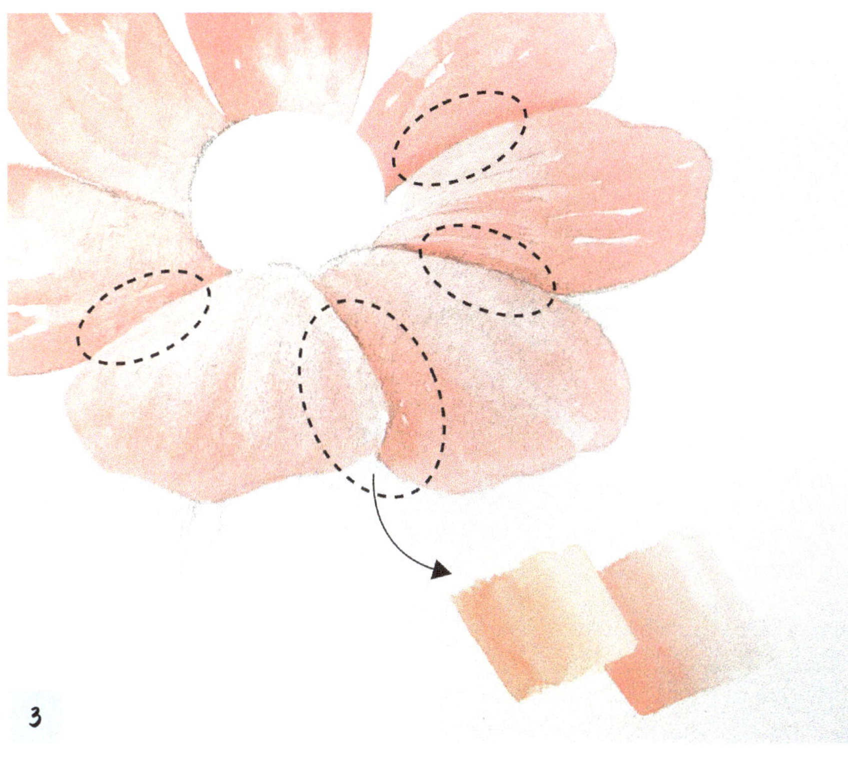

3

3 Notice where the petals overlap. Paint the top petal with Level 1 density Shell Pink, and paint the overlapped area on the bottom petal with Level 4 density Shell Pink. Refer to the gradient color swatch to see the differences in the values of the colors.

4 Color the stem using Level 4 density Hooker's Green.

While painting, the watercolor paper doesn't always have to face the same direction. Move the paper if needed to make it easier and more comfortable to create the brushstrokes.

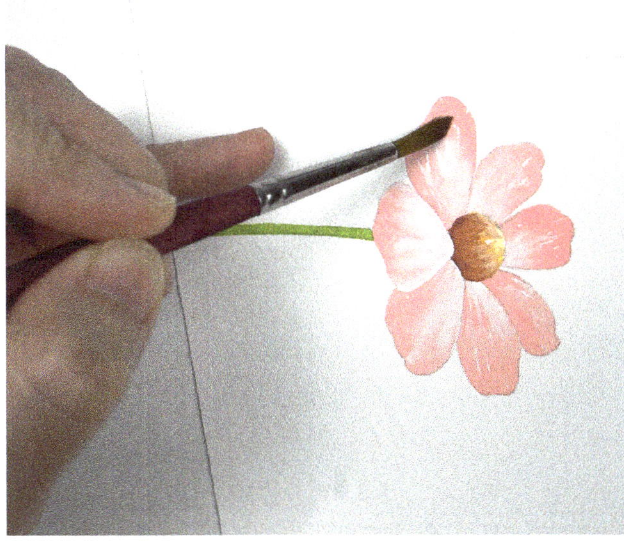

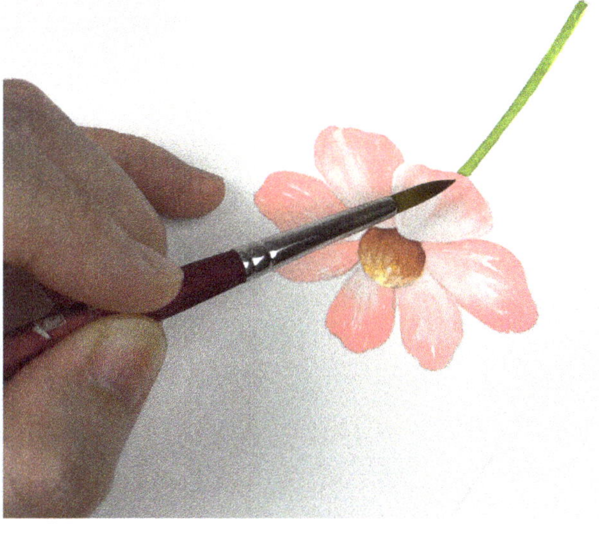

Angles C and D

Sketch the Angle C and D flowers lightly on watercolor paper. Angles C and D show more of the backs of the petals, but the techniques are similar to what you've learned in Angles A and B. After painting the Angle C cosmos, try painting Angle D on your own.

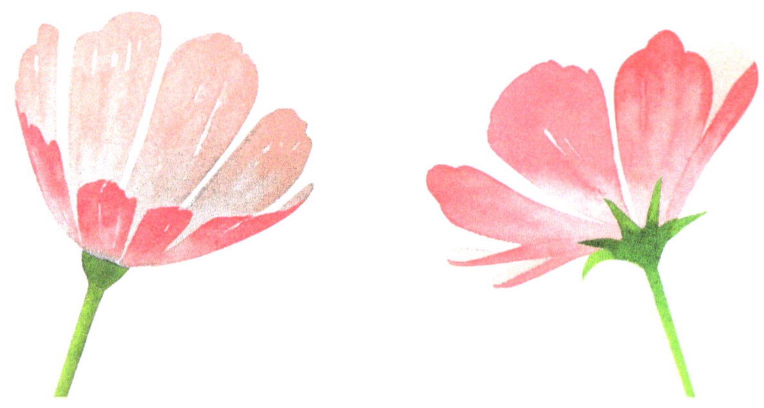

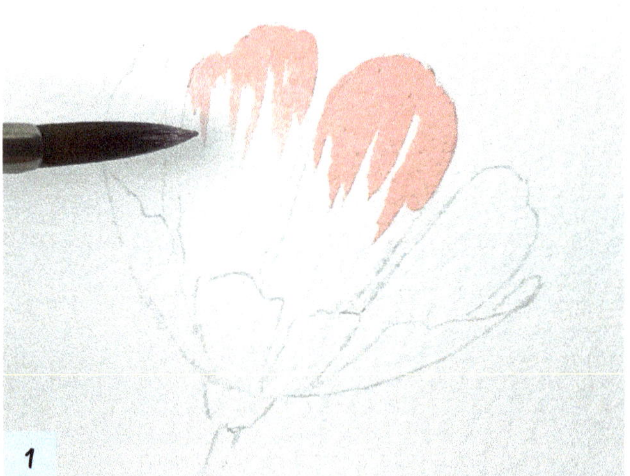

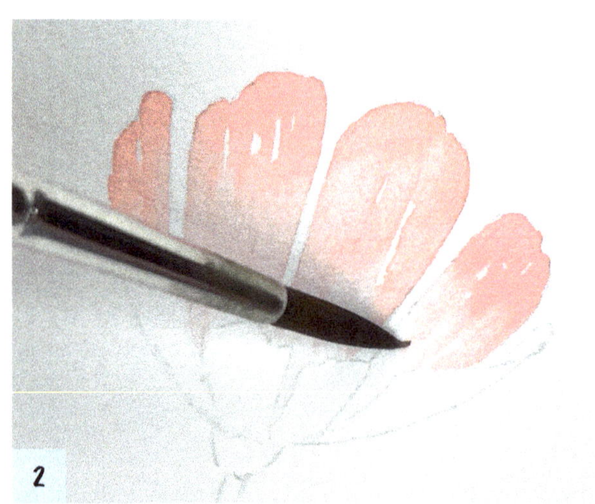

1 Color the top portion of the flower petal using Level 4 density Shell Pink, using the gradient technique. Once you get used to this method, you can color two or three petals together, as shown.

2 Thoroughly wash the brush and absorb most of the water with a paper towel, as before. Move the brush down the petal vertically, dragging the color to create the gradient.

3 Create the same dark pink shade as in Angle A, step 4. Color the top half of the backs of the flower petals using Level 4 density dark pink.

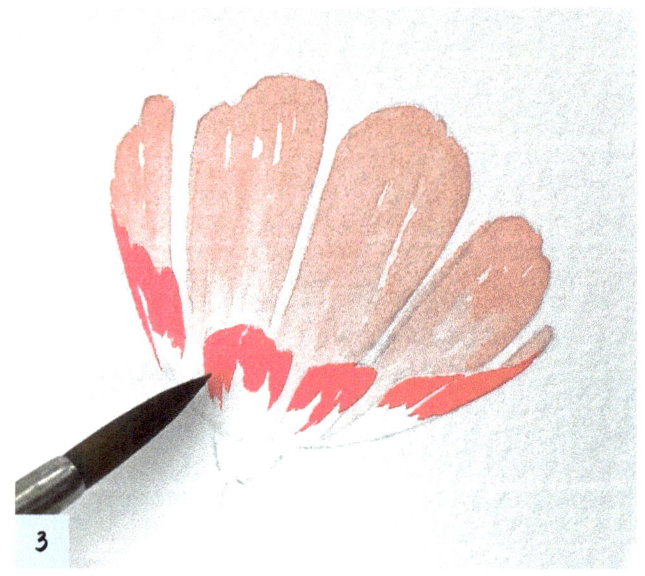

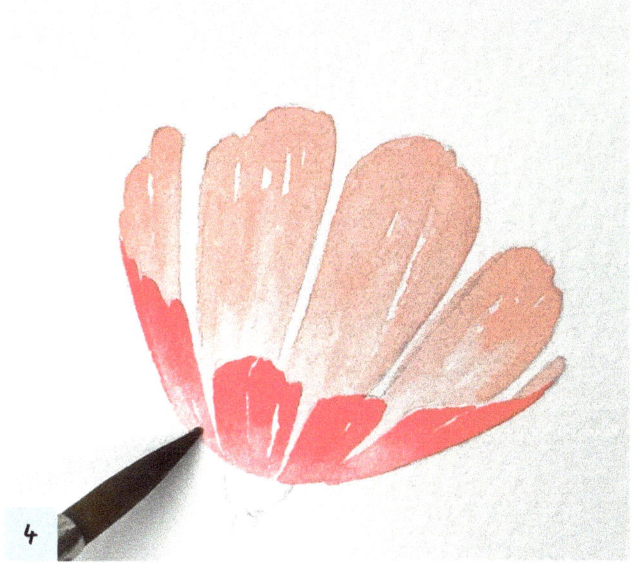

4

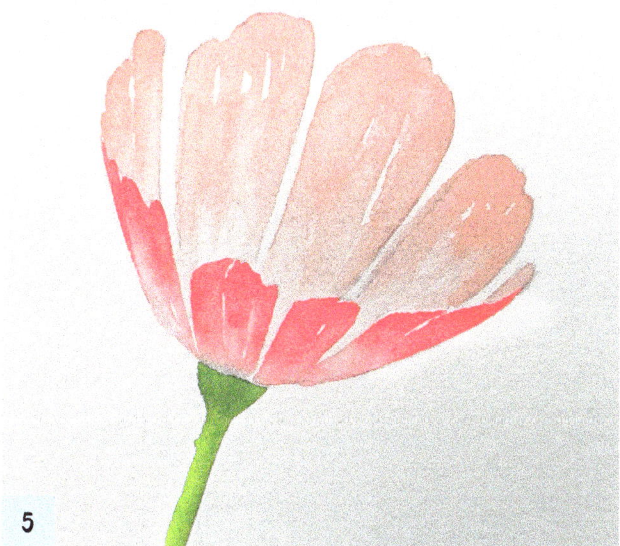

5

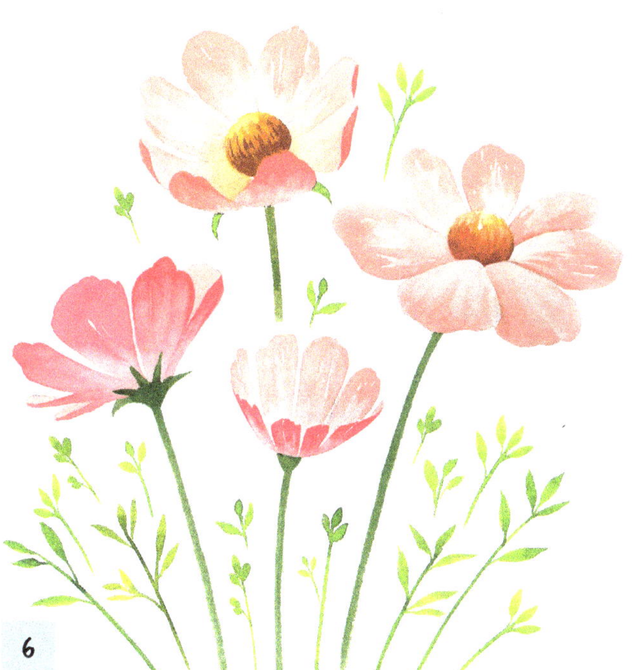

6

4 Wash and semi-dry the brush as before and brush the color from the top of the petal down, creating a gradient. The color should begin to fade as you go toward the bottom of the petal.

5 Color the stem and sepal using Level 4 density Hooker's Green (see the finished image on opposite page).

6 After you've practiced painting the cosmos from different angles, add small leaves to the background and paint them together.

You can easily paint leaves using only brushstrokes without creating any initial sketches. Instead of using one color, use Hooker's green, sap green, and olive green alternately (see "Brush Control," page 34).

Lily

For the lily, you'll paint a blossom that is slightly tilted, like the daffodil (see page 26). This best shows the characteristics of the trumpet shape, which is the basic form of the lily. Afterward, you'll draw the front side of the lily.

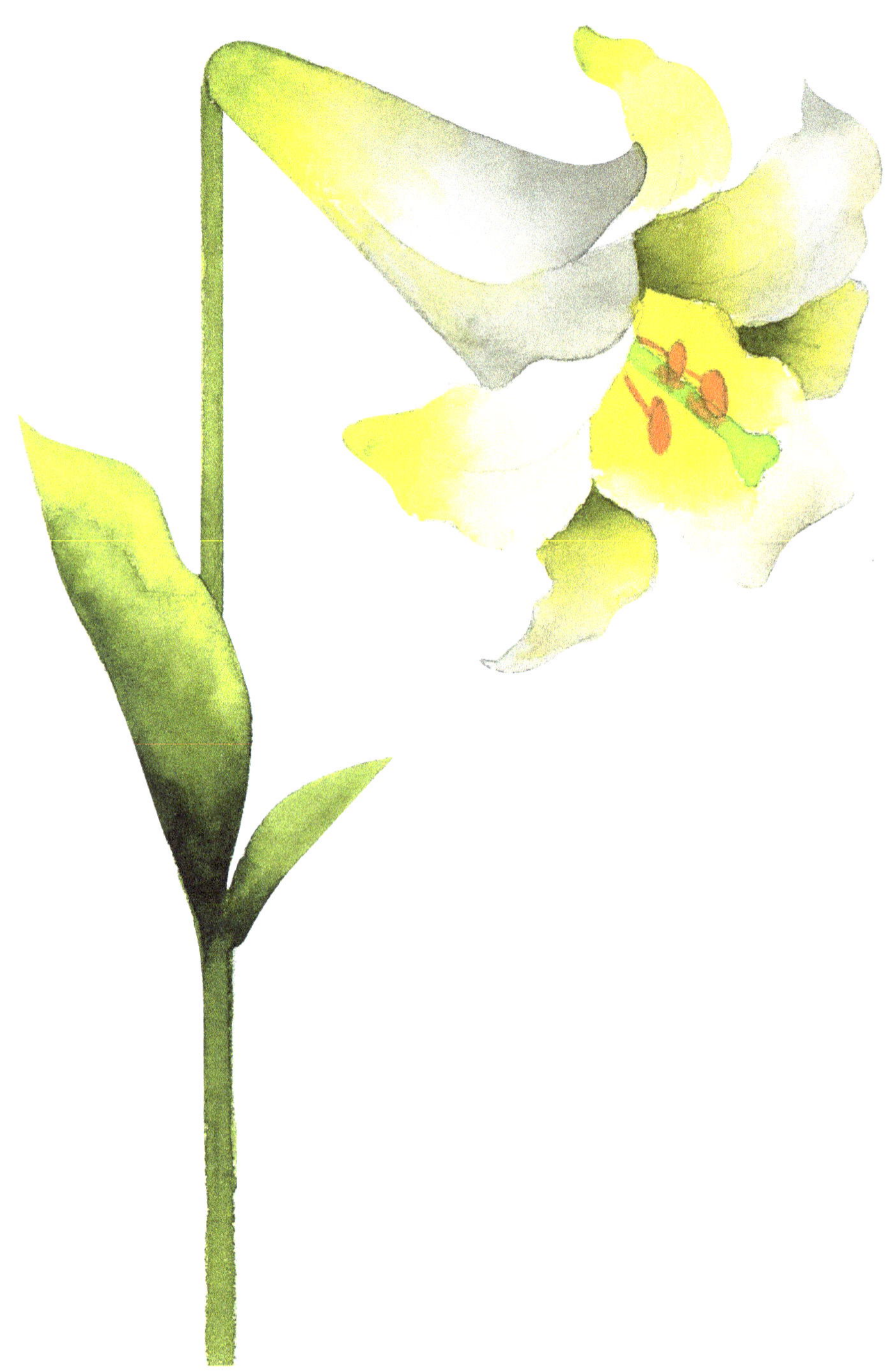

SKETCH THE FLOWERS

You'll learn how to sketch a lily in two different angles using the three-step method.

Angle A

1 The basic shape of a lily is a trumpet, so you'll first need to draw an oval with an elongated cone. Draw a smaller oval inside the larger one, and draw six guidelines to mark the positions of the flower petals. Note that the guidelines alternate between solid and dotted lines, and that they curve outward. Draw a slightly curved stem that ends at the base of the cone.

2 Draw flower petals using the solid guidelines first, making note of the angles of the petals and the way they curve. Draw petals on the dotted lines the same way. This creates layered petals, with the top layer overlapping the bottom layer.

3 Add details to the outlines of flower petals, creating wavy lines to indicate ruffles, and draw stamens. Next, add thickness to the stem and draw leaves to complete the lily. Erase the guidelines.

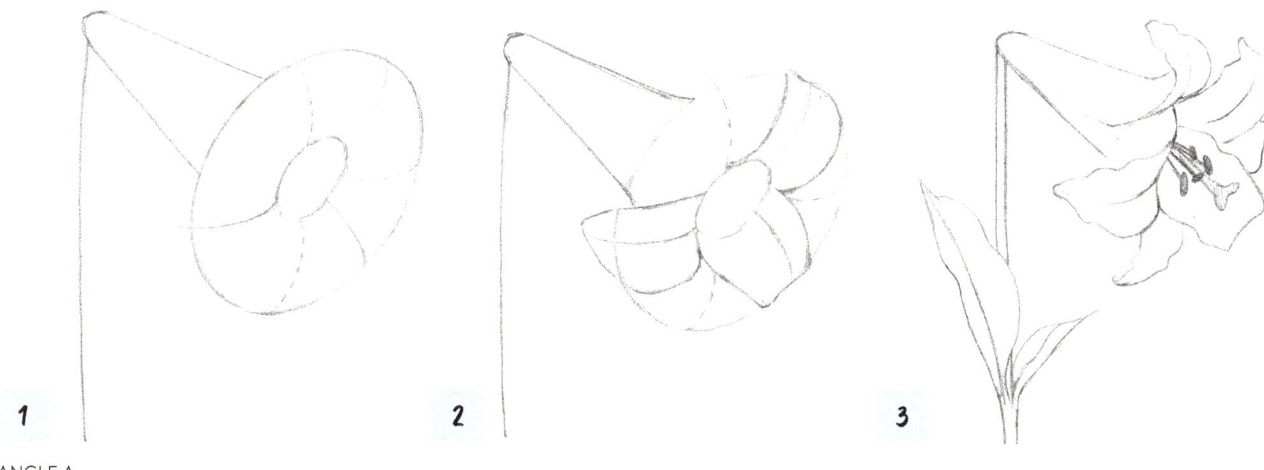

ANGLE A

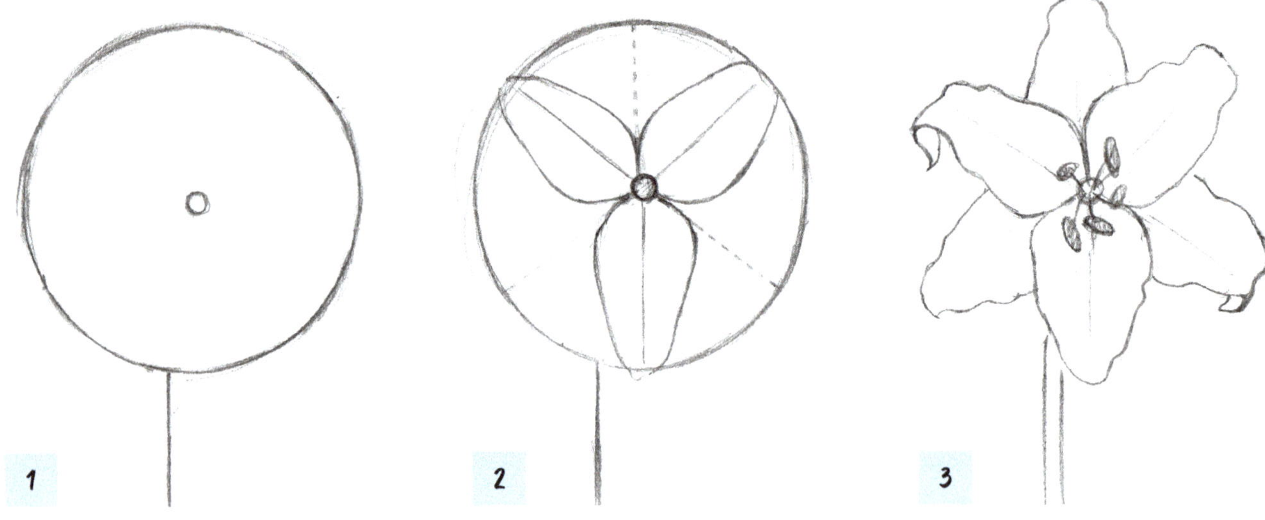

ANGLE B

Angle B

1. For a lily viewed from the front, use a circle for the base, and draw a straight line for the stem.
2. Draw six guidelines, alternating solid and dotted, to mark the positions of the flower petals. Draw flower petals around the solid lines first. Draw flower petals on the dotted lines; these will appear to be underneath the first layer of petals.
3. Add details to the outlines of the petals using wavy lines. Draw some flower petals with curved tips, indicating dimension. Draw small ovals to create stamens in the center of the flower. Add thickness to the stem.

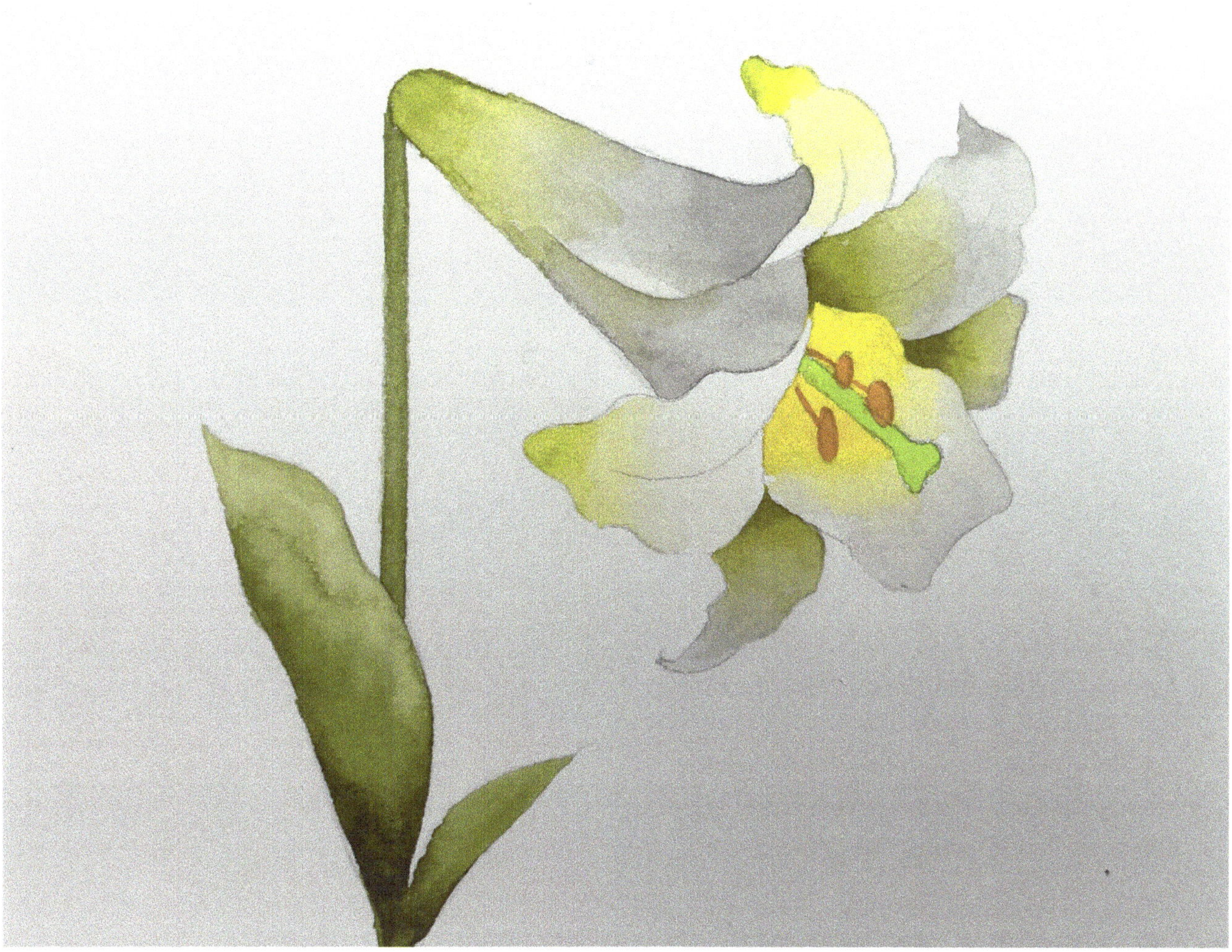

PAINT THE FLOWERS

Angle A

Creating white flowers isn't difficult when you mix subtle shades of gray and yellow that add vitality to the painting (see "Mixing Neutral Colors," page 52).

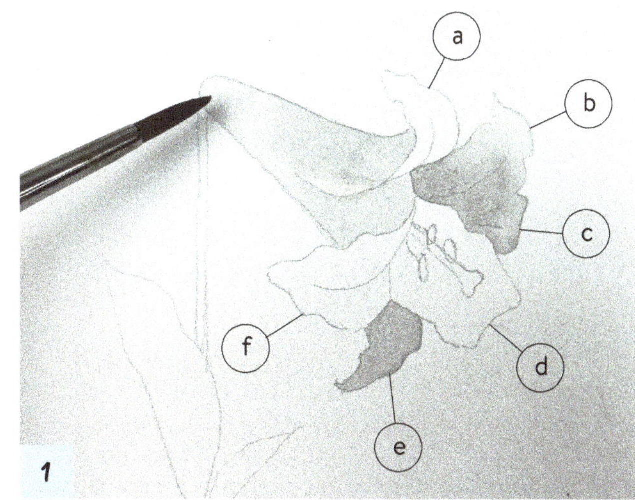

1 Sketch the Angle A flower lightly on watercolor paper. Working wet-on-dry, apply Level 2 density black to the cone and petals b, c, and e, using the flat wash technique (see page 40).

(continued)

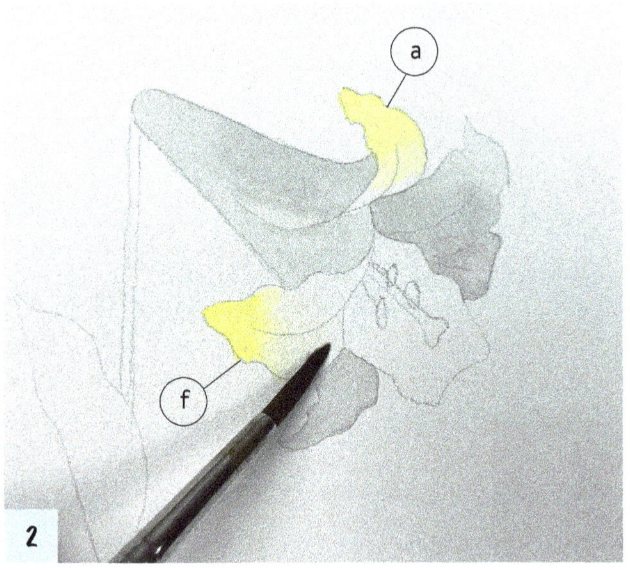

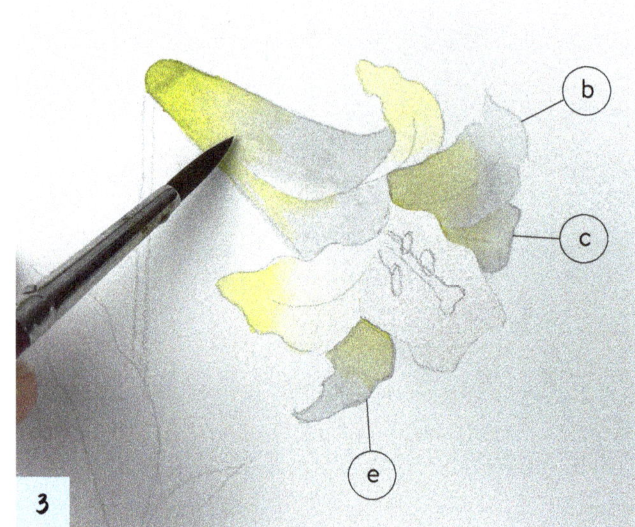

2 Working wet-on-dry, apply Level 3 density greenish-yellow to the tips of petals a and f. Apply the paint at the tips of the petals and use the gradient technique so the petals have a lighter shade near the center. (See "Wet-on-Dry Gradient," page 43.)

3 Use Level 3 density greenish-yellow to glaze petals b, c, and e, and the left side of the cone (see "Glazing Technique," page 45).

4 Still working wet-on-dry, apply Level 3 density Permanent Yellow Light around the stamen area, but don't paint the stigma, the tall spike in the middle of the flower. Paint Level 2 density black on the edge of the petals to create a two-color gradient with Permanent Yellow Light (see page 43, image B).

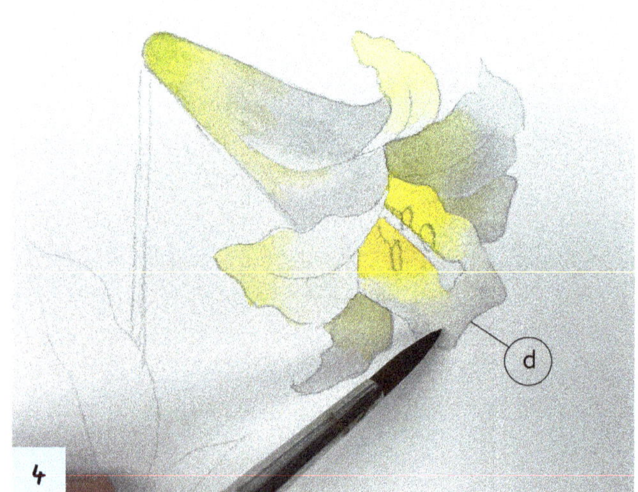

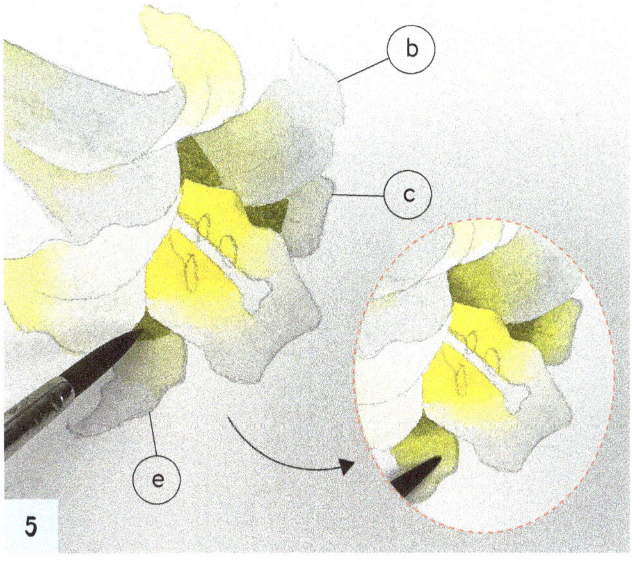

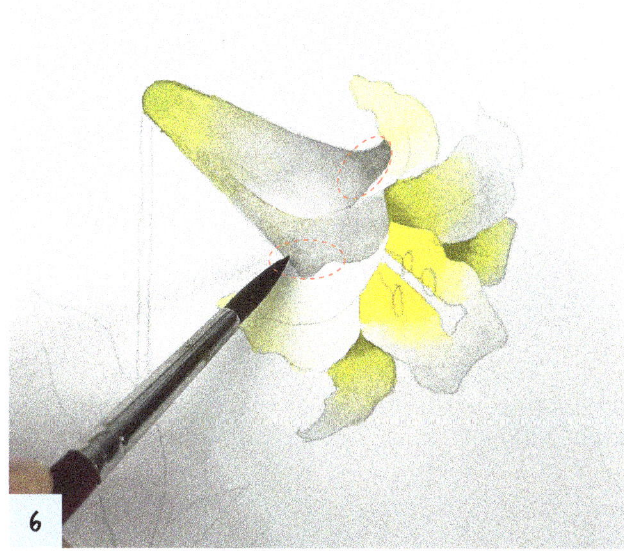

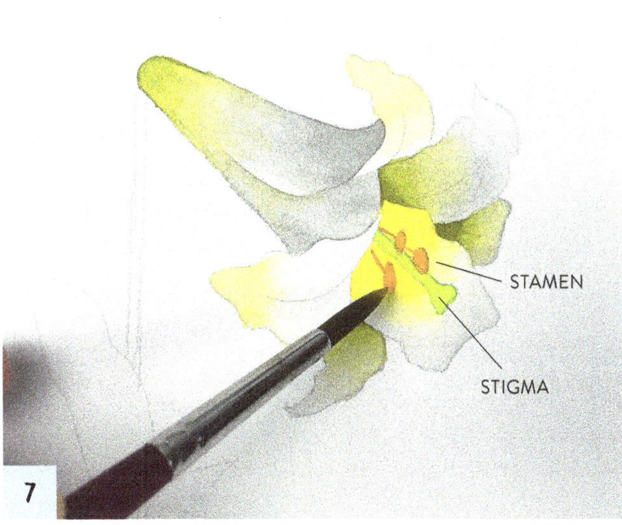

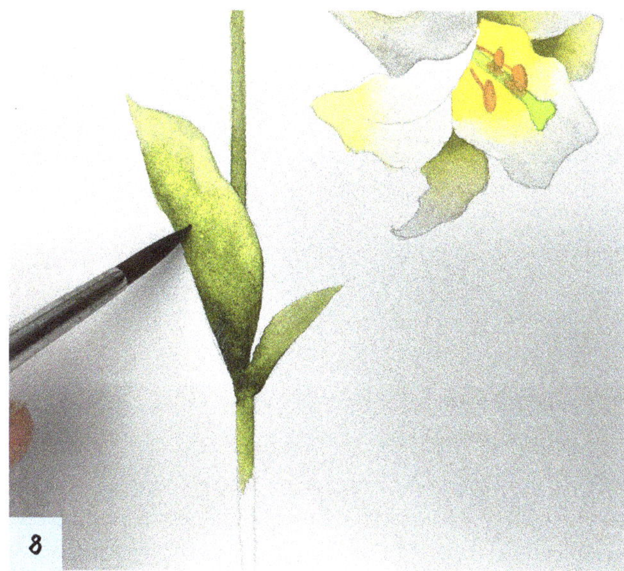

5 To emphasize the contrast between bright and dark, use Level 5 density greenish-yellow to add extra glazing in the interior of flower petals b, c, and e. As indicated in the close-up, use the brush to blend the edge of those areas; there shouldn't be a harsh line.

6 Using the same method as in the previous step, glaze the red dotted area with Level 3 density black to add shading.

7 Apply Level 5 density yellow-green on the stigma. Paint the stamens with Level 3 density yellow-orange.

8 Color the stem with Level 3 density olive green. Use the same color for the leaves. Create a gradient, with a lighter color at the top of the leaf and a darker shade toward the bottom.

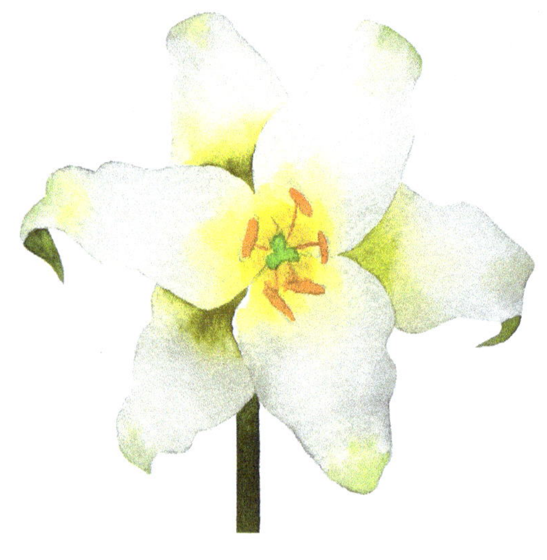

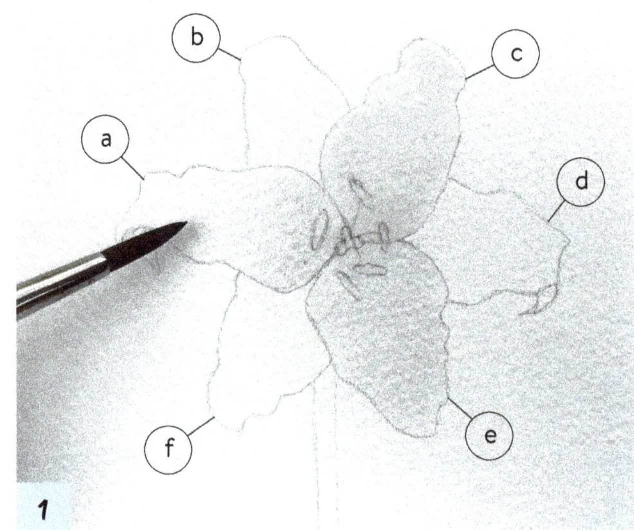

Angle B

You'll combine the wet-on-wet technique and the wet-on-dry technique to color the front of the lily using shades of yellow and green to indicate depth and dimension.

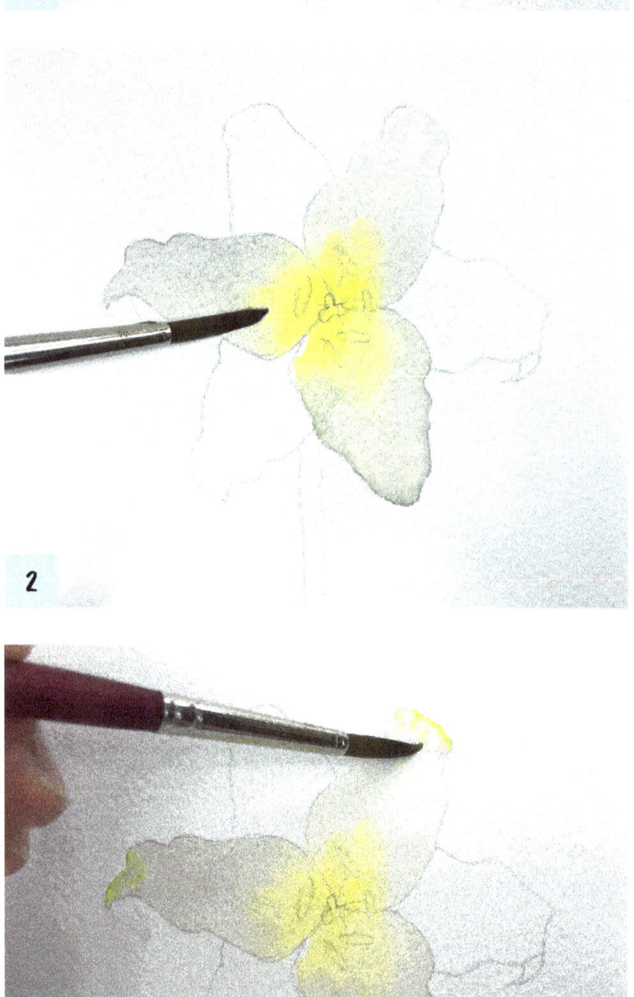

1 Sketch the Angle B flower lightly on watercolor paper. Working wet-on-wet (see page 36), brush water on petals a, c, and e, and apply Level 1 density black to the petals, using a flat wash (see page 40).

2 Before the water dries, apply Level 3 density Permanent Yellow Light in the center of the same three petals. Wash the brush, remove any excess water, and blend out the edge of the yellow area so there is no hard edge.

3 While the paper is still wet, apply Level 3 density yellow-green on the tip of the same petals. If the paper has dried, add the paint, wash and semi-dry the brush, and blend the edge of the area so there is no hard edge.

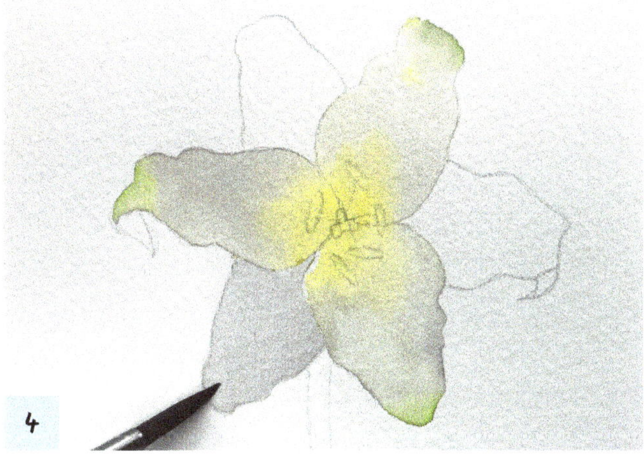

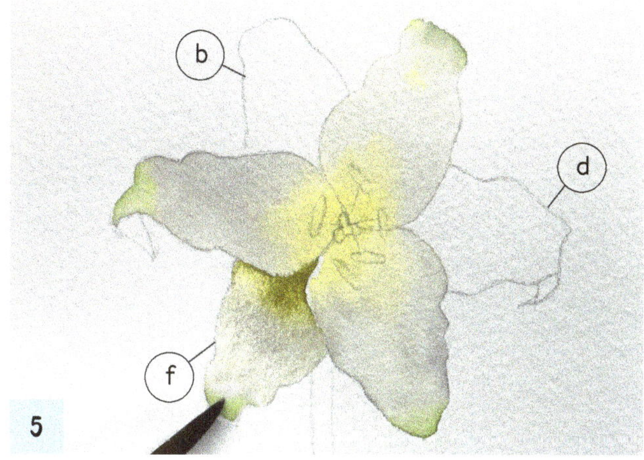

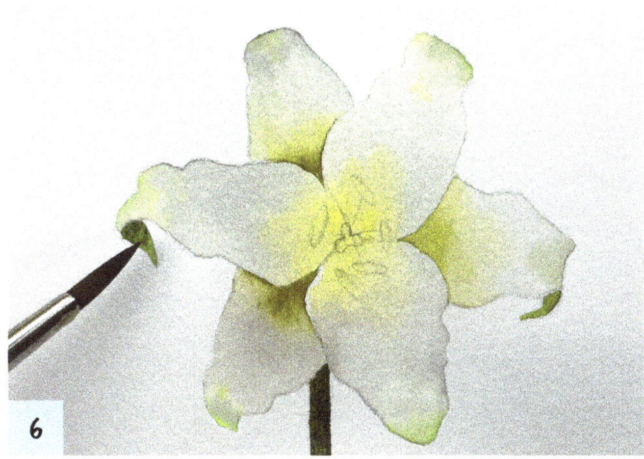

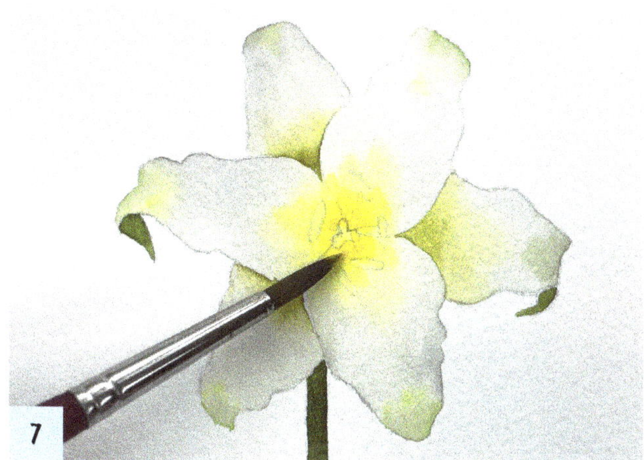

4 Working wet-on-dry (see page 38), apply Level 1 density black on petal f, using a flat wash (see page 40).

5 Before the paint dries, apply Level 4 density greenish-yellow on the portion of the petal closest to the center of the flower. Apply Level 3 density yellow-green on the outer portion of the petal. Repeat for flower petals b and d.

6 Apply Level 3 density olive green on the undersides of the petals and use the same color to paint the stem.

7 At this stage, the center of the flower looks flat because paint lightens as it dries. Before painting the stamens, shade the flower center by glazing it with Level 3 density Permanent Yellow Light.

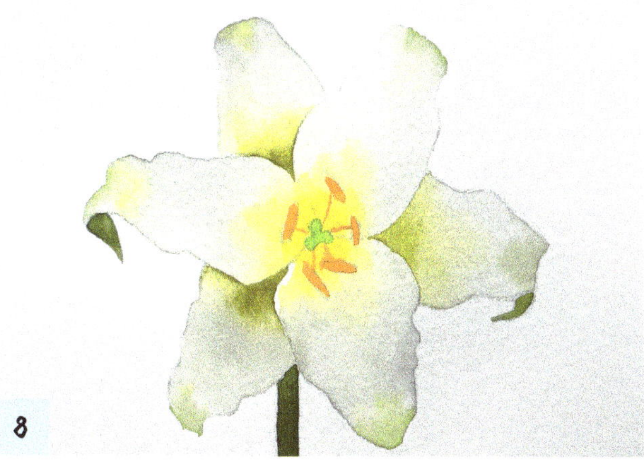

8 Paint the stamens with Level 5 density yellow-orange. Paint the stigma with Level 5 density yellow-green.

Balloon Flower

Balloon flowers have an interesting star shape. When drawing this flower, be mindful of the proportion of the shapes. The three-step sketching method makes it easy to render this attractive flower.

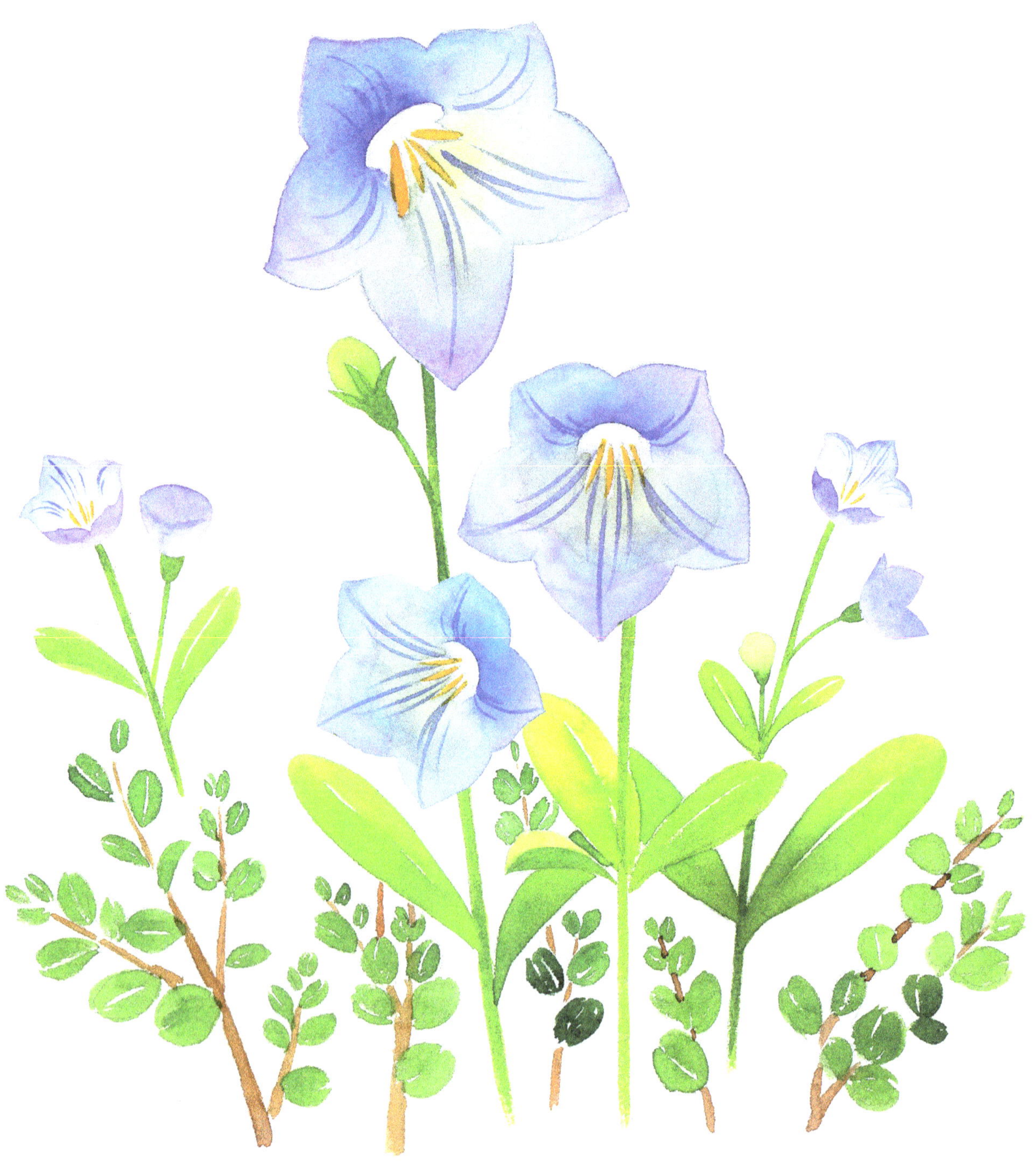

SKETCH THE FLOWERS

You'll learn how to sketch a balloon flower in four different angles using the three-step method.

Angle A

1. Draw a large circle with vertical and horizontal guidelines that bisect the circle evenly. Draw a smaller circle within the larger one using a dotted line, making it off center. Draw an off-center oval within the smaller circle. This forms the base for a flower angled to the right. Draw a line indicating the stem.

2. Draw five guidelines that radiate from the inner oval, noting how they curve outward. Create pointed, connected petals around the guidelines.

3. Draw stamens in the center of the flower and thicken the stem. Erase the circular guidelines but leave the five petal guidelines; these will be useful when coloring the flower petals.

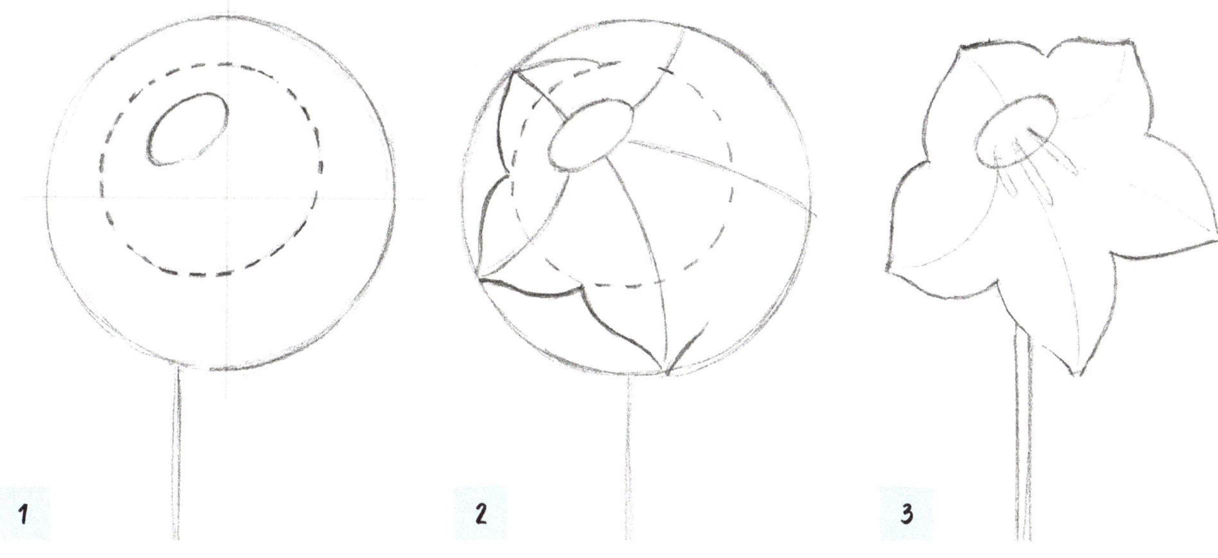

ANGLE A

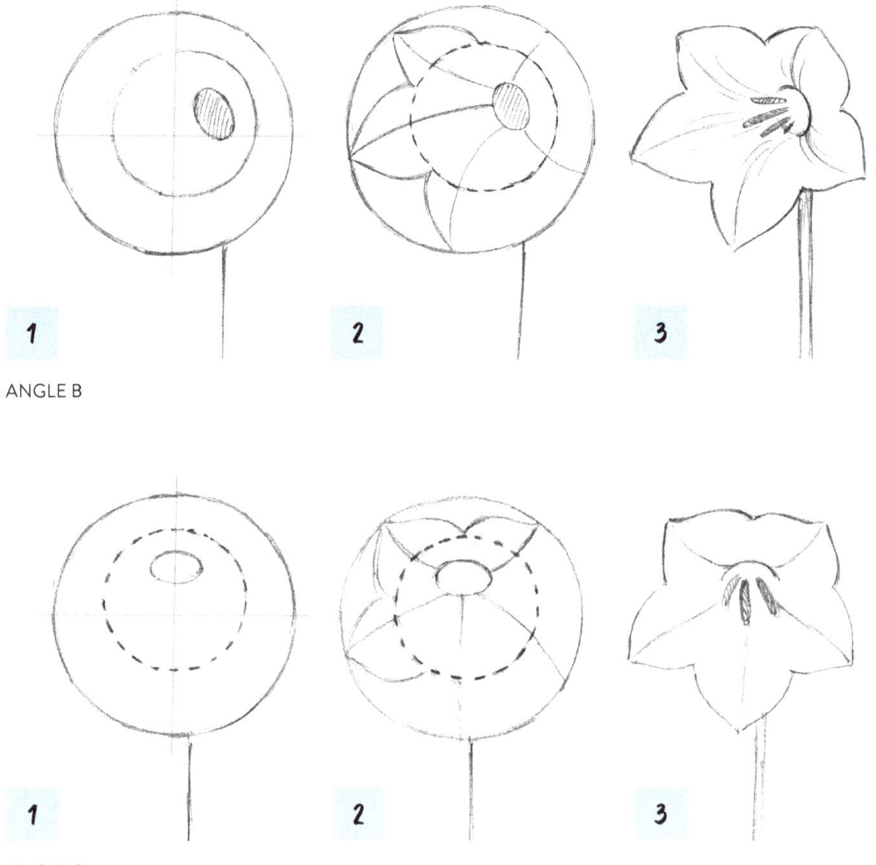

Angle B

1 Repeat Angle A, step 1 to create the flower, but this time flip the positioning of the circles, oval, and petal guidelines so the flower faces left. Draw a line indicating the stem.

2 Repeat Angle A, step 2 to create the five petal guidelines, and draw the curved, connected petals.

3 Draw stamens in the center of the flower and add thickness to the stem to complete the sketch. Erase the circular guidelines but, as before, don't erase the petal guidelines.

Angle C

1 For a front-facing flower, draw a large circle and add horizontal and vertical guidelines that bisect the circle evenly. Draw a smaller, slightly offset circle with a dotted line inside the larger one. Draw an oval inside the smaller circle, also making it offset. Draw a line to create a stem.

2 Draw five guidelines that radiate from the oval, noting how they curve. Draw the outlines of the pointed petals, connecting them.

3 Draw tiny elongated ovals to indicate stamens in the center of the flower. Thicken the stem. As before, erase the circular guidelines but leave the five petal guidelines.

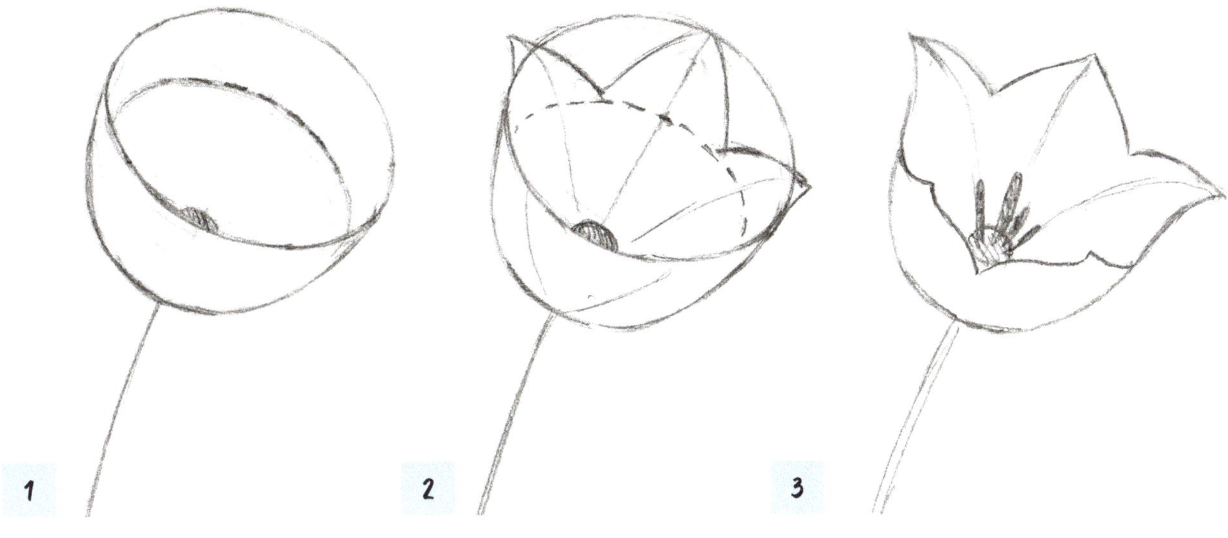

ANGLE D

Angle D

1. To sketch a flower facing upward and to the right, draw a basic cup shape. Start with an oval and add a curved line underneath. Draw a curved line underneath and parallel to the topmost oval line; this indicates volume. Draw a tiny mark at the bottom of the oval for the flower center. Add a stem by drawing a slightly curved line.
2. Draw five petal guidelines, noticing the direction of each curved line. Connect the outlines of the pointed flower petals.
3. Enlarge the flower center and add thickness to the stamens and the stem. Erase the circular guidelines but leave the flower petal guidelines.

PAINT THE FLOWERS

Angles A, B, and C

Practice changing colors in this lesson by using periwinkle, which is the combination of blue and violet. You'll learn to convey brightness and darkness by glazing areas with purple tones. The coloring methods used in Angles A, B, and C are all the same. Practice Angle A first, then move on to Angles B and C.

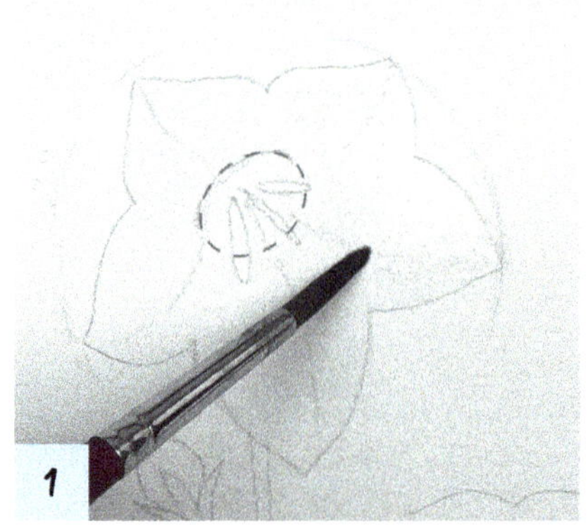

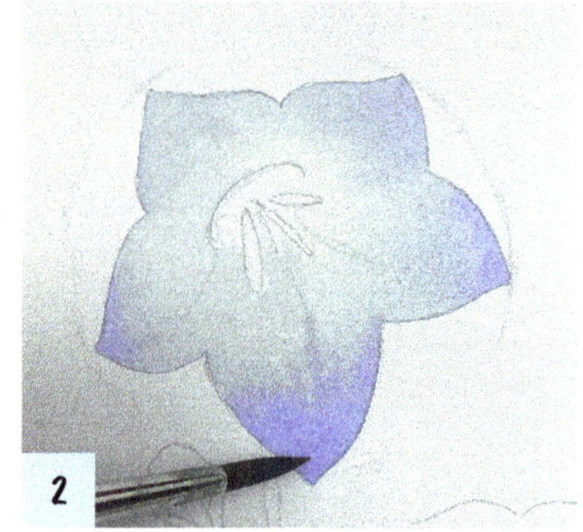

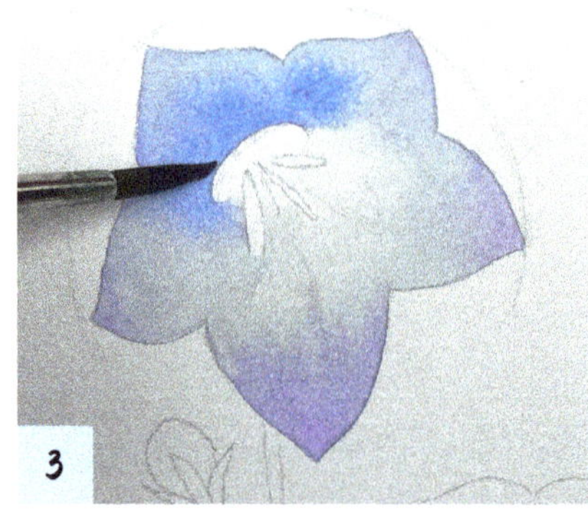

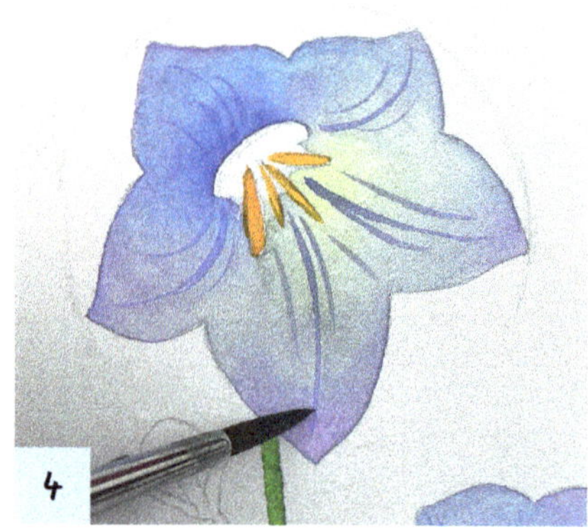

1 Sketch the Angle A , B, and C flowers lightly on watercolor paper. Working wet-on-wet (see page 36), brush water on the petals but leave the stamens and the center oval dry (indicated by the dotted line). Leave the center oval unpainted for now, and paint the stamens last.

2 Before the water dries, mix a vibrant pink (I used Opera Pink) and cobalt blue in an approximately 3:2 ratio to make a red-violet color. Apply Level 1 density paint on the petals, again avoiding the center oval. Mix the same colors in a Level 3 or 4 density and apply this shade on the edges of the petals.

3 Brush Level 4 density cobalt blue on the innermost part of the top petals, along the top of the oval center. This creates a shadow effect. Make sure the paint doesn't bleed into the center. The paper should still be wet enough at this stage to allow the colors to blend nicely.

4 While the paper is still wet, apply Level 1 density yellow-green paint to the area below the center oval. Allow the paint to dry. Paint the stamens with Permanent Yellow Deep (golden yellow). Create thin lines in the petals with Level 2 or 3 density cobalt blue, going from the center outward. Follow the curve of the individual petals, referring to the pencil drawing if necessary. Apply Level 5 density medium green on the stem.

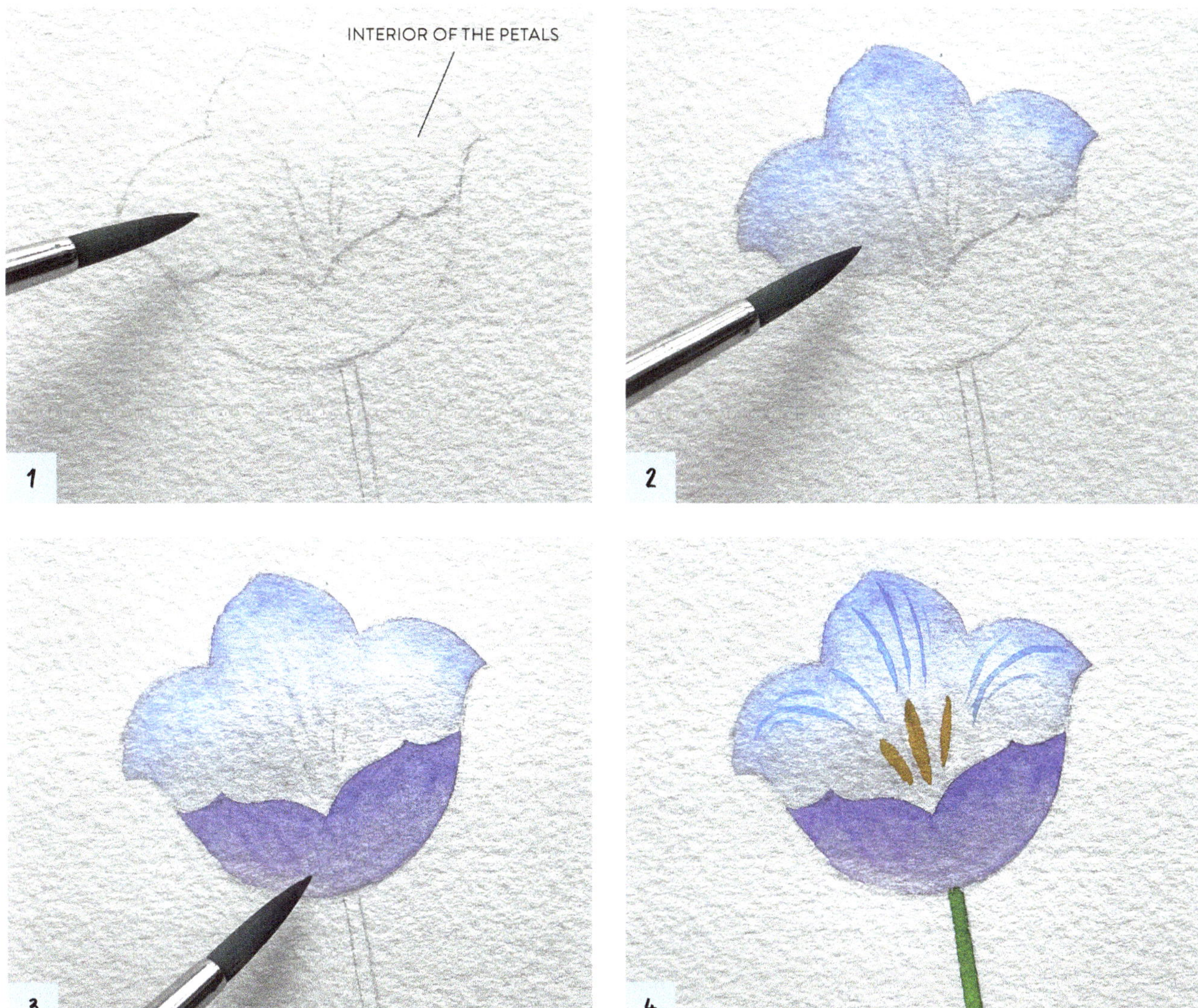

Angle D

1. Sketch the angle D flower lightly on watercolor paper. Working wet-on-wet, brush water on the interior of the petals only.
2. Before the water dries, apply Level 3 density cobalt blue on the edge of the interior petals and create a gradient. Allow the paint to dry.
3. Mix a vibrant pink (I used Opera Pink) and cobalt blue in an approximately 3:2 ratio to make a red-violet color. Apply Level 3 density paint on the upper edge of the outer petals. Working wet-on-dry, make a gradient.
4. Paint the stamens with Permanent Yellow Deep. Create thin lines in the petals with Level 2 or 3 density cobalt blue, going from the center outward. Apply Level 5 density medium green on the stem.

Hibiscus

The hibiscus is a beautiful tropical flower characterized by its protruding stamen. This is an excellent flower to sketch because it's easy to render from various angles.

SKETCH THE FLOWERS

You'll learn how to sketch the hibiscus in three different angles using the three-step method.

Angle A

1 For a front-facing flower, draw a large circle and create horizontal and vertical guidelines that evenly divide the circle. Draw a tiny circle at the intersection of the guidelines.

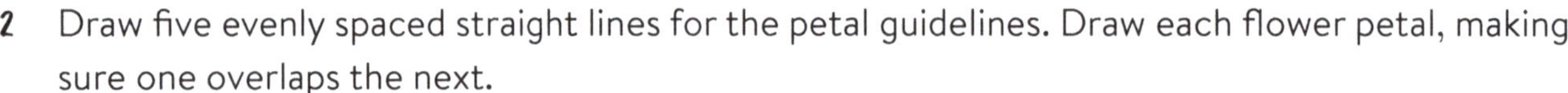

2 Draw five evenly spaced straight lines for the petal guidelines. Draw each flower petal, making sure one overlaps the next.

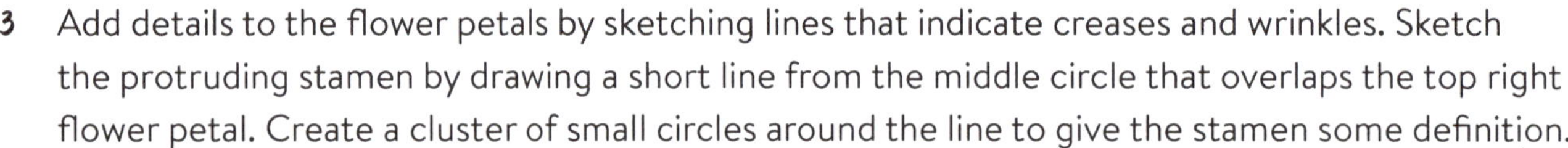

3 Add details to the flower petals by sketching lines that indicate creases and wrinkles. Sketch the protruding stamen by drawing a short line from the middle circle that overlaps the top right flower petal. Create a cluster of small circles around the line to give the stamen some definition.

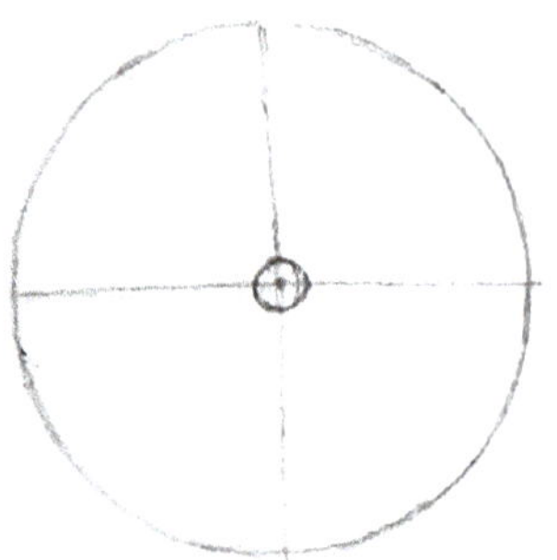

1

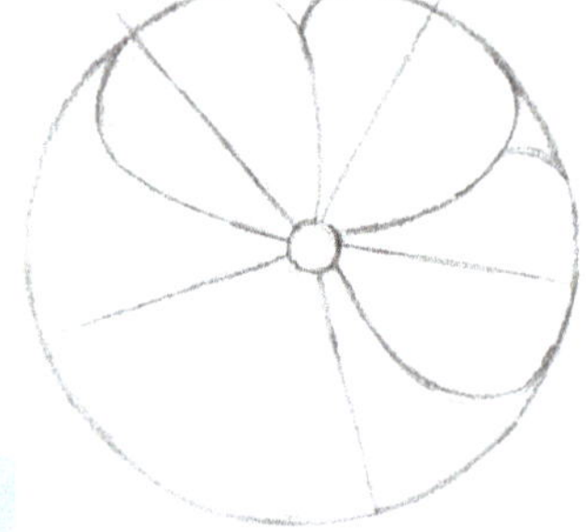

2

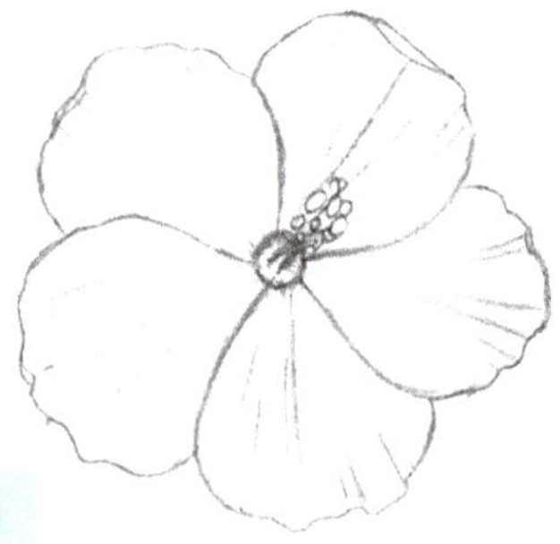

3

ANGLE A

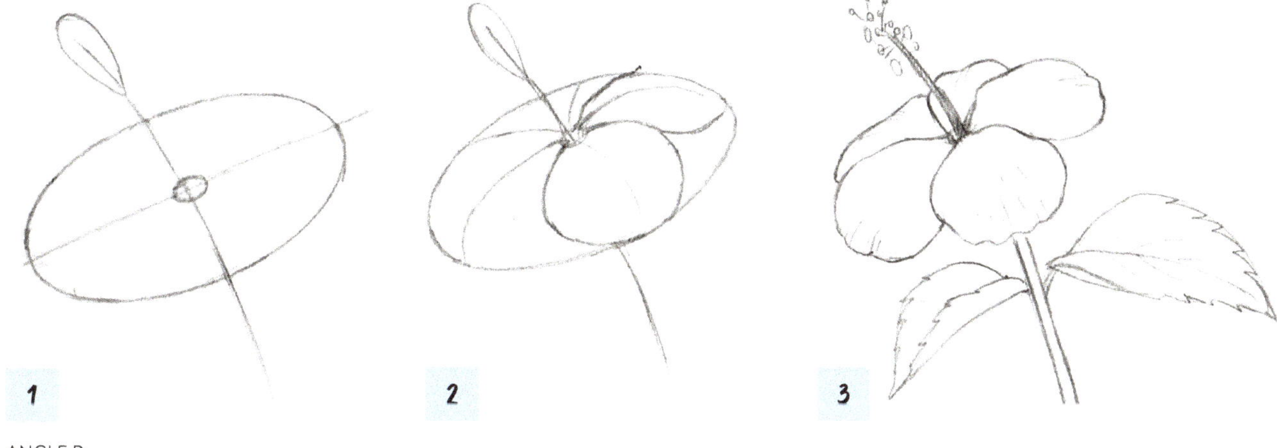

ANGLE B

Angle B

1 Draw a vertical line slightly curving to the right. Draw a horizontal line perpendicular to the vertical line. Using these as guidelines, draw a larger oval with a smaller oval in the center. Sketch a teardrop shape on the top of the vertical line to mark the stamen.

2 Draw five curved guidelines to create the placement of the flower petals. Using the guidelines, draw each flower petal, noting how the petal shapes become wider or more narrow, or shorter or longer, according to the perspective. Also indicate how the petals overlap.

3 Add details to the petals by sketching lines that indicate wrinkles. Add random small circles to the stamen. Thicken the stem and add jagged-edged leaves to complete the sketch.

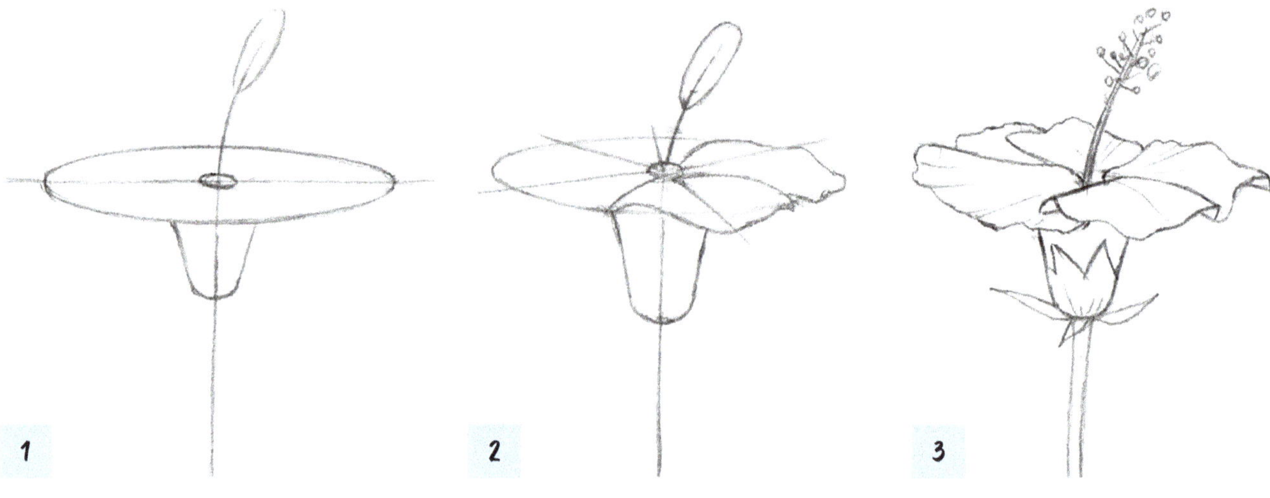

ANGLE C

Angle C

1 Draw a vertical line slightly slanting to the right, and a perpendicular line intersecting it. Draw a narrow horizontal oval using the intersecting lines as guidelines. Create a tiny oval in the middle of the larger oval and draw a cone at the base. Sketch a teardrop shape at the top of the vertical line; this forms a side view of the hibiscus.

2 Draw five guidelines indicating the positions of the flower petals. Use straight lines for the petal guidelines instead of the curved ones in Angle B. Draw flower petals one by one, following the guidelines. Here, the perspective flattens the petals, but they still overlap, with some petals curving.

3 Draw lines in the petals to create wrinkles and a cluster of random small circles for the stamen. Add a pointed layer to the base of the cone, draw a sepal, and thicken the stem to complete the flower.

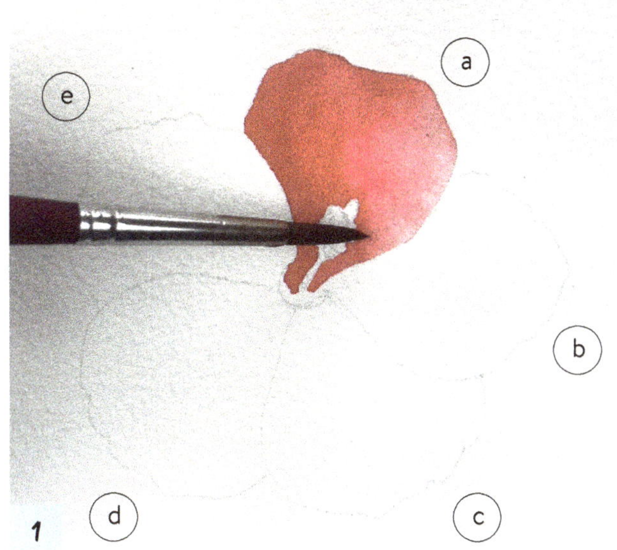

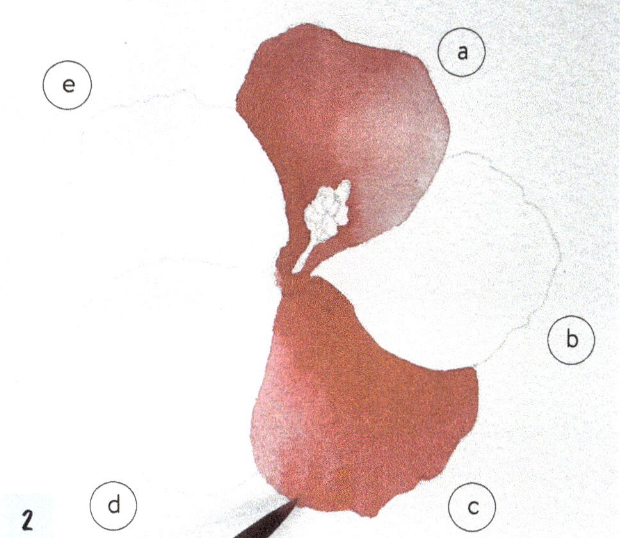

PAINT THE FLOWERS

Painting hibiscus flowers is an excellent way to practice using the color red. In this lesson, you'll learn how to provide enough contrast to express the intensity and the light texture of the flower petals.

Angle A

1 Sketch the Angle A flower lightly on watercolor paper. For this flower, paint each petal separately. Working wet-on-dry (see page 38), use Level 5 Permanent Red (medium warm red) to paint the left portion of flower petal a. Create a gradient (see page 43) by moving the color horizontally with the brush so that it fades out on the right side of the petal.

2 Follow the instructions in step 1 to color flower petal c. I recommend you color alternate petals instead of consecutive ones; this way the colors won't mix, and you'll save time because you won't have to wait for the previous petal to dry.

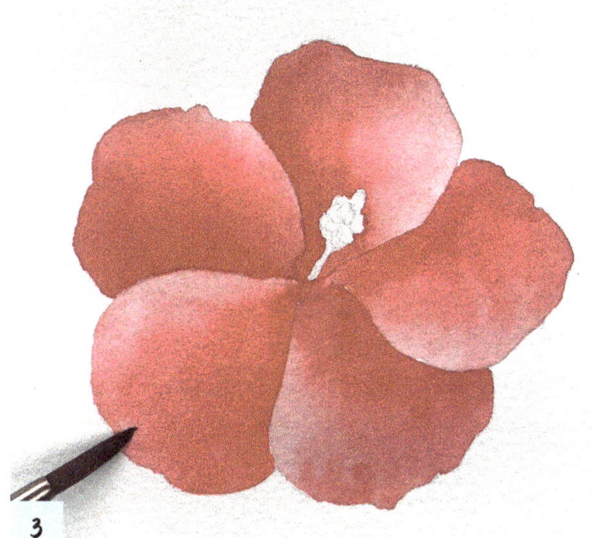

3 Paint the remaining petals using the same technique (avoid painting the stamen). By doing this, you'll notice that each flower petal includes dark and bright areas. Although the red is intense, the petals don't look stuffy or heavy.

(continued)

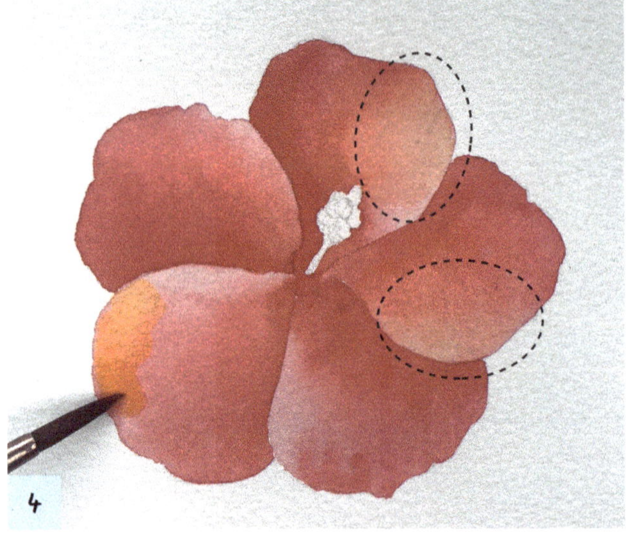

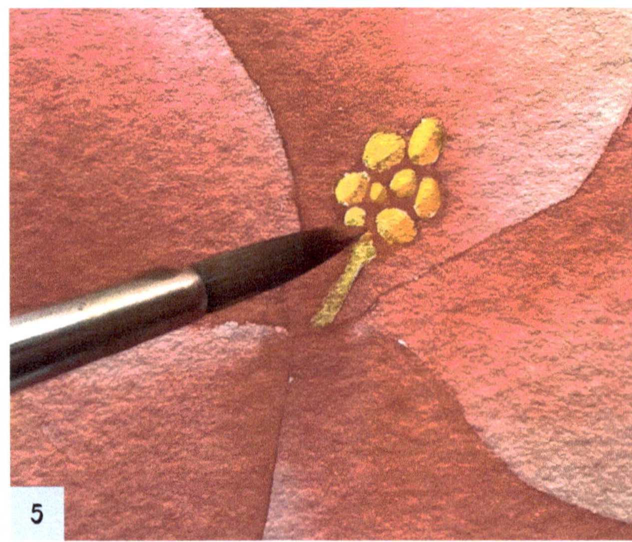

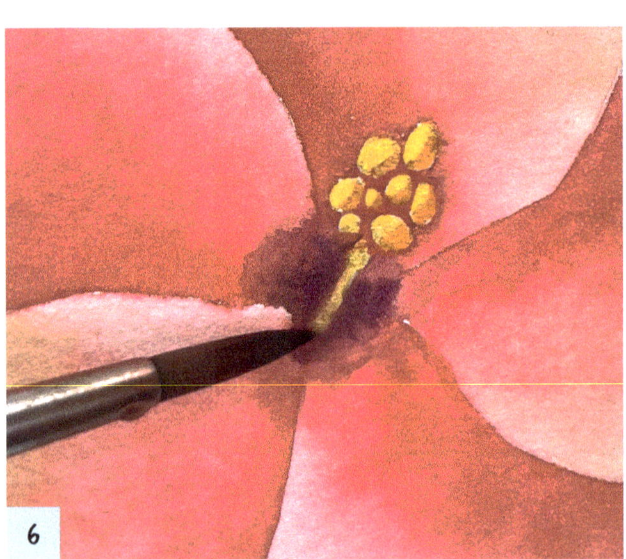

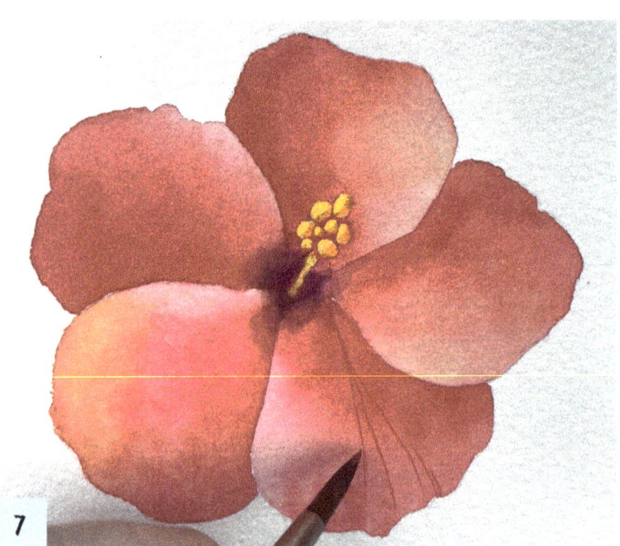

4 Make the red hue even more dynamic by glazing (see page 45) the brighter portion of the flower petals with Level 1 density yellow-orange, indicated by the dotted lines. Glaze only a couple of the petals. If all petals are glazed, the dynamic effect will be lost.

5 Color the stamen by painting dots with Level 5 density yellow. Use just the tip of the brush to color the dots. Allow the paint to dry. Shade the stamen by brushing yellow-orange on one side of the dots. The area is relatively small, but these color details make a big difference.

6 Create depth in the flower center by adding shading. Paint the area around the stamen using Level 4 density Bright Clear Violet (blue-purple). Avoid painting the stamen violet. Softly blend the edges with the brush.

7 Create patterns of thin lines on the petals with Level 5 Permanent Red. Hold the brush straight up and use just the tip to make the lines. Increase the amount of lines toward the outer part of the petals (see the finished image, page 87).

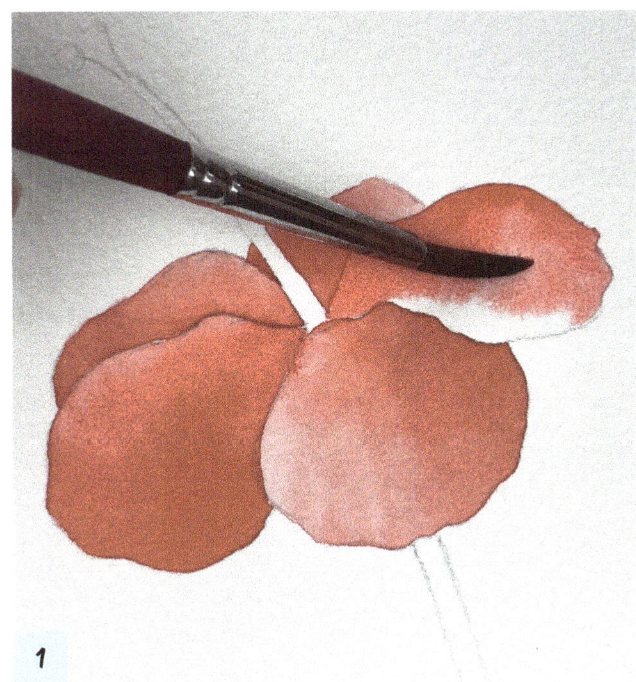

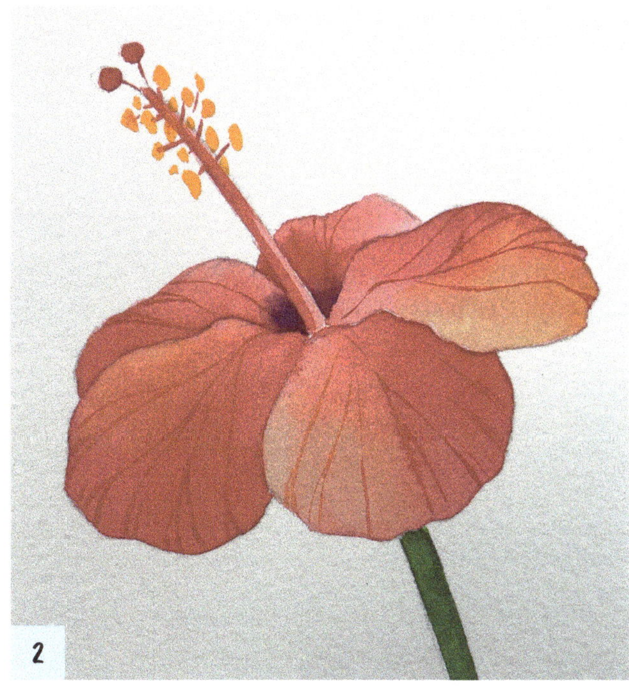

Angle B

1 Sketch the Angle B flower lightly on watercolor paper and paint the petals following steps 1 to 4 for the Angle A flower.

2 Color the stamen using the gradient technique (see page 43) and Level 5 density red. Apply the color near the upper part of the stamen, moving it down to make it fade. Use Level 5 density yellow to color the stamen dots, making random strokes with the brush tip. Add shading to the center of the flower petals by glazing the area with Level 3 density violet. Paint thin lines on each petal with Level 5 Permanent Red (warm, bright red). Complete the flower by coloring the stem with Level 4 density Hooker's Green.

Be sure to paint curved thin petal lines (a) instead of straight ones (b) for the Angle B flower. This helps create a more natural-looking flower.

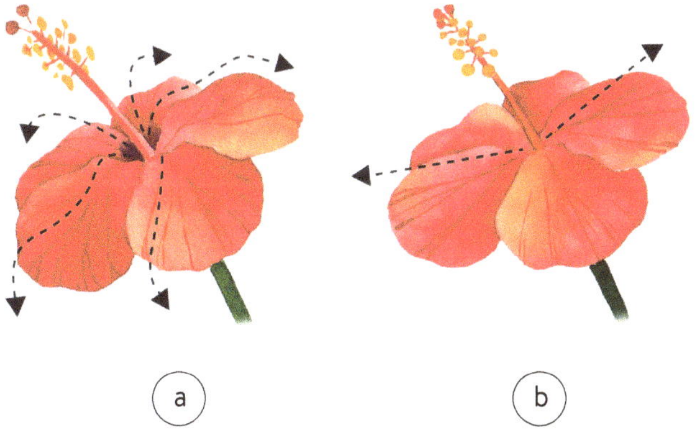

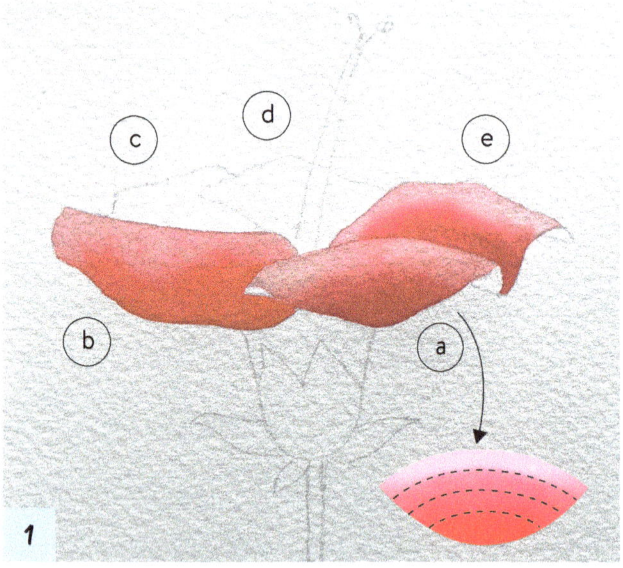

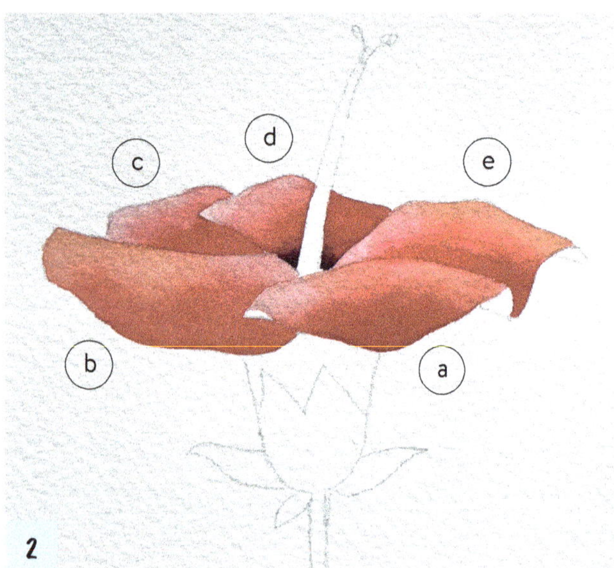

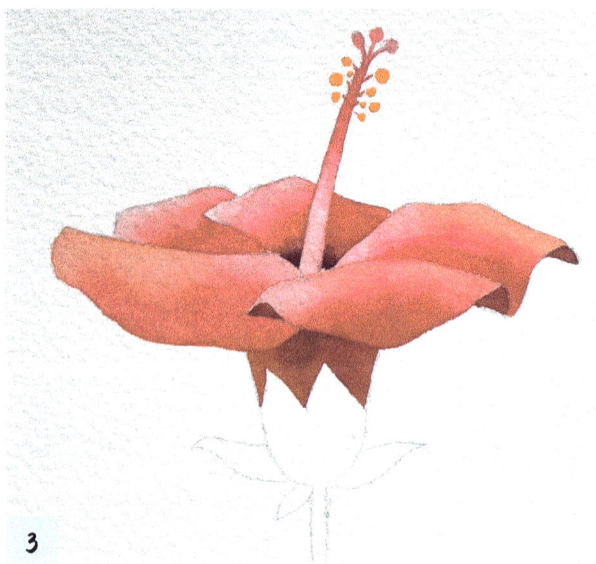

Angle C

1 Sketch the Angle C flower lightly on watercolor paper. Working wet-on-dry, paint Level 5 density Permanent Red (medium warm red) on the bottom edge of petal a. Wash the brush with clean water, then lightly blot it with a paper towel. Then create a curved gradient along the top edge of the petal as shown in the picture. Allow the paint to dry. Paint petal e in the same way. Paint petal c in the same way and create a horizontal gradient.

2 Working wet-on-dry, paint Level 5 density Permanent Red (medium warm red) on the right side of the petal d and create a gradient as shown in the picture. Before the paint dries, add Level 4 density Bright Clear Violet (bluish-purple) around lower stamen of the petal d. Allow paint to dry. Paint petal c in the same way, but do not add purple shading. Add a glazing layer using Level 1 density yellow-orange on the right upper portion of the petal a and e. For petal b, add glazing in the upper left.

3 Working wet-on-dry, use Level 5 density Permanent Red (medium warm red) to color the upper part of the stamen, then move it down to make it fade. Use the same color to paint the small dots at the top of the stamen. Use Level 5 density yellow to color the remainder of the circles on the stamen, using random brushstrokes. Color the underside of the petals and the cone-shaped petal with Level 5 density red-brown.

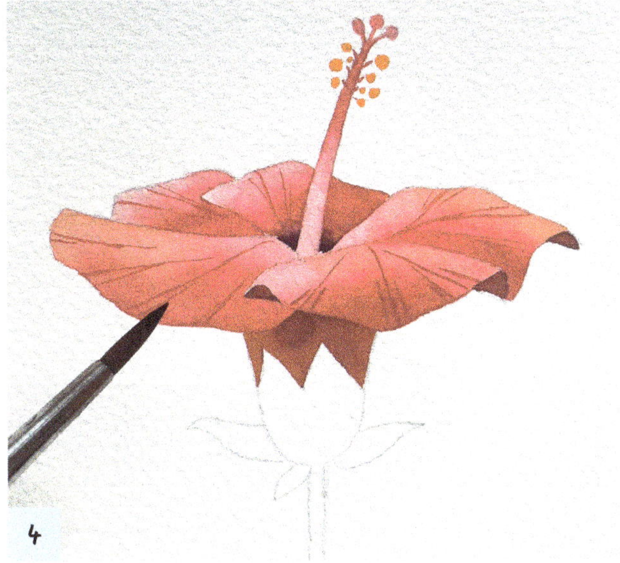

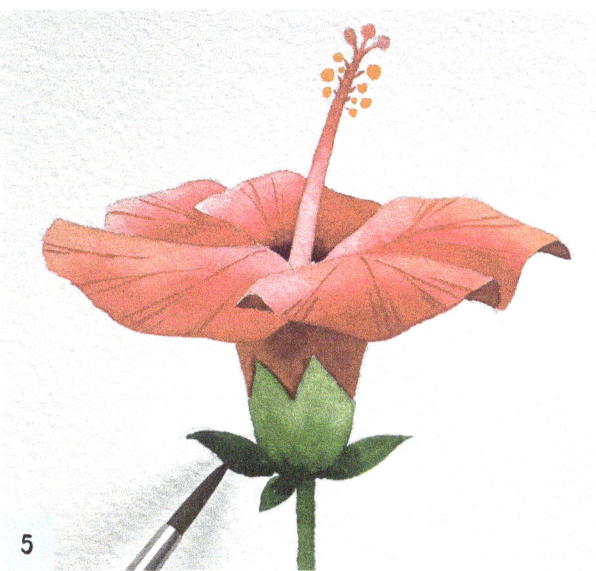

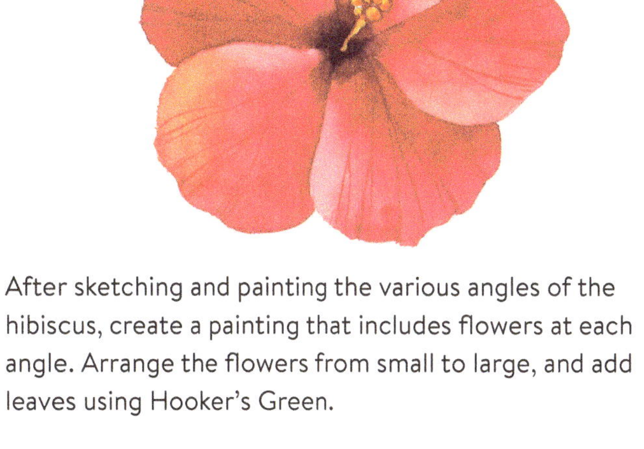

After sketching and painting the various angles of the hibiscus, create a painting that includes flowers at each angle. Arrange the flowers from small to large, and add leaves using Hooker's Green.

4 Paint thin lines on each flower petal with Level 5 Permanent Red. For this perspective, the lines should be straight.

5 Color the stem and the leaves with Level 4 Hooker's Green. Create a gradient for the bottom of the sepal using Level 4 density Hooker's Green. The color should be lighter near the top and darker at the base.

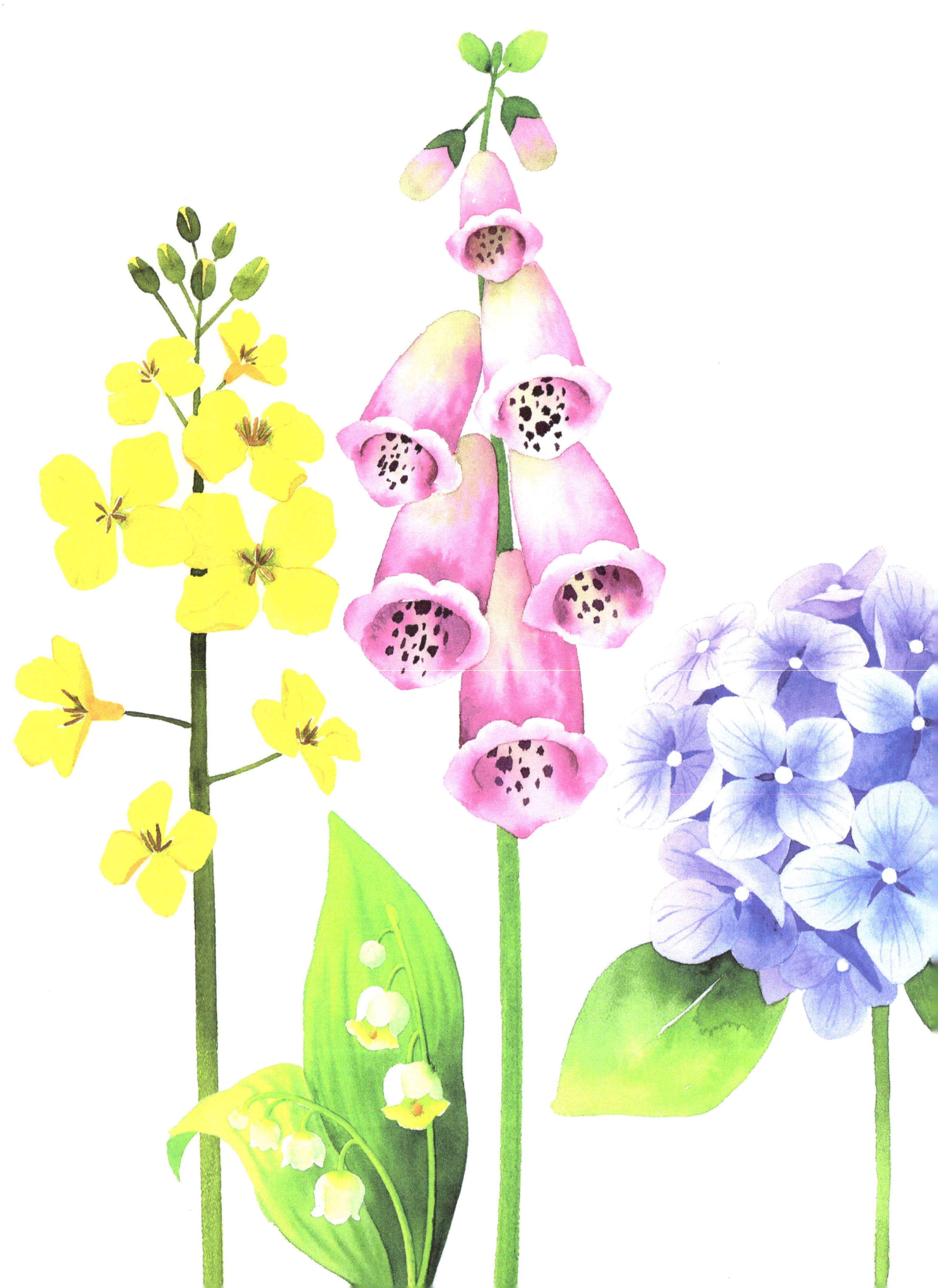

5

Flower Clusters

In the previous chapter, you practiced drawing and painting simple flowers. In this chapter, you'll work on more complex flowers. Cluster-type flowers have several blossoms on one stalk. But don't be nervous. If you follow along with my steps, you will easily create these florals. You'll learn to render a canola, lily of the valley, hydrangea, and foxglove. The emphasis will be on learning how to simplify the form by breaking down the flower arrangement. Also, you'll learn interesting coloring methods that incorporate masking fluid.

Canola Flower

The bright yellow blossoms of canola flowers grow in clusters. This type of flower has a complex structure, and it would be challenging to draw all the features you see. In this lesson, you'll learn how to remove the unnecessary parts and make the drawing simpler by realigning the structure. This method maintains the canola flower's basic form. Remember, you're realigning the structure, not creating a new flower.

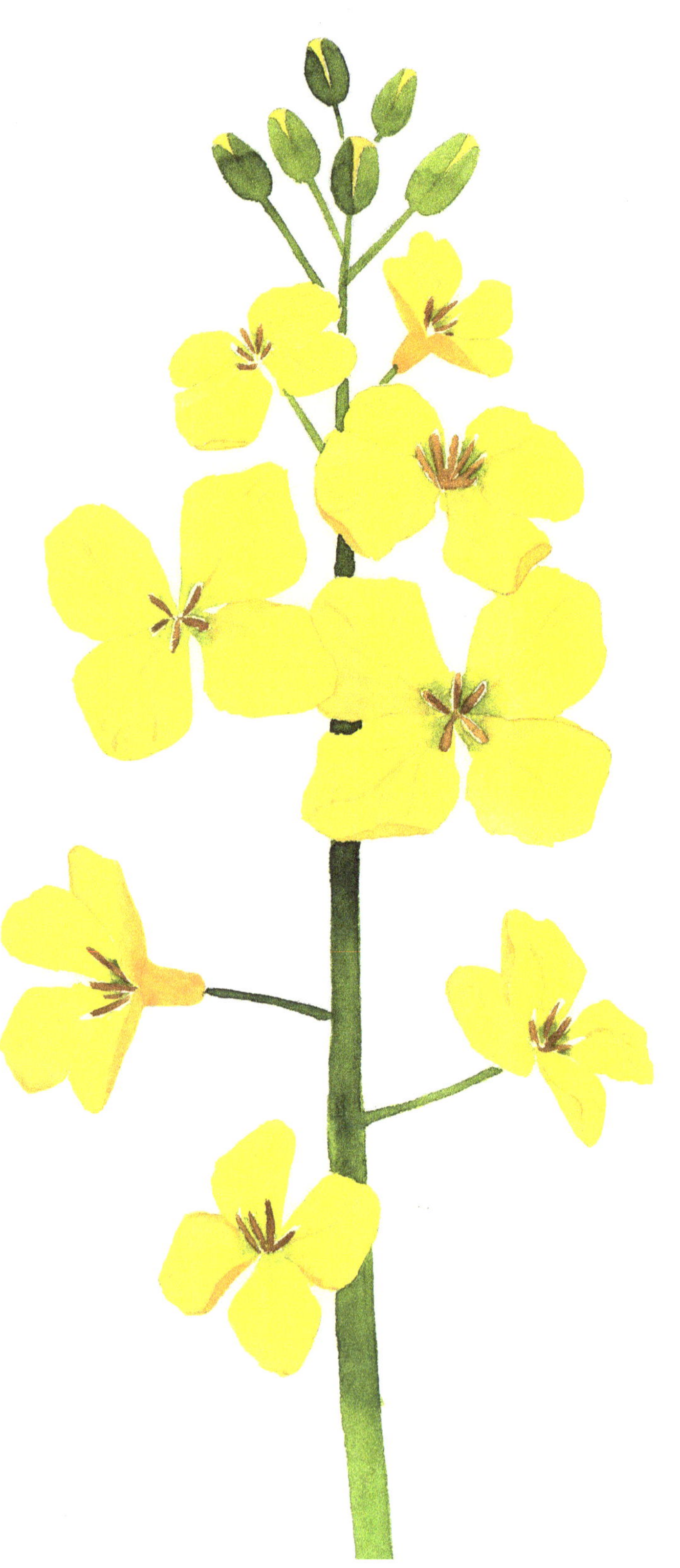

SKETCH THE BLOSSOMS

Use the three-step sketching method to practice drawing the four-petal blossoms from different angles. Notice the curve of the petals and how some turn upward at the edge. The stamens also point upward, which you can see in Angle C.

These sketching diagrams will help you draw the main blossoms of the flower.

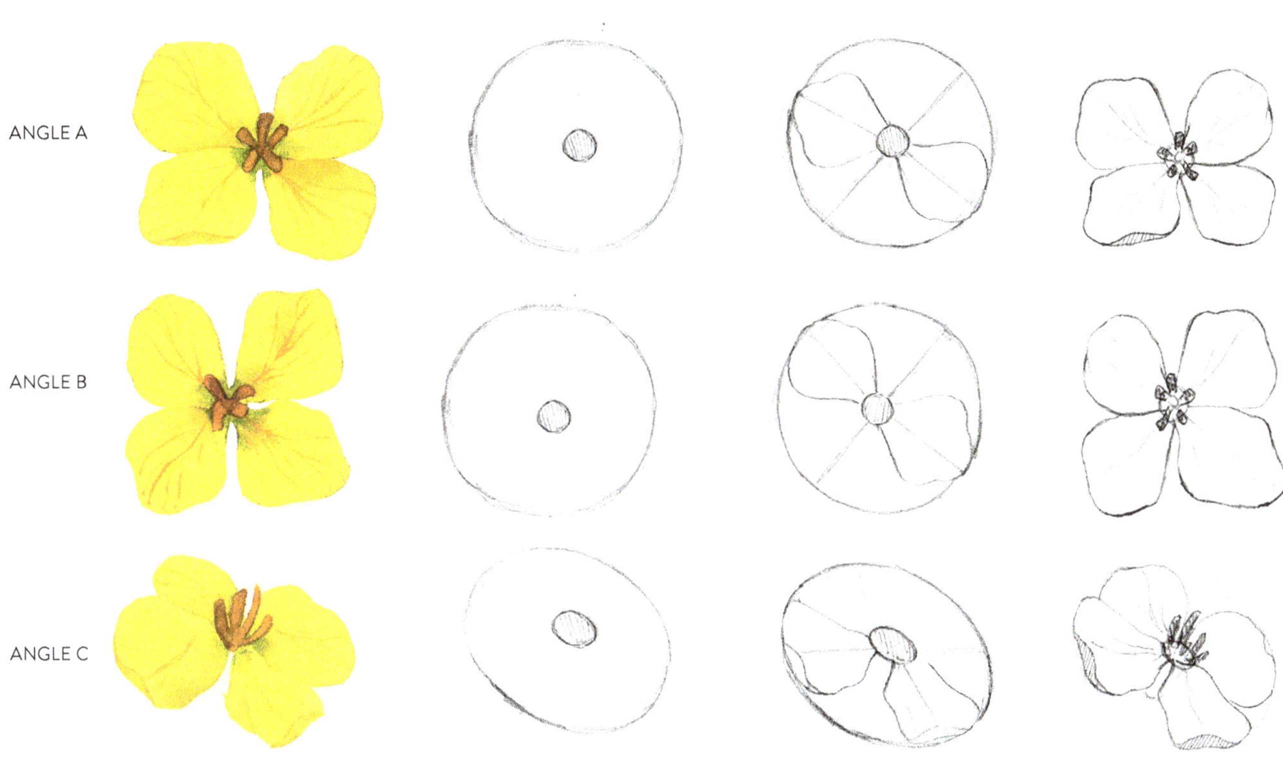

More blossom variations

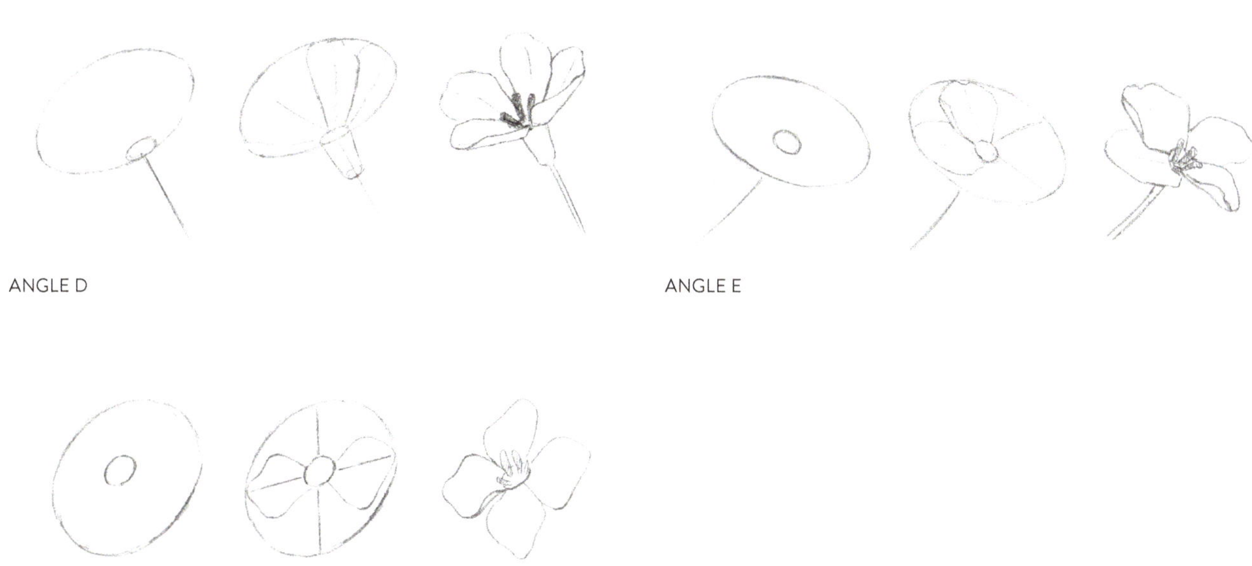

SKETCH THE FLOWER

1 Draw a center stem for the three main blossoms. Draw circles and ovals for the blossom placement. Creating blossoms in different sizes and at different angles makes them more visually interesting. Remember that circles are bases for flowers viewed straight on, and ovals indicate flowers that are at an angle.

2 Choose the placement of the other blossoms and buds, being aware of angles and positioning. As in step 1, draw them as circles or ovals first to determine the angle. The blossoms will appear more natural if you change the angles and have them face in different directions rather than having them all facing the same way. Use the three-step sketches (page 91) to draw the blossoms and their guidelines on the stem. Make sure some of the blossoms overlap, adding to the natural look.

3 Continue to draw more blossoms, referring again to the three-step sketches. Draw some buds as well to complete the flower. Notice that from some angles you can see short stems attaching the blossoms to the main stem, as well as a cone-shaped blossom base.

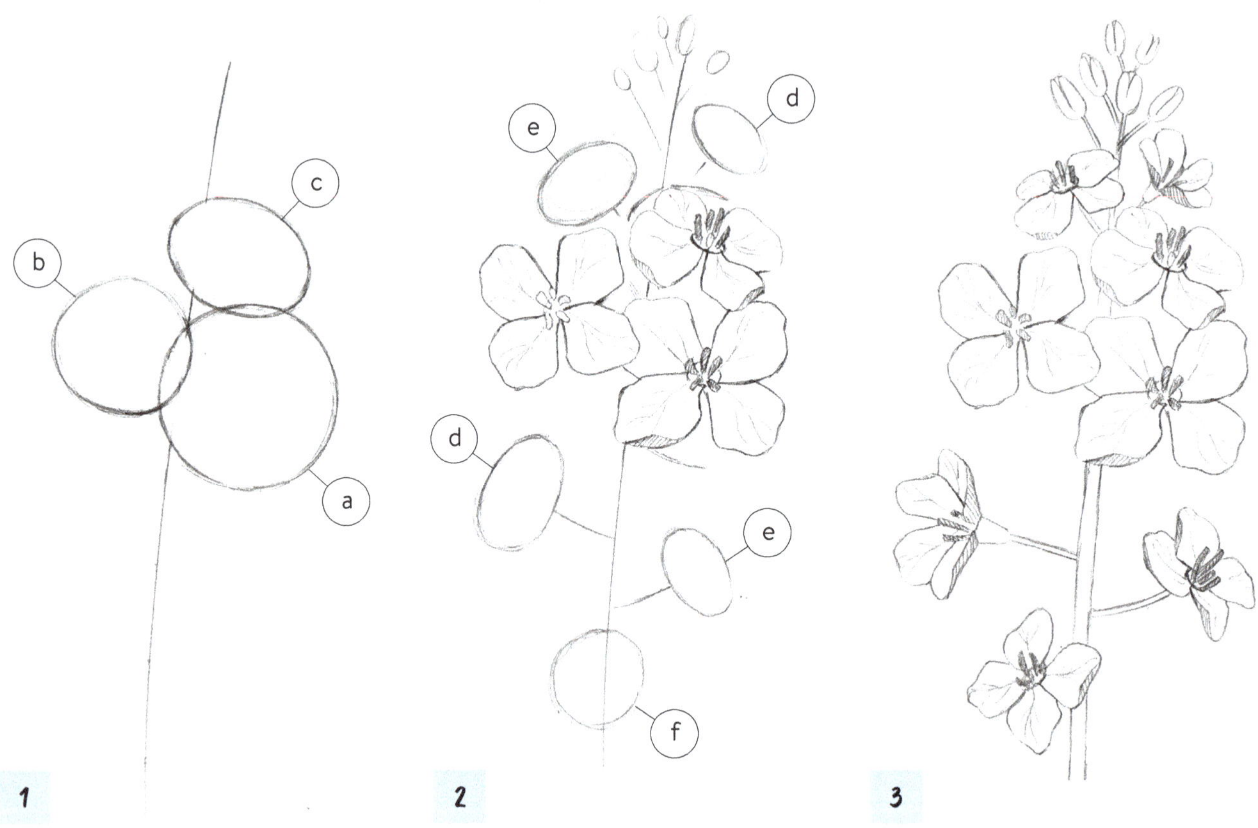

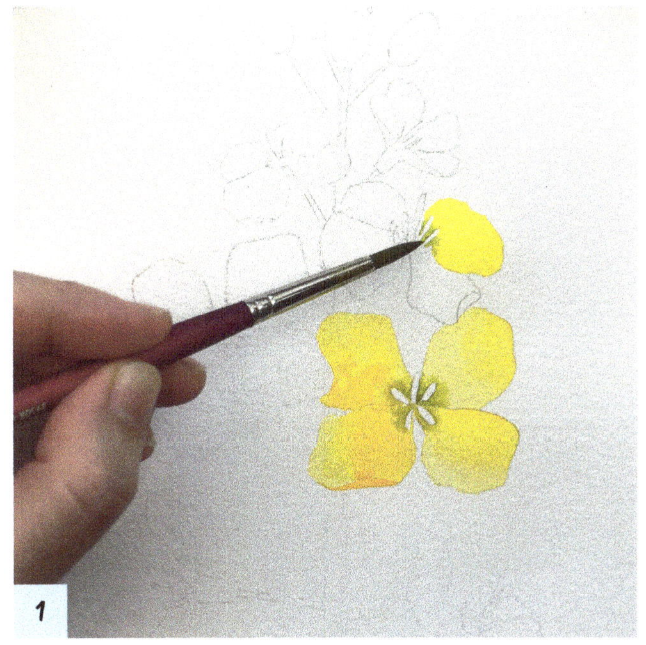

1

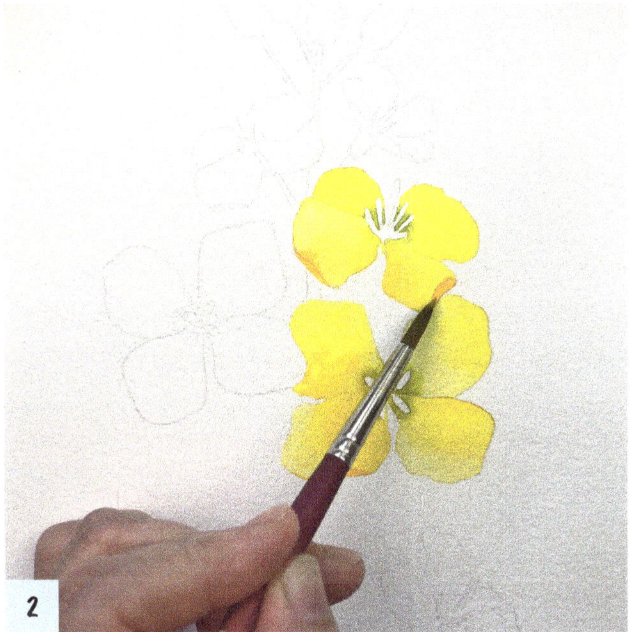

2

PAINT THE FLOWER

These flowers are painted in analogous shades of yellow, green, and gold, producing lovely gradations of color. To achieve the deep golden shade for the flowers, I used Permanent Yellow Light (bright yellow) as the base color, greenish-yellow for the flower centers, and Yellow Ochre (mustard yellow) for the stamens.

1 Apply Level 3 density Permanent Yellow Light on four petals with a small round brush. Before the paint dries, apply greenish-yellow to the center where the petals begin. Avoid painting the stamens for now. Allow the paint to dry.

2 Apply Level 4 density Permanent Yellow Deep to the back of petals that curl up. This adds dimension to the petals. Waiting until the previous layer of paint is dry allows you to color these areas more precisely. Allow the paint to dry.

(continued)

When adding the greenish-yellow to the flower centers, don't overdo it—the area is very small, so refer to the image for guidance.

3 Color the stamens with Level 5 density Yellow Ochre. Allow the paint to thoroughly dry.

4 Use Level 5 density Permanent Yellow Deep to paint the veins on each petal with the tip of the brush, following the petal's natural curve. Make sure the color isn't too dark, or it will stand out too much.

5 Complete the flower by coloring the stem and the buds with Level 4 density olive green (see the finished image, page 90).

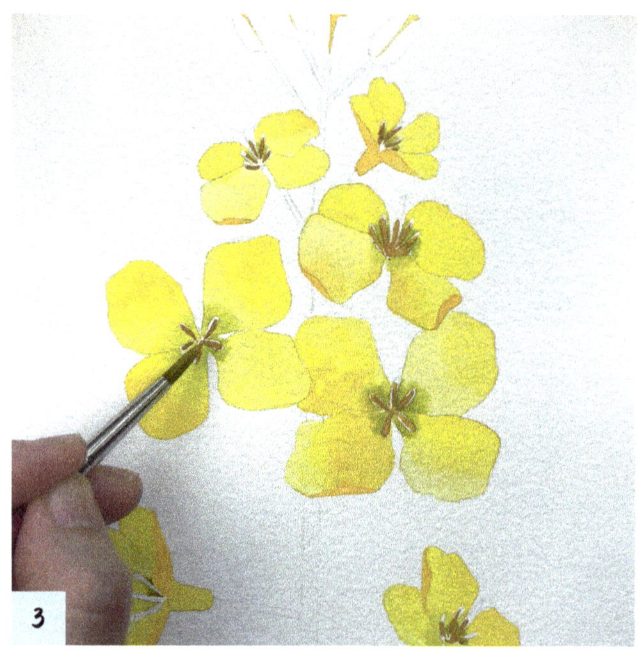

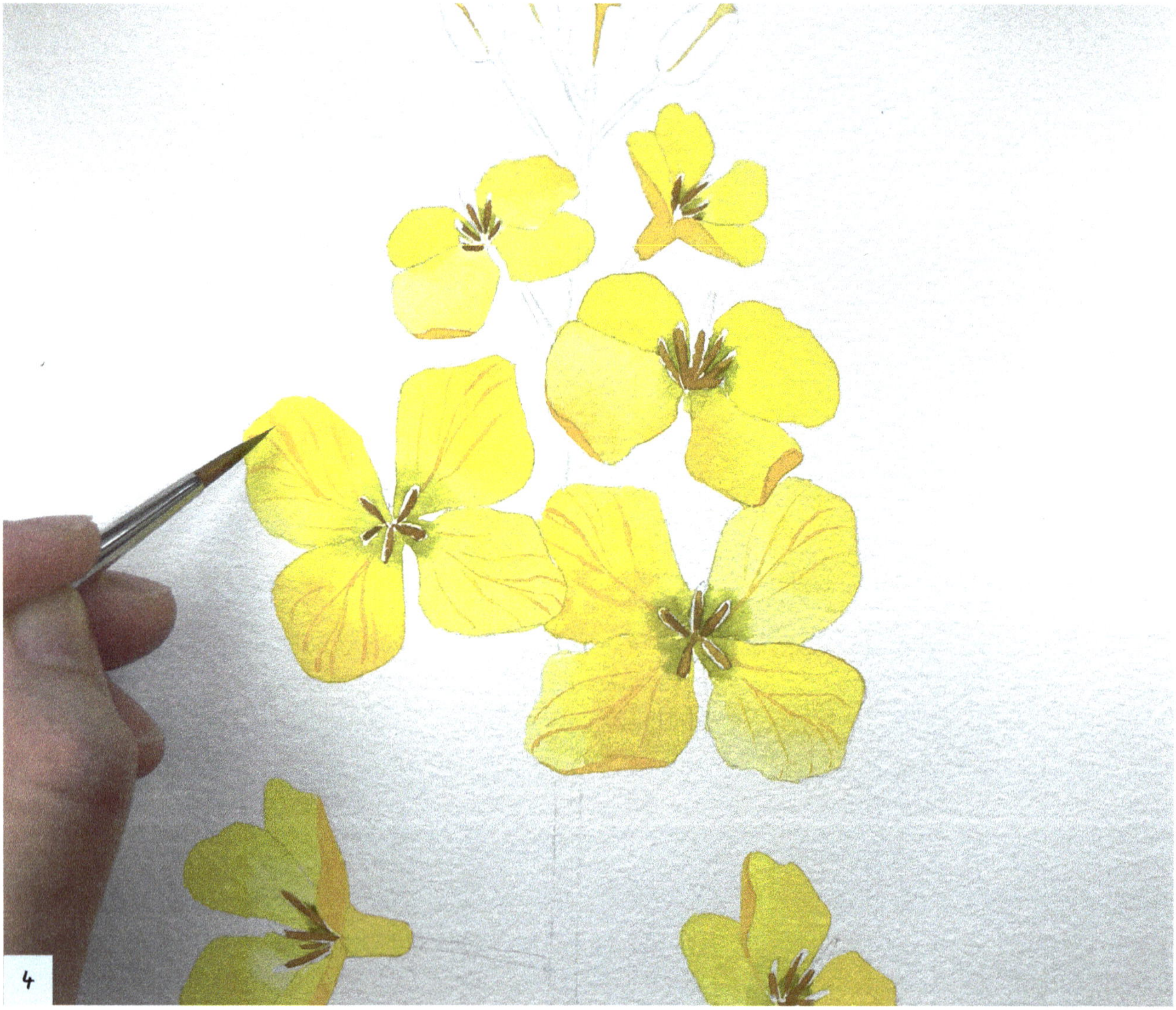

Lily of the Valley

The lily of the valley's rounded blossoms resemble little fruits, and they're petite and cute. The flower also has an interesting structure, with groups of small blossoms that are surrounded by relatively large leaves. In this lesson, you'll learn how to color white blossoms by using masking fluid to keep the paper white, then removing the dried fluid and adding pale layers of watercolor.

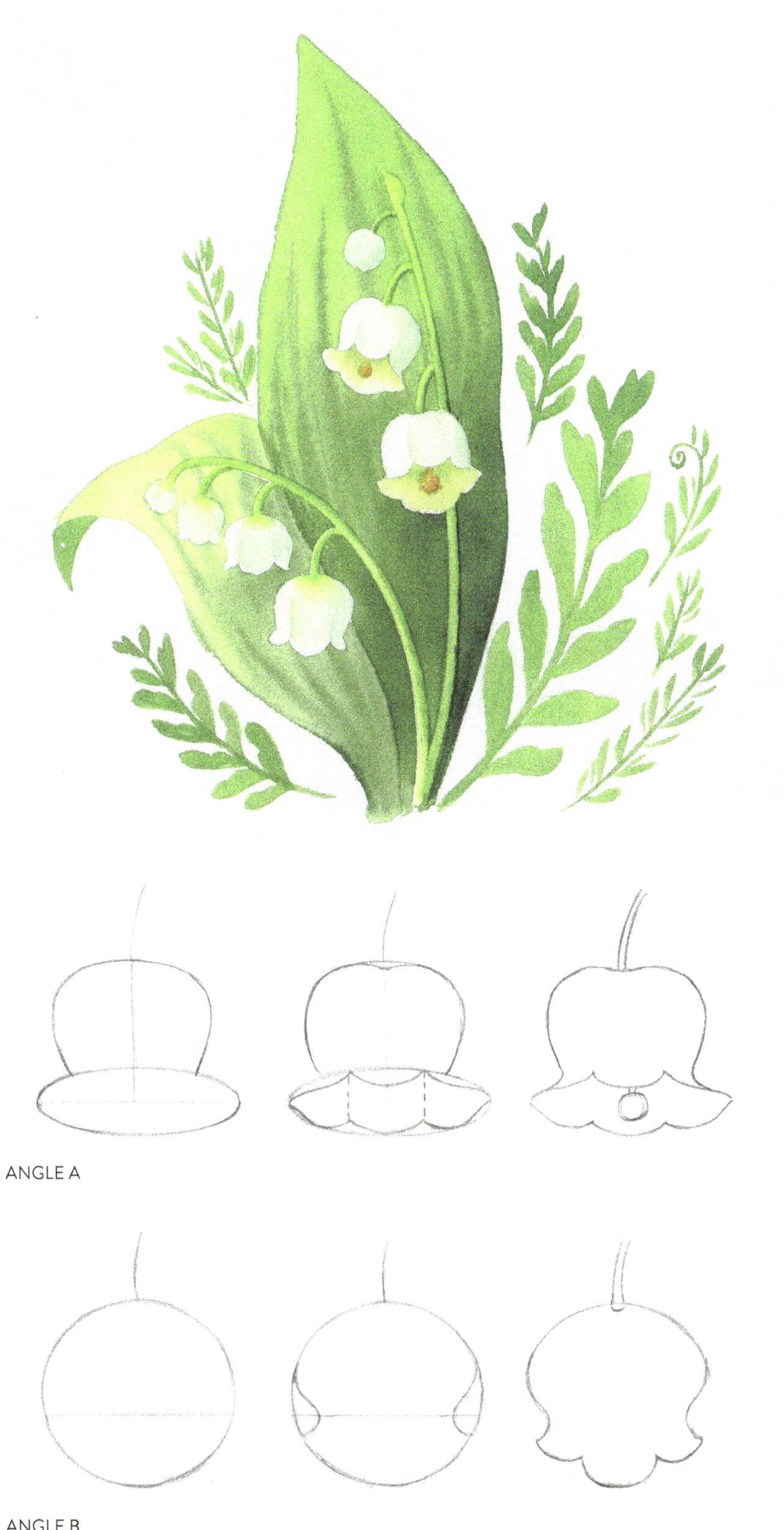

SKETCH THE BLOSSOMS

Use the three-step sketching method to draw the lily of the valley blossoms in two different positions. Angle A reveals the bottom of the blossom petals and some of the interior, while Angle B shows only a side view.

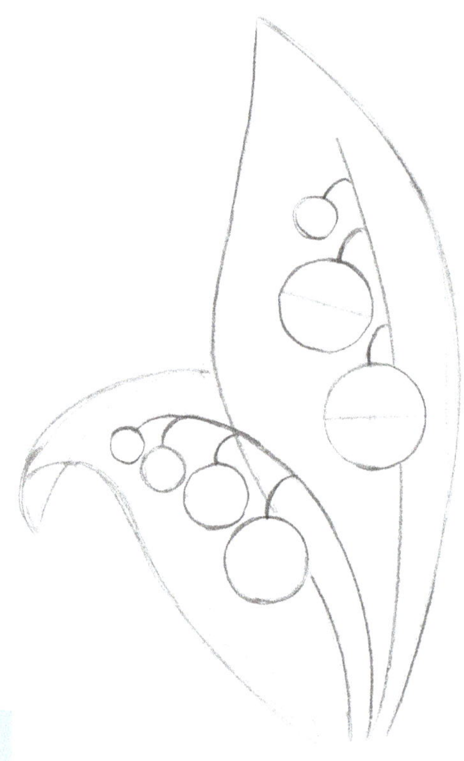

1

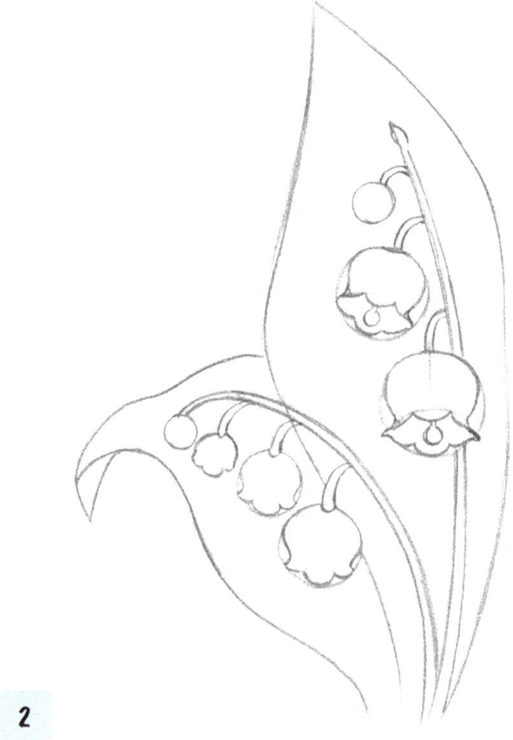

2

SKETCH THE FLOWER

1 Draw two curved lines for the stems, making the left stem more curved than the right. On the right stem, draw three different-size circles to create Angle A blossoms. On the left stem, draw four circles to create Angle B blossoms. Draw two large leaves behind the stems, noting that the tip of the left leaf curls under.

2 Add details to the blossom petals as you did in the initial sketches, such as creating scalloped petals, stamens, and showing the interiors of the Angle A blossoms. Add thickness to the stems.

3 Add leaves in various shapes surrounding the flowers to complete the drawing. Make sure your pencil lines are clear and precise so that it will be easier to apply the masking fluid.

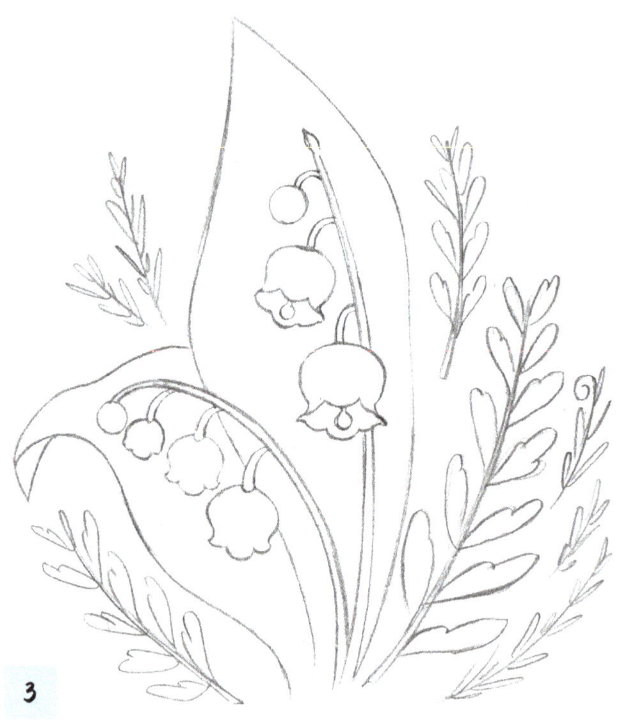

3

PAINT THE FLOWER

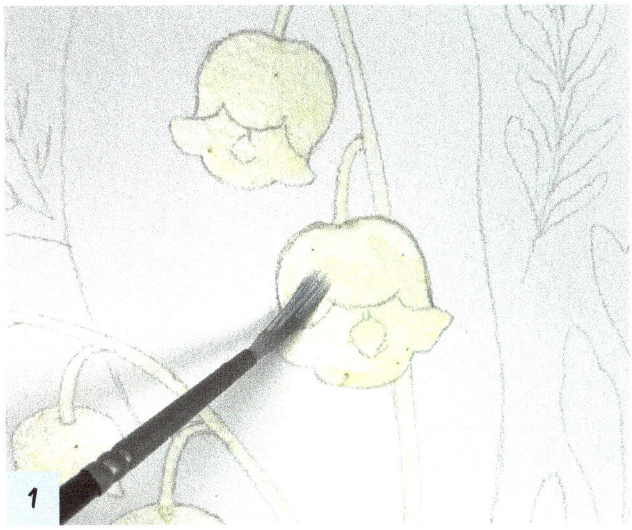

1

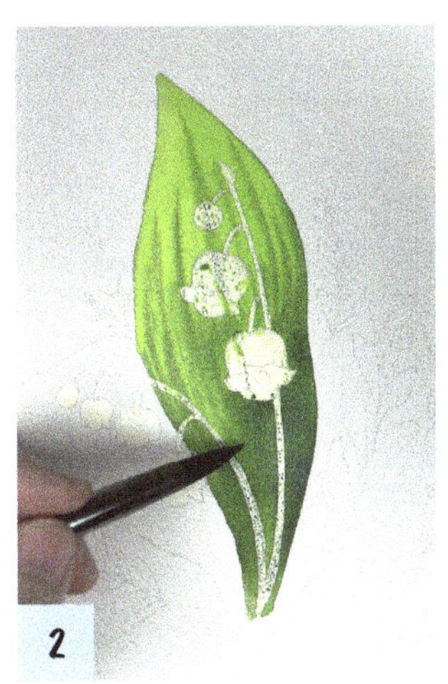

2

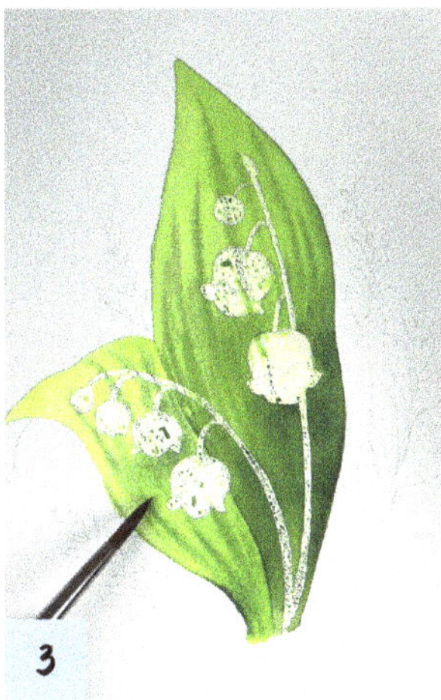

3

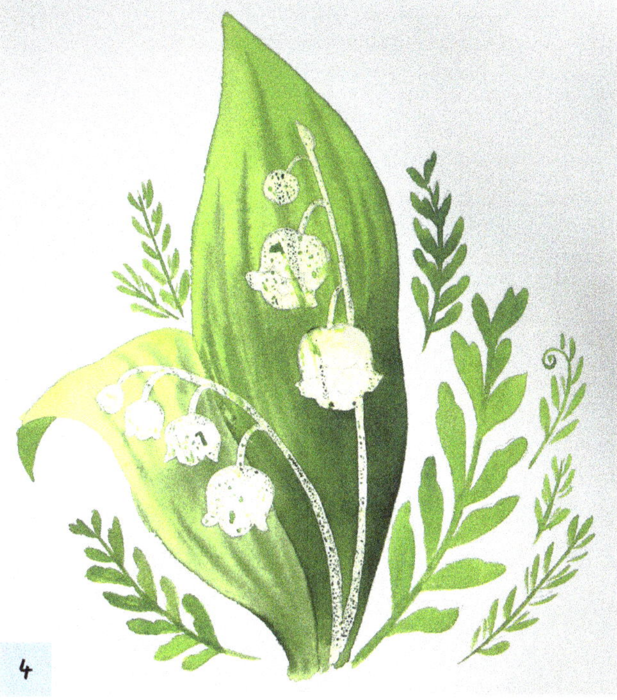

4

In this lesson, you'll learn how to paint lily of the valley, small white cluster flowers surrounded by large leaves. In this case, using masking fluid is an effective way to paint white flowers quickly and easily. (For more information on masking fluid, see page 19.) I suggest drawing a delicate pencil line to sketch the area that will be brushed with masking fluid.

1 Thoroughly apply the masking fluid on the blossoms and stems that will be left white. Apply the fluid lightly and allow it to dry completely. Aim for a delicate but thorough application, even if the masking fluid layer is thin.

2 Working wet-on-wet (see page 36), brush water on the leaves and use Level 3 density sap green for the top part of the right-hand leaf. For the bottom of that leaf, use Level 5 density Hooker's Green and create a gradient (see page 41). Before the colors dry, use Level 5 density Hooker's Green to draw long vertical lines with the brush tip. Extend the lines into the top area to indicate the texture of the leaves.

3 Repeat step 2 to color the left-hand leaf. When the paint is completely dry, color the underside of the curled leaf with a flat layer of Level 5 density sap green.

4 Working wet-on-dry (see page 38), paint the background leaves using sap green or Hooker's Green. Use a flat layer of color with no gradient.

(continued)

5 Remove the masking fluid with a rubber cement eraser by placing it on the masking fluid and gently pressing down. The masking fluid will come off when you lift the eraser.

6 Paint the interiors of the blossoms on the right. Working wet-on-dry, mix yellow-green and olive green in a ratio of 1:1. Use Level 3 density paint and work in a gradient, using the darkest value at the top of the interior area.

7 Paint the blossom's exterior. Mix yellow-green and Cerulean Blue (sky blue) in a 2:1 ratio to make green-blue. Use Level 1 density paint to create a flat layer on petal a. Leave the tip of petal a white, as seen in the area marked by dotted lines. Create a hard edge on the left side of petal b and let the color fade toward the right side, where it connects with petal a. As before, leave the dotted line area white.

8 Color the stamens using Level 5 density Permanent Yellow Deep (golden yellow). Color the buds by working on a gradient with the green-blue, as shown.

Color the stem by painting it with Level 2 density yellow-green first, then create a gradient to shade it using Level 5 density Hooker's Green.

9 Color the blossoms on the left using the methods in step 7. Use yellow-green for the flower peak, fading the color where it connects to the stem.

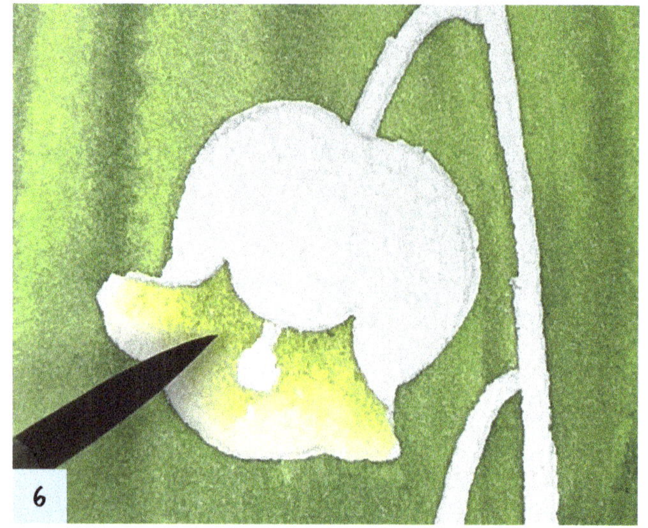

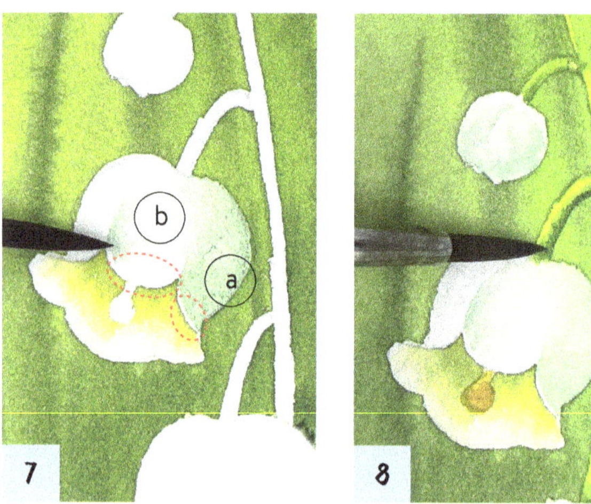

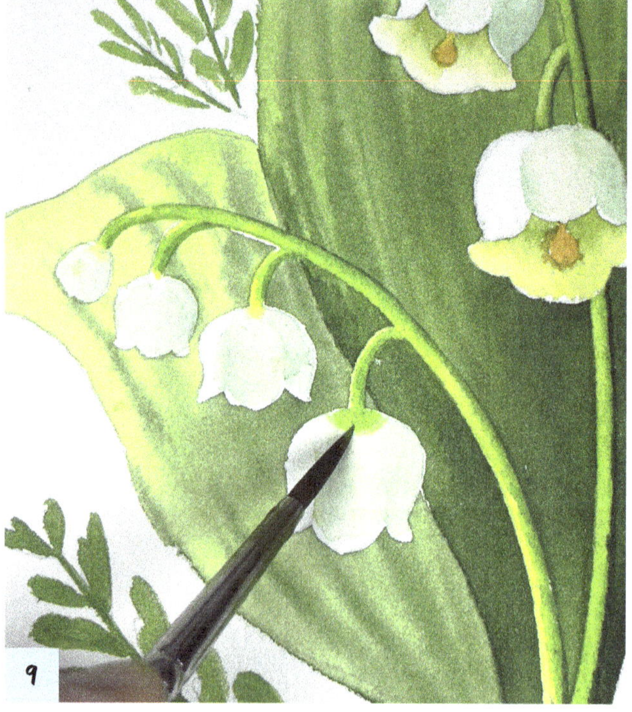

Hydrangea

Hydrangea flowers have a spherical shape made from a collection of many tiny blossoms. Because of its complex structure, many people consider this a challenging flower to draw. However, I rearranged and simplified the structure so beginners can sketch it easily.

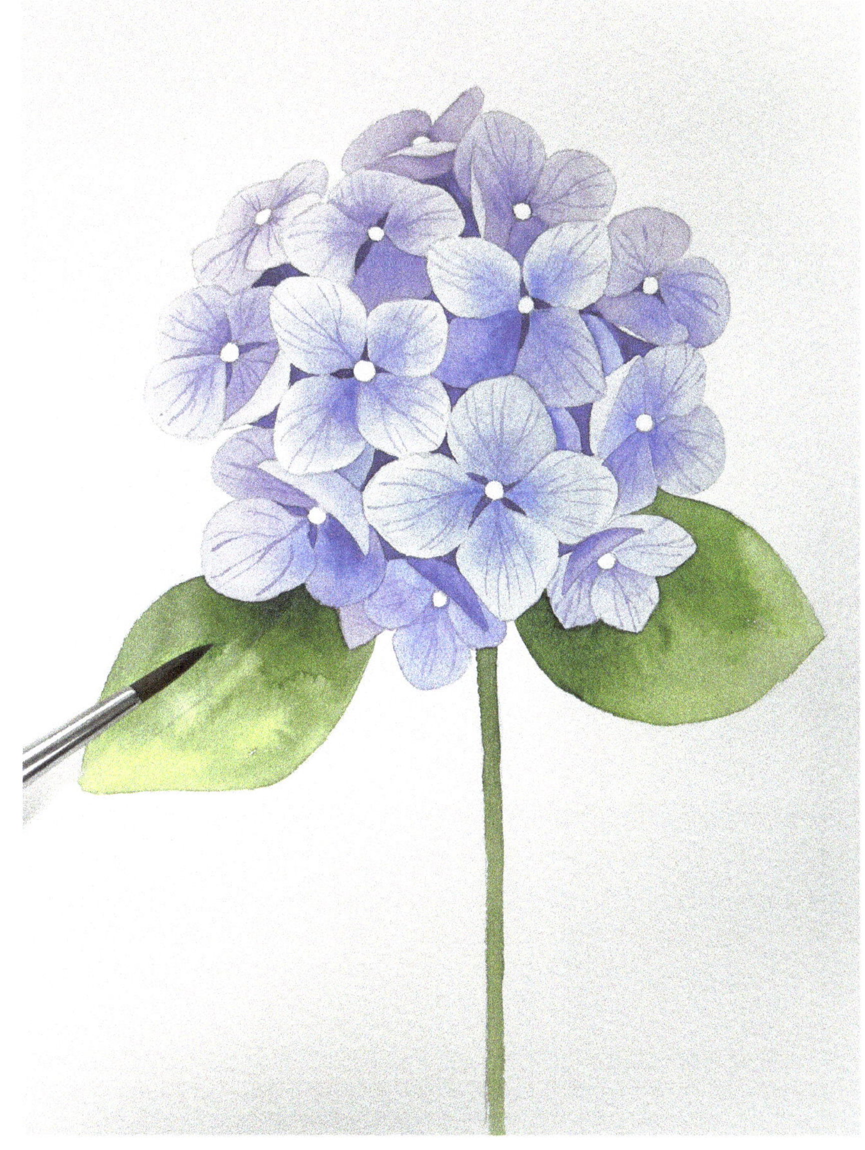

SKETCH THE BLOSSOMS

Practice sketching the main Angle A blossoms in the center and the Angle B blossoms on the side by referring to the three-step sketch. Angle A blossoms face the front, and Angle B blossoms feature a flattened side view with petals in a variety of angles.

The angles and shapes of the petals may change a bit, but the sketching method is the same for all. Practice sketching blossoms in various side-view angles by referring to the illustrations.

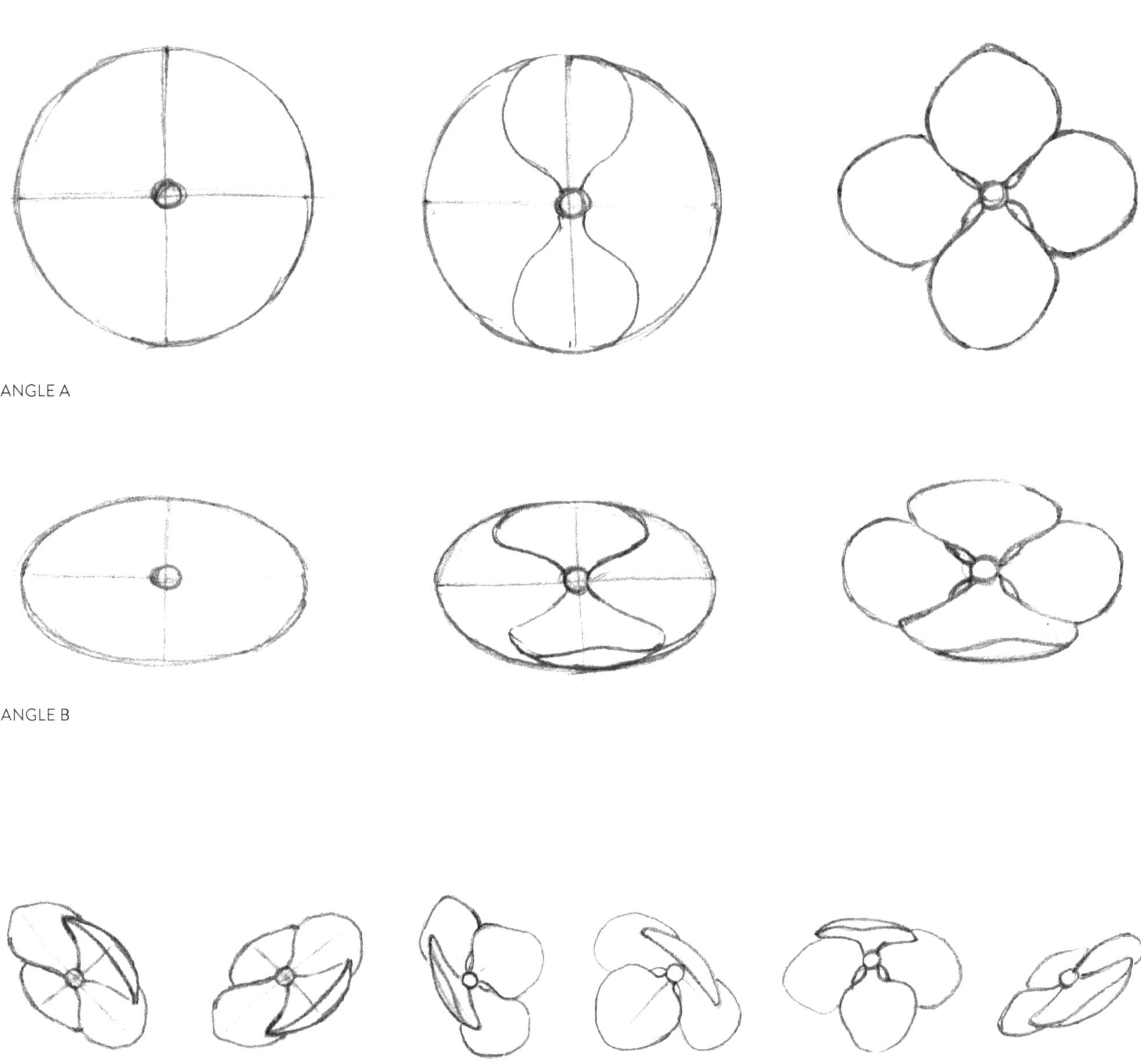

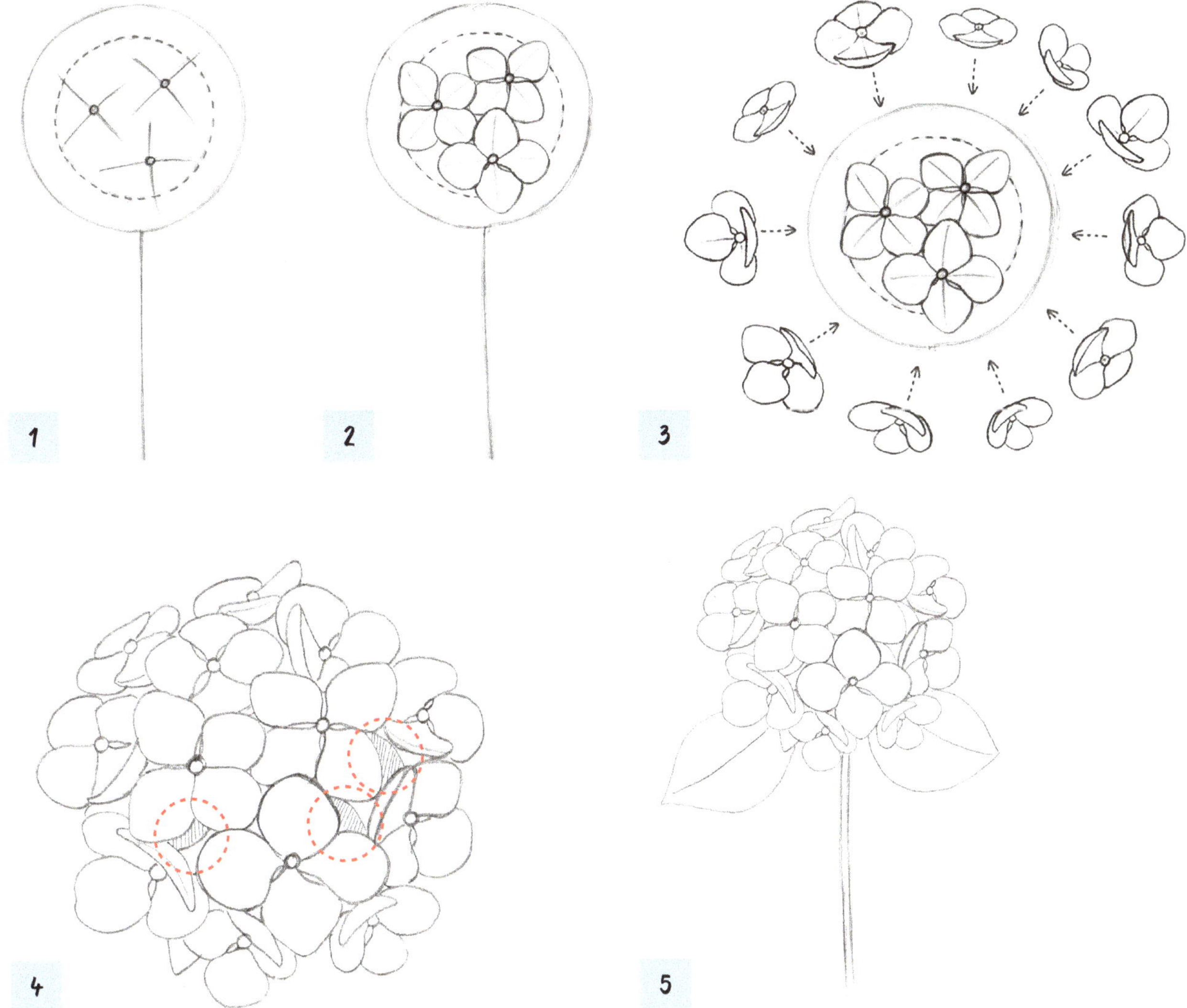

SKETCH THE FLOWER

1. Draw a large circle. Draw a smaller circle inside with a dotted line. Mark the placement of three main blossoms in the center and add very slightly curved perpendicular guidelines. Draw a line for the stem.
2. Draw three Angle A blossoms inside the smaller circle, making them overlap a little.
3. Draw blossoms on the positions marked by arrows between the two circles and be aware of the angles. Notice how some of the petals overlap, lending a natural look.
4. You'll see empty spaces between some of the blossoms. Draw single petals behind the blossoms to fill in the gaps.
5. Add thickness to the stem and draw two leaves to complete the hydrangea.

PAINT THE FLOWER

The simplified painting below represents the gradient of Ultramarine Deep (deep ocean blue) and Bright Clear Violet (medium purple) for the hydrangea. Refer to this color scheme when painting the flower.

1 Start painting with blossom a. Working wet-on-wet, brush water on the petals but leave the center circle dry. Apply Level 2 density Ultramarine Deep on all the petals. Color the interior of the petals with Level 3 density Ultramarine Deep. If edges form where the two areas meet, blend them with the brush.

2 Color blossoms b, c, k, and j using the method in step 1.

3 Mix Ultramarine Deep and Bright Clear Violet in a ratio of 1:3 to create blue-violet. Working wet-on-wet, brush water on the petals of blossom d, leaving the center circle dry. Apply Level 2 density blue-violet evenly on the petals. Deepen the interior of the petals with Level 3 density blue-violet, again blending any edges that appear.

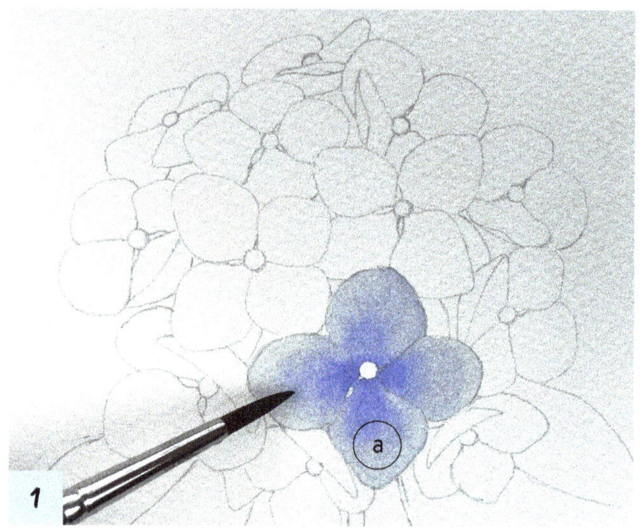

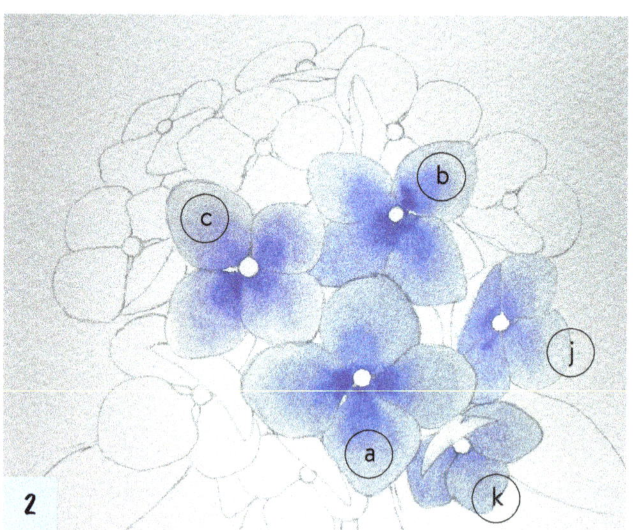

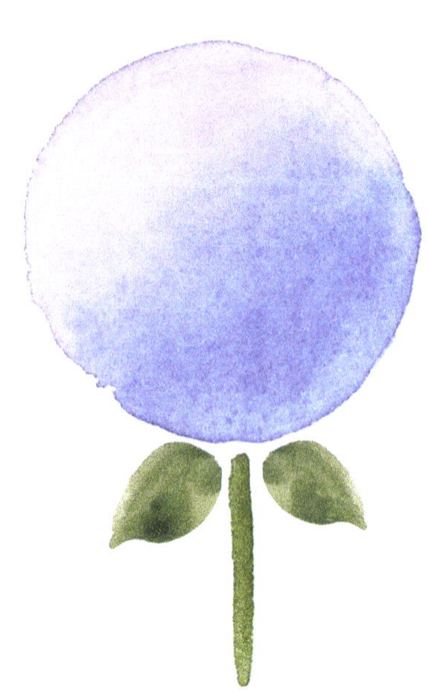

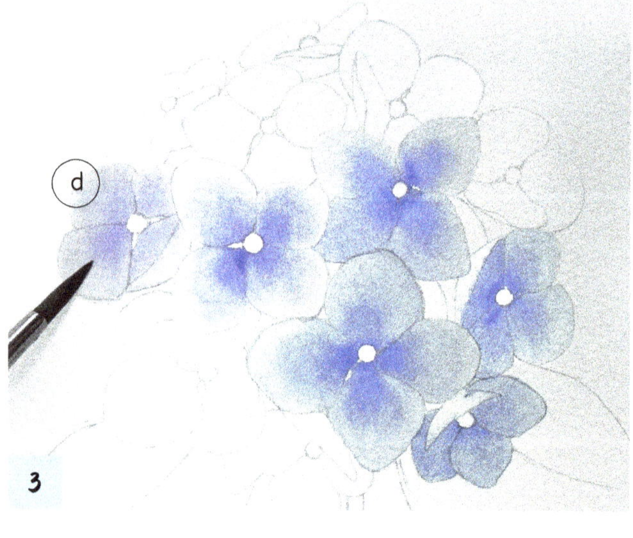

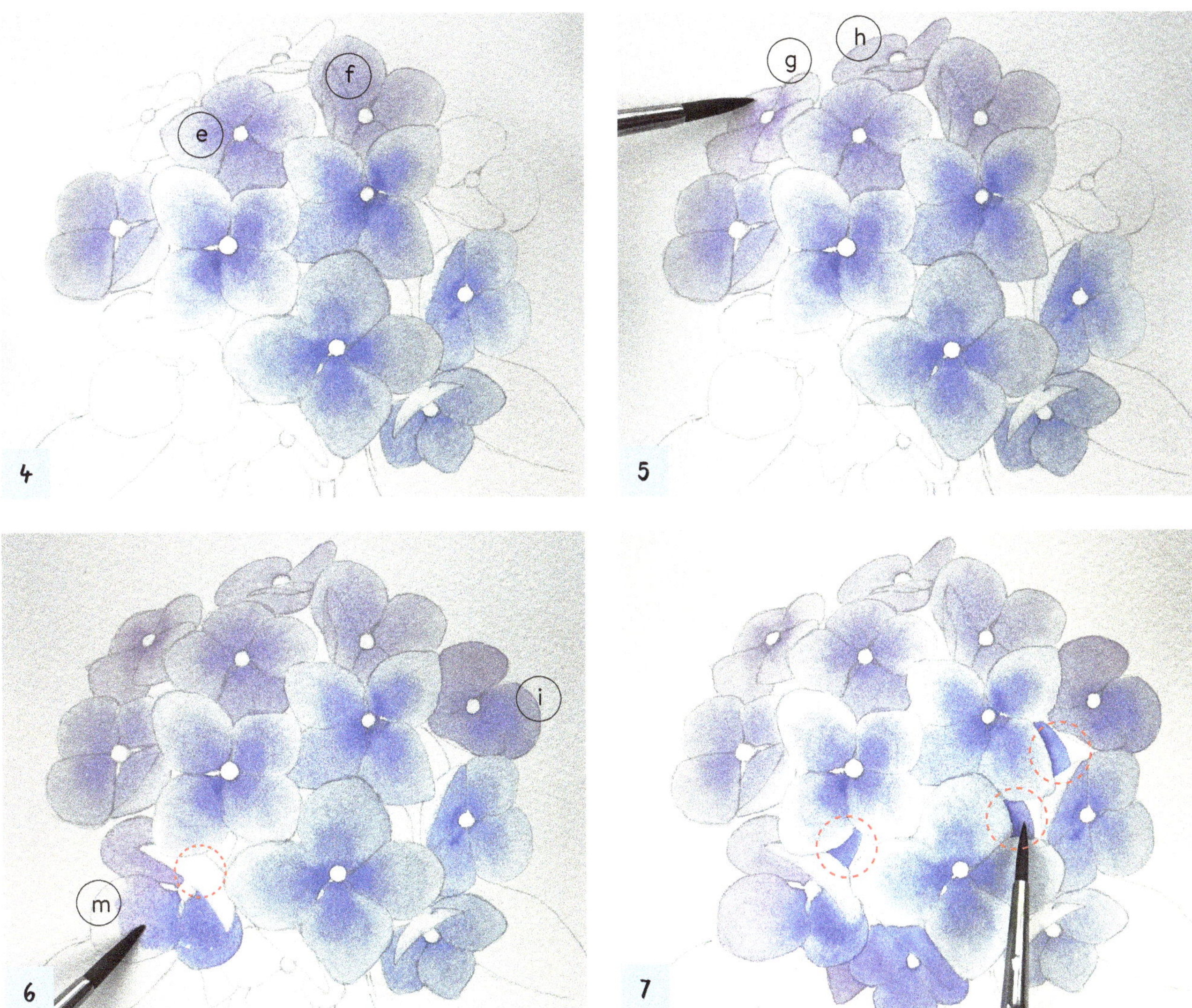

4 Color blossoms e and f using the methods in step 3.

5 Working wet-on-wet, brush water on the petals of blossoms g and h, except for the center circle. Apply Level 2 density Bright Clear Violet over the petals evenly. Color the interior of the petals with Level 3 density of the same color. Blend any edges.

6 Paint blossoms m and i, working wet-on-dry. Create a gradient on the three blossom petals except for those in the dotted lines. Use Level 2 density Bright Clear Violet for the top petals, and Level 3 density Ultramarine Deep for the petals at the bottom. Blend the edges in the center of the blossom. Allow the paint to dry. Apply Level 2 density Ultramarine Deep over the blossom petals within the dotted lines.

7 Finish coloring the main components by painting the areas noted by the dotted circles. Work wet-on-dry, using Level 4 density Ultramarine Deep.

(continued)

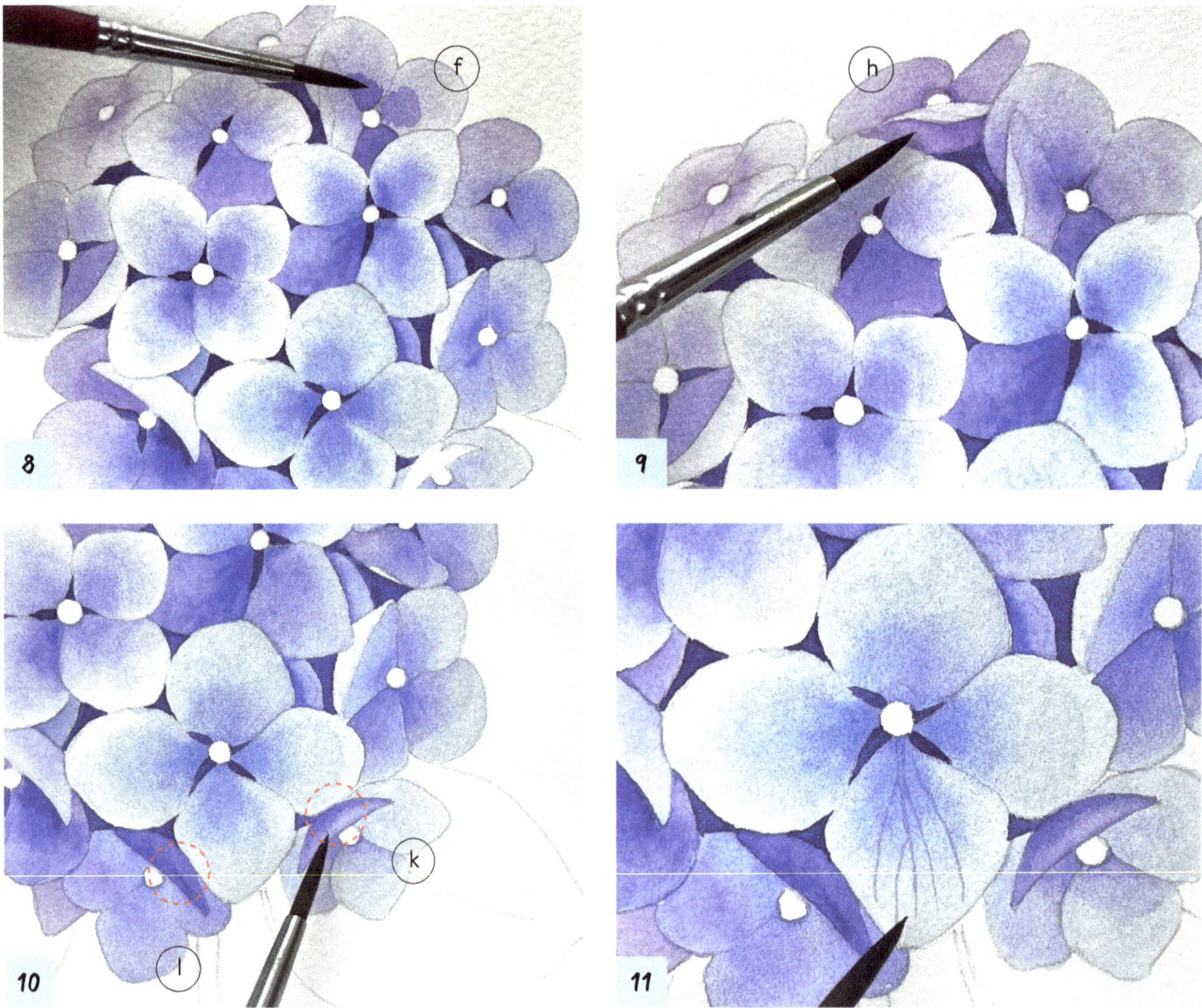

8 Add depth by coloring the gaps between the petals. Mix Ultramarine Deep and Bright Clear Violet in a ratio of 1:1. Apply the color in Level 5 density in the white areas between the blossom petals. Add a glaze (see page 45) to some areas to adjust the color or shade the areas overlapped by the petals. Apply Level 3 density bluish-violet in the center of blossom f, softly fading the edges.

9 Apply Level 3 density Bright Clear Violet on the underside of the petal of blossom h.

10 Apply Level 4 density Ultramarine Deep on the petals of blossoms l and k, noted by the dotted circles.

11 Paint thin lines on each petal using Level 2 or 3 density Ultramarine Deep, as shown.

12 Color the stem using the wet-on-dry technique with Level 3 density sap green. Paint the leaves with the same color. Create a gradient near the petals before the paint dries, using Level 5 density paint near the petals. Blend and fade the color as you move downward on the leaf (see finished image, page 99).

Foxglove

Sketching and painting a foxglove is easier than it seems, although its structure looks complex. This is a flower you'll enjoy creating.

SKETCH THE BLOSSOMS

Draw a cone-shaped blossom using the three-step sketching method. Note that the end of the blossom has upturned, scalloped edges and that the angle shows some of the interior.

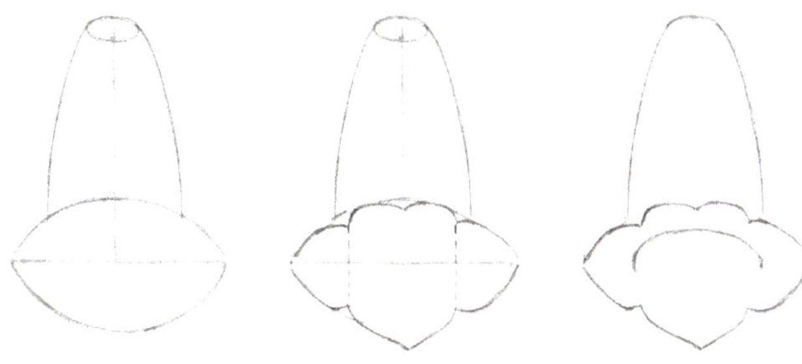

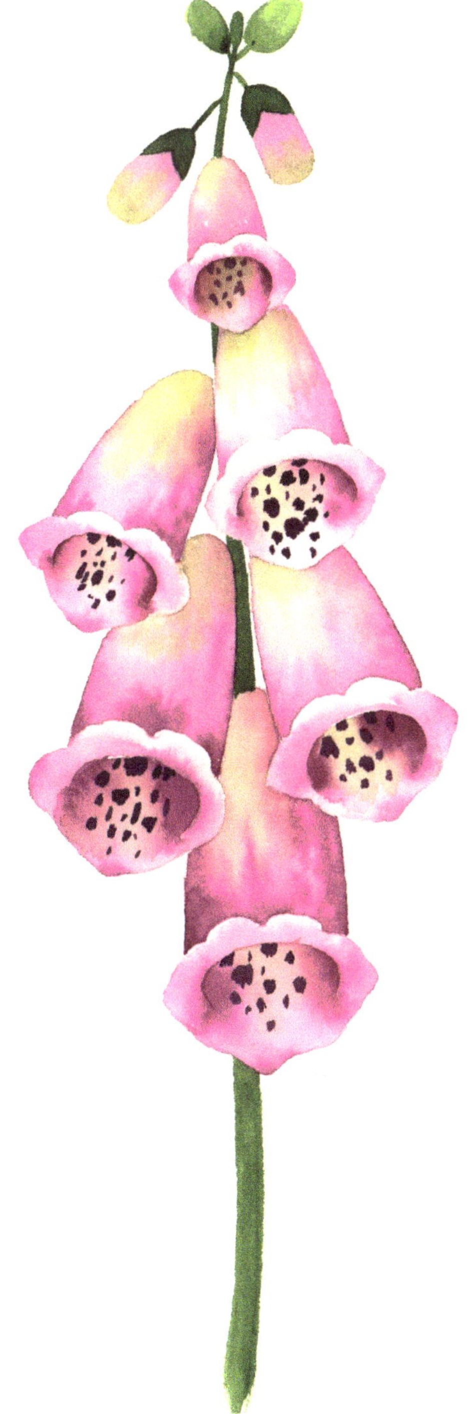

SKETCH THE FLOWER

1 Draw a long, slightly curved line for the stem. Draw guidelines branching out on either side of the stem's center. Draw three ovals (a, b, and c, as shown) to mark the placement of the blossoms. Blossom a will be the largest one, and b and c will be smaller.

2 Draw the basic shape of two smaller blossoms on top of and overlapping blossoms b and c. Draw two more even smaller blossoms on top of those. Create oval-shaped buds with short stems at the top of the main stem. Add scalloped edges to the bottoms of blossoms a, b, and c. Draw curved lines at the openings of all of the blossoms. Thicken the stem to complete the sketch.

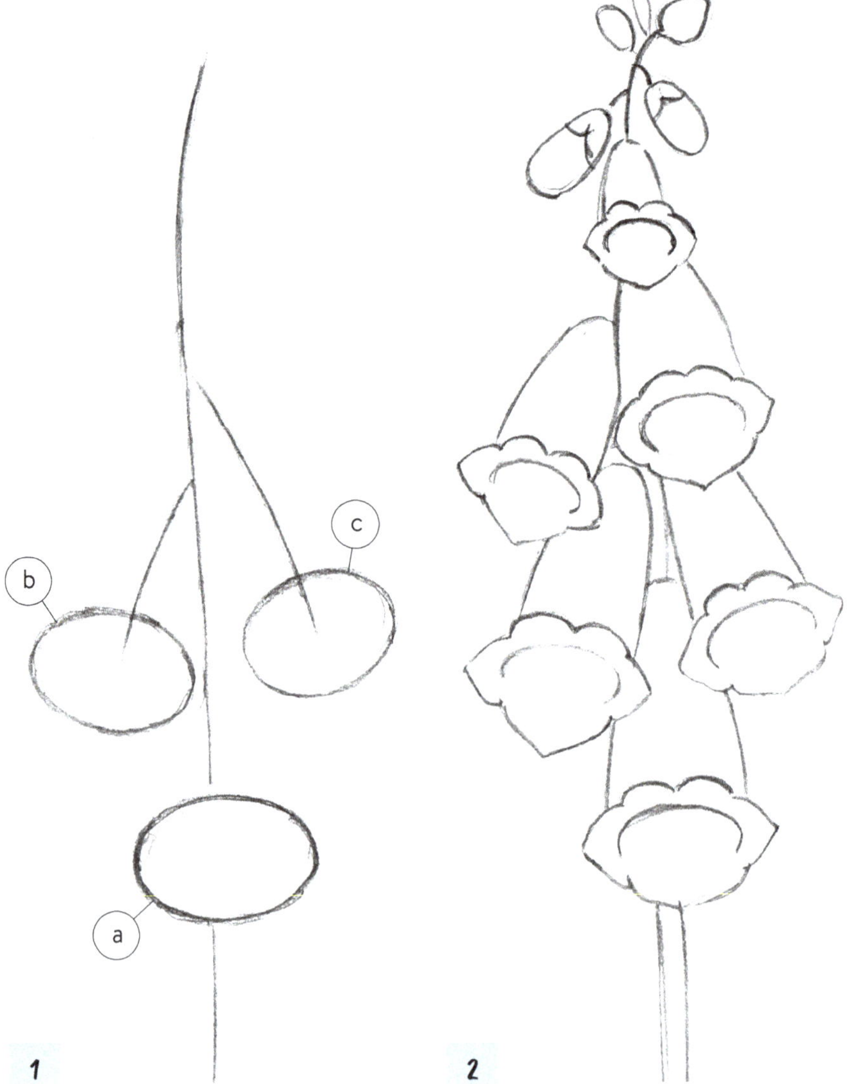

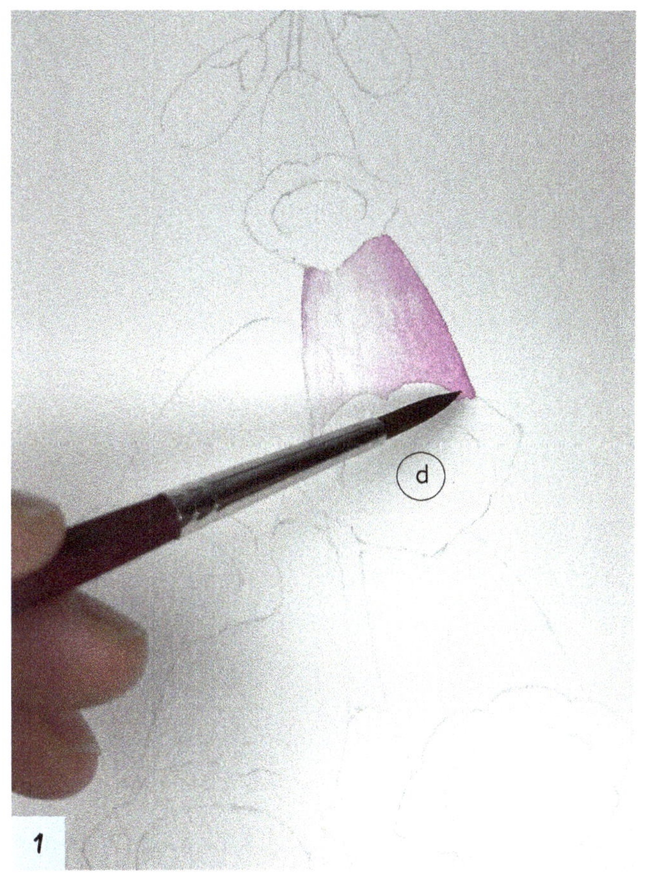

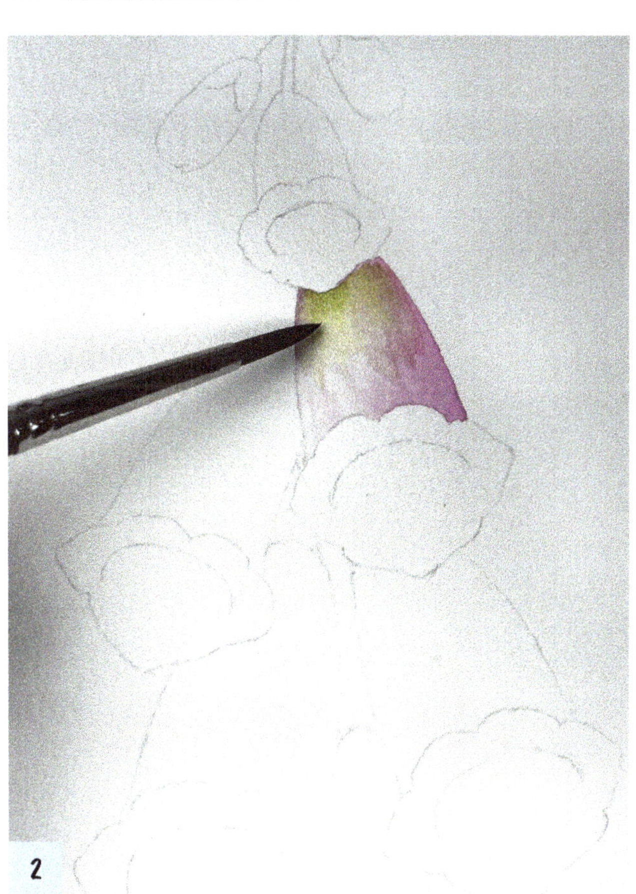

PAINT THE FLOWER

Foxglove features a variety of stunning colors. Red-violet, a shade introduced with this lesson, is the main color. In this lesson, you'll learn how to use complementary colors to make hues more dynamic.

1 Brush water on the cone of blossom e, using the wet-on-wet technique (see page 36). Use Level 3 density red-violet on the right side. Create a smooth, light gradient as you move the brush to the left side of the blossom. Apply a heavy layer of Level 3 density red-violet to the right edge.

2 While the paint is still wet, apply a thin layer of Level 2 density Phthalo Yellow Green to the cone's peak and the bright left-hand portion of the blossom.

(continued)

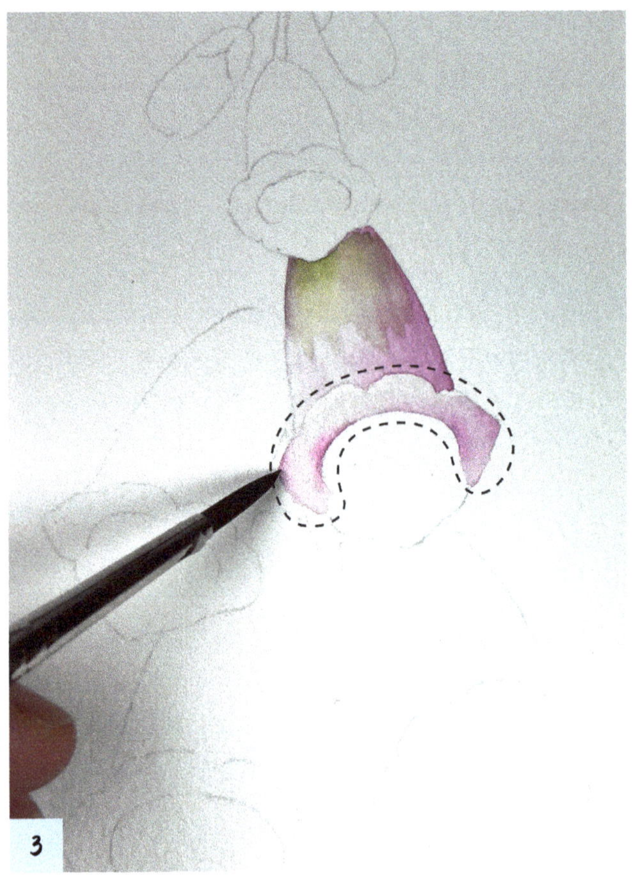

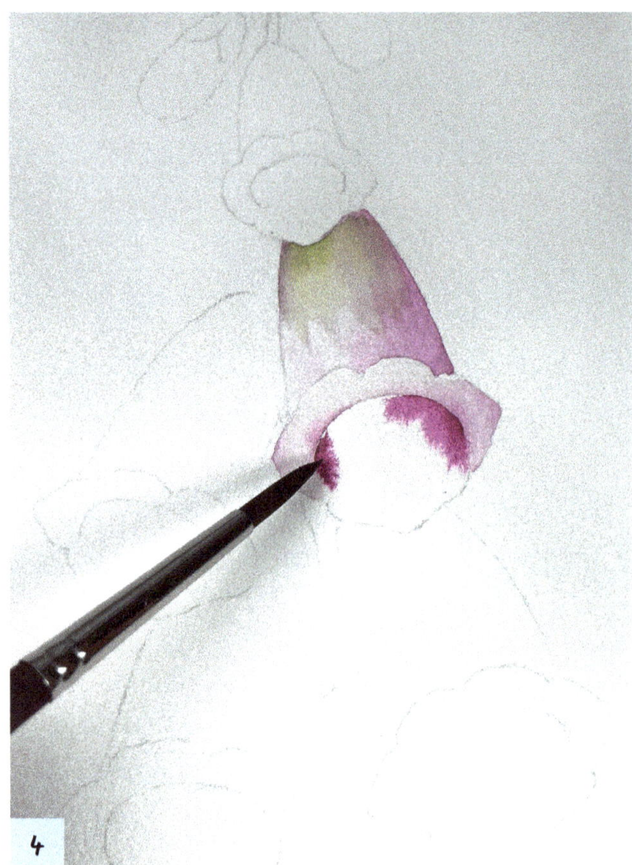

3 Brush water in the upturned part of the blossom in the area marked with dotted lines. Color the area with Level 2 density red-violet. Apply another layer of the color on the edges of this area, as shown. Use the brush tip to apply the paint, moving it as if making small dots on the paper.

4 Brush water over the interior of the blossom, using the wet-on-wet technique. Use Level 4 density red-violet to apply a little color on the right and left sides, as shown. Do not make strokes. After applying paint to the paper, leave the color to spread naturally.

5 Add a thin layer of Level 2 density yellow-green over the bright portion of the interior, in the top left area.

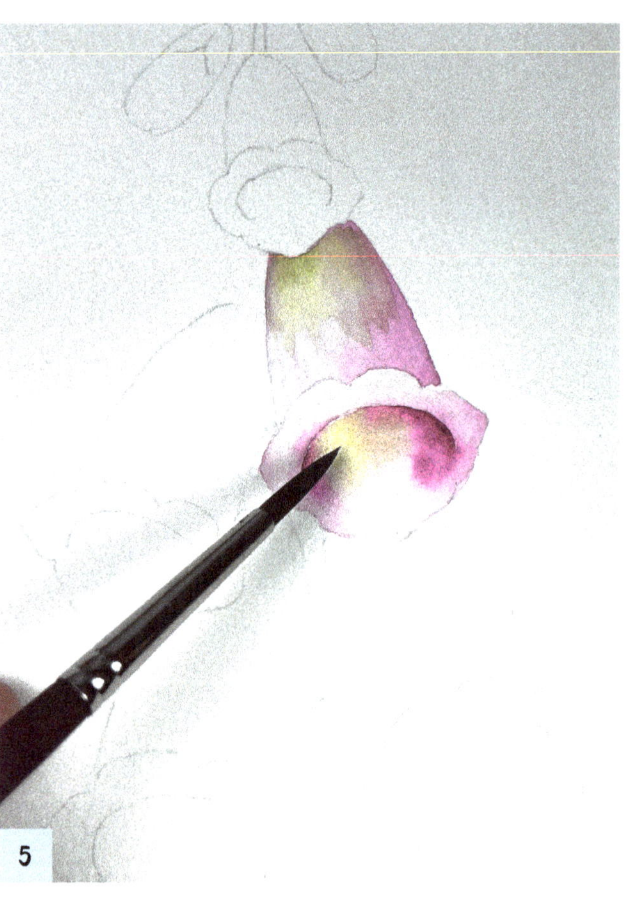

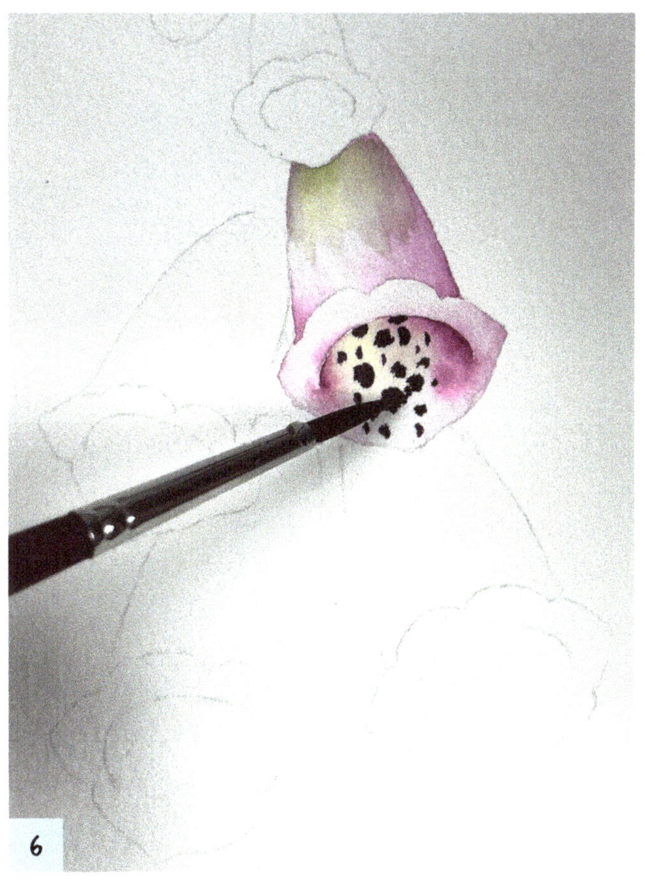

6

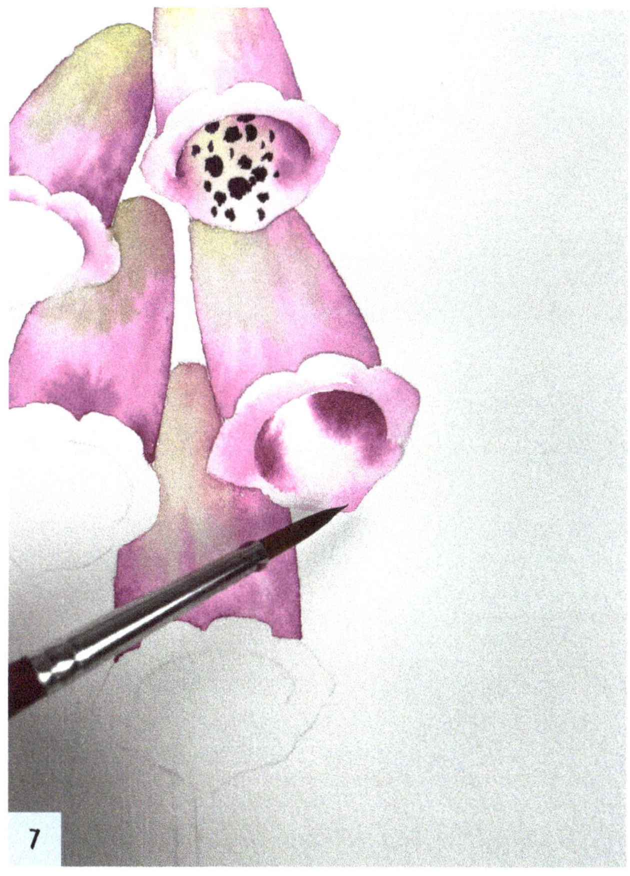

7

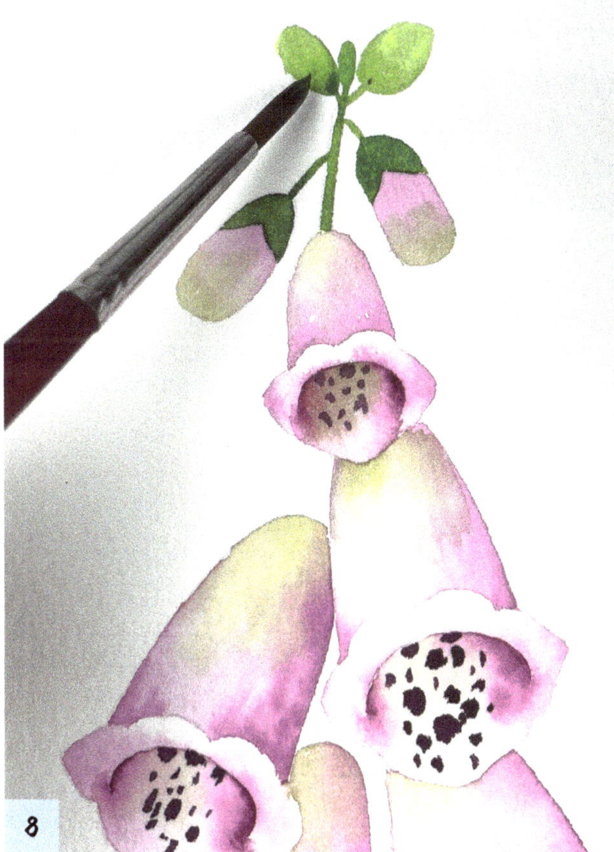

8

6 Mix red-violet and black in an approximate ratio of 1:2. Working wet-on-wet, create random patterns inside the cone using Level 5 density paint. Repeat steps 1 to 5 to color the other blossoms on the stem.

7 Use Level 2 density red-violet to color the interiors where the blossoms don't overlap. Apply the paint and leave it to spread naturally.

8 Color the base of the buds (nearest the sepal) with Level 2 density red-violet. Create a gradient with Level 2 density yellow-green applied to the top of the buds. Color the sepal and stem of the flower with Level 3 density Hooker's Green.

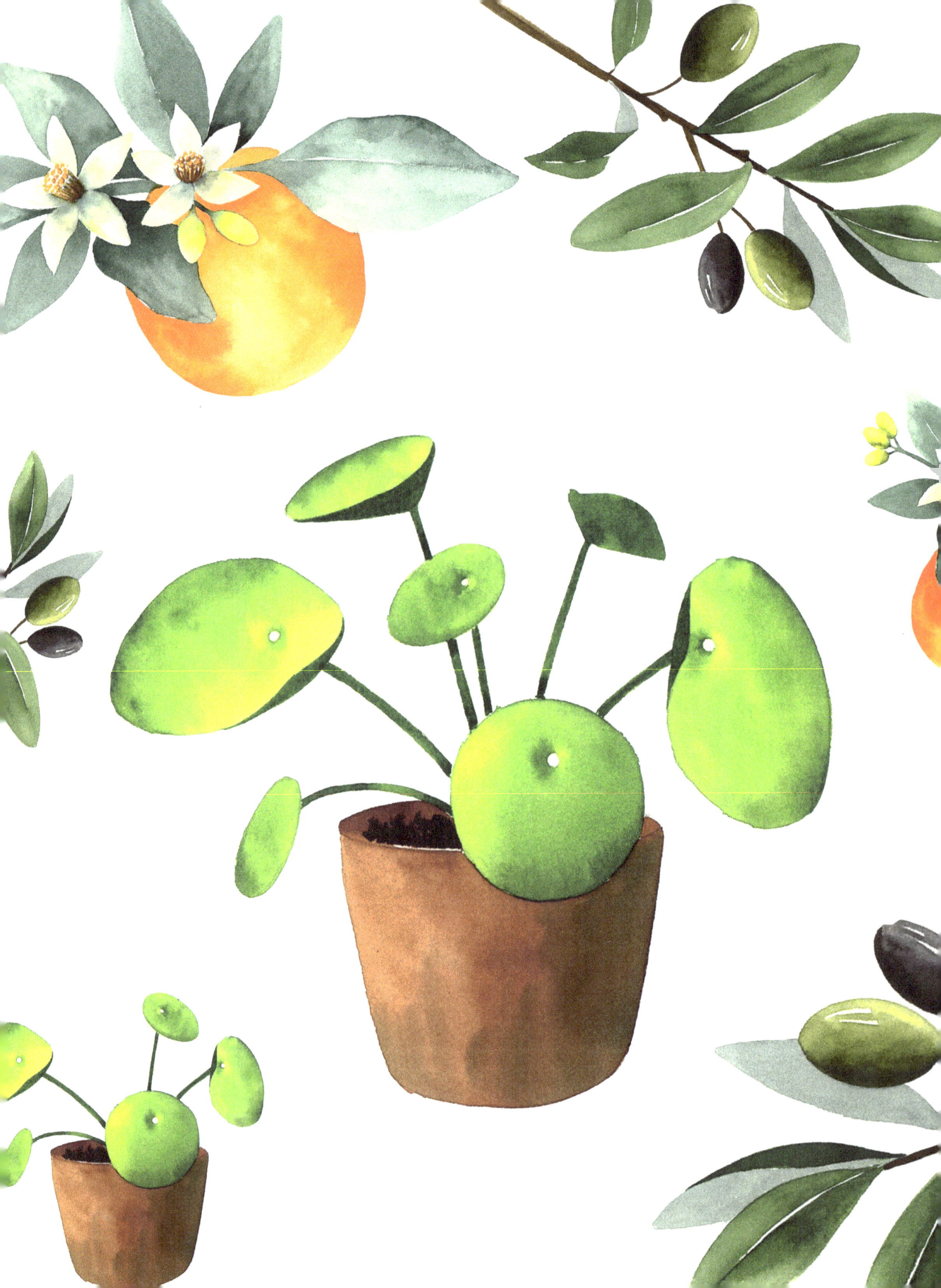

6

Fruits and Potted Plants

In this chapter, you'll increase your skills as you learn to draw and paint fruits and potted plants. Fruits are wonderful to paint on their own, but they also pair well with flowers, especially for still life paintings—flowers and fruits are frequently together. You'll discover how to create balanced arrangements and pleasing color palettes for flowers, leaves, and fruits, specifically orange blossoms, olive branches, and a potted pilea plant. Plant drawings and paintings look more attractive when they're paired with props, such as pots. The pilea is an especially good subject for beginners.

Orange Blossom

To be successful at creating orange blossoms and oranges, use the three-step sketch method to draw the blossoms first, adding leaves and the fruit afterward. In this example, the key point is to arrange leaves and fruits as the background of the blossoms. In this way, coloring white flowers will become much more manageable.

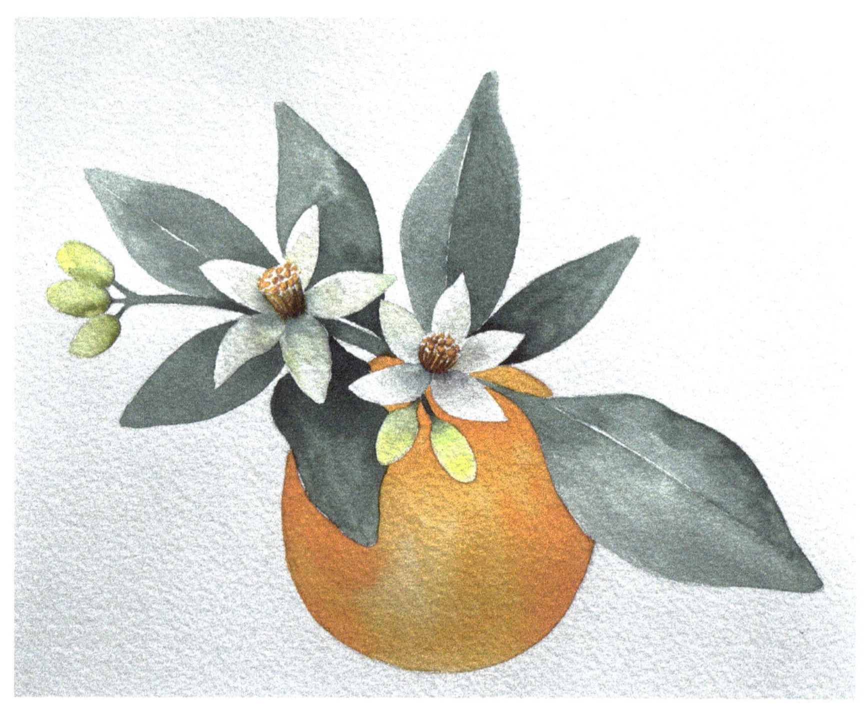

SKETCH THE BLOSSOMS

Sketch five-petal orange blossoms in two different angles using the three-step sketch method.

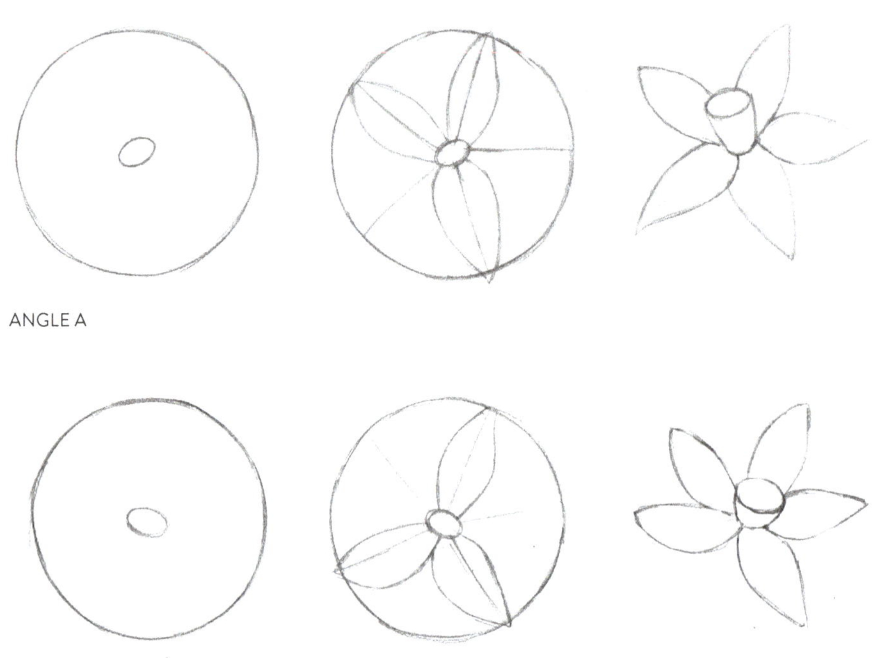

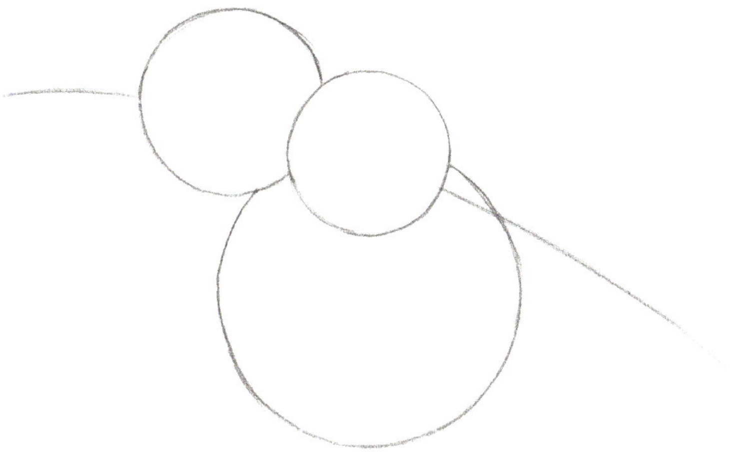

1

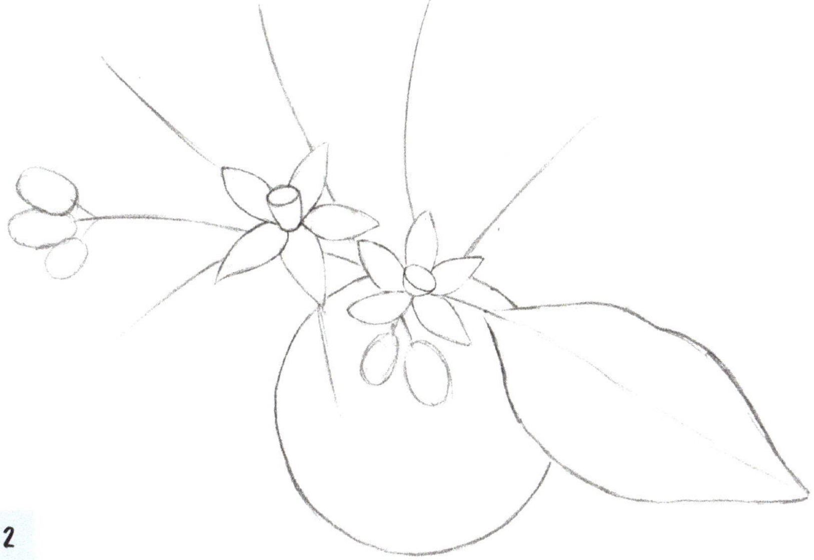

2

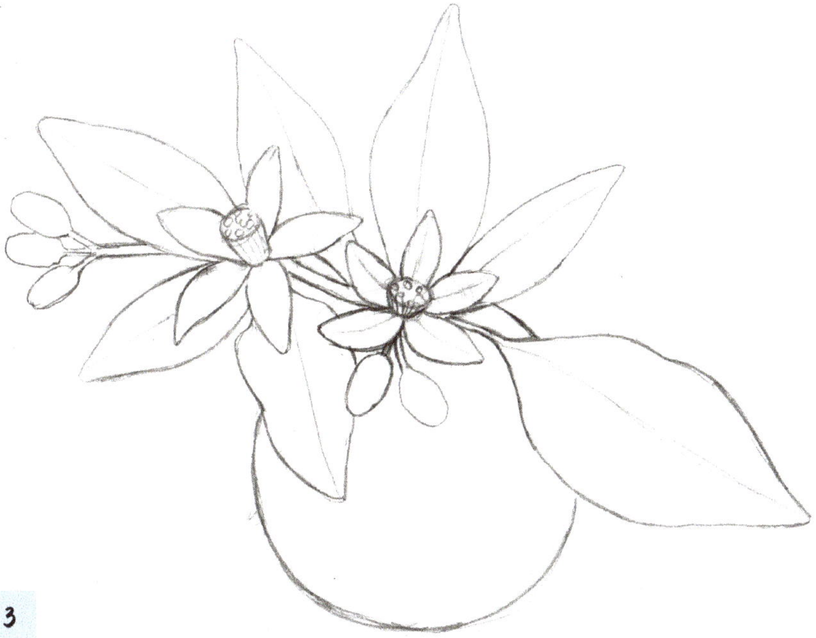

3

SKETCH THE BLOSSOMS, LEAVES, AND FRUIT

1 Draw a line indicating the branch, slanting it downward to the right. Draw a large circle at the bottom right for the basic shape of the orange. Draw two small circles to mark the placement of the blossoms. Note how the shapes overlap.

2 Draw one angle A and one angle B blossom in the two small circles. Draw guidelines for the leaves branching out from the stem. Note the number and location of leaf guidelines. Draw ovals to mark the placement of buds at the left end of the branch and at the top of the orange. Draw a large leaf on the right of the branch.

3 Draw four leaves on the upper part of the branch and two leaves under the left flower. All the leaves are surrounding the blossoms. An effective way to paint white flowers is to use leaves as a background. Add details to the stamens and the branch.

PAINT THE BLOSSOMS, LEAVES, AND FRUIT

In this lesson, you'll use a new color: Van Dyke Green. When used alone, it creates a gloomy, vintage feel. However, when used alongside high-saturation colors such as orange, it creates a unique mood by adding weight to the lightness of the orange. While working on this piece, observe how challenging colors can make a big difference to a painting. After working with these colors, challenge yourself to use diverse colors to express your individuality.

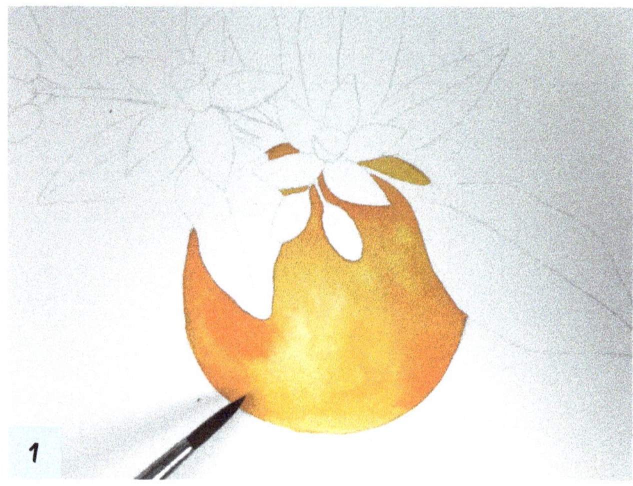
1

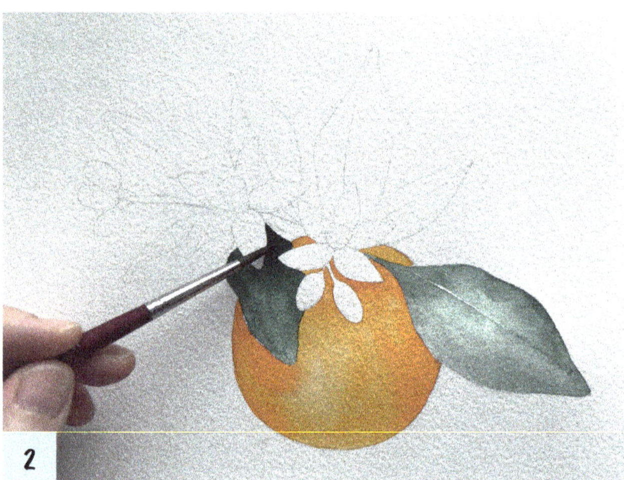
2

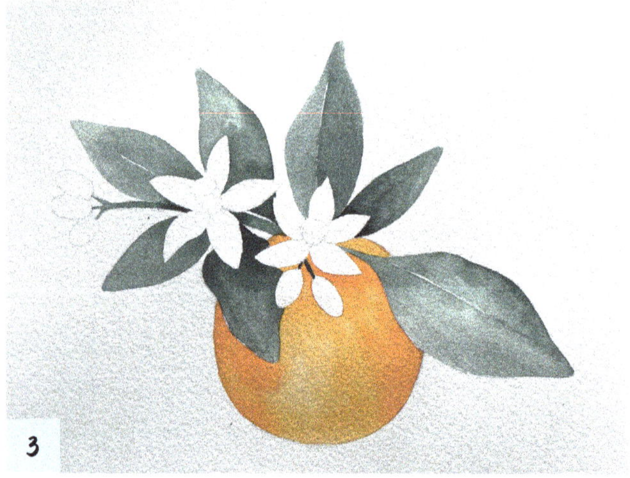
3

1 Begin by painting the orange. Working wet-on-wet (see page 36), brush water on the circle and apply Level 2 density orange paint. While the paint is still wet, apply a layer of Level 4 density orange over the left side, the right edge, and at the bottom of the petals. Leave the paint to spread naturally; don't blend the edges.

2 Working wet-on-dry (see page 38), use Level 2 density Van Dyke Green to color the large leaf on the right, leaving the middle vein of the leaf white. While the paint is still wet, apply the same color in Level 3 density over the top of the leaf and the area near the stem. Blend the edges smoothly.

Working wet-on-dry, use Level 5 density Van Dyke Green to color the top portion of the leaf resting on top of the orange. Use Level 3 density of the same color near the bottom of the leaf, and create a light gradient between the two shades.

3 Color the rest of the leaves and the stem by repeating step 2, noting placement of the shadows.

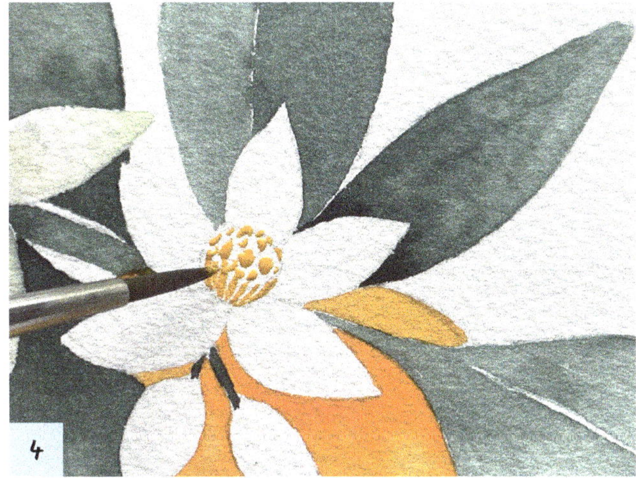

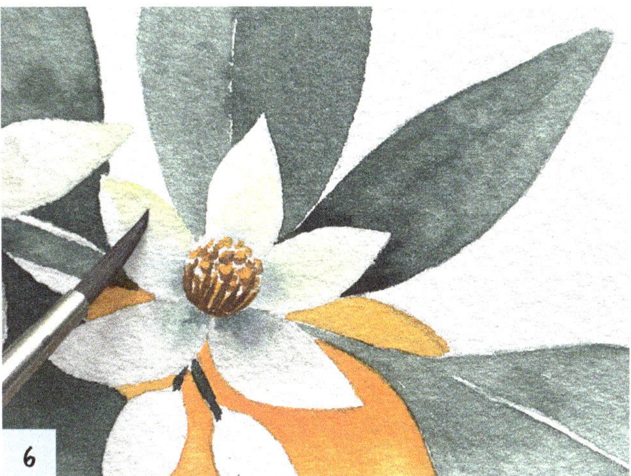

4 Color the stamens. Working wet-on-dry, use Level 5 density Permanent Yellow Deep (golden yellow) to add details to the stamen by drawing vertical lines and dots using the brush tip.

5 Color the two front petals of the Angle B blossom. Working wet-on-dry, color the interior of the petals using Level 2 density Indigo. Create a light gradient toward the edges of the petals. Make smooth strokes, using the brush tip on the interiors. The color should spread naturally.

Apply Level 3 density Indigo to the petals closest to the stamen. Use Level 1 density yellow-green to color the edges of the petals. Color the remainder of the petals following steps 6 and 7.

6 Fill the gaps between the yellow lines of the stamens with Level 4 density Burnt Umber. Paint a line at the bottom right of each dot.

Color all buds completely with Level 1 density yellow-green. Apply a glaze (see page 45) of Level 1 density olive green near the stem.

Use Level 1 density yellow-green to color the exterior of the petals. Color the rest of the petals using the same method.

Olive Branch

Olive trees are among the best small-fruit plants that beginners can practice painting. Since olives don't grow in bunches, like blueberries or grapes, coloring them is quite simple.

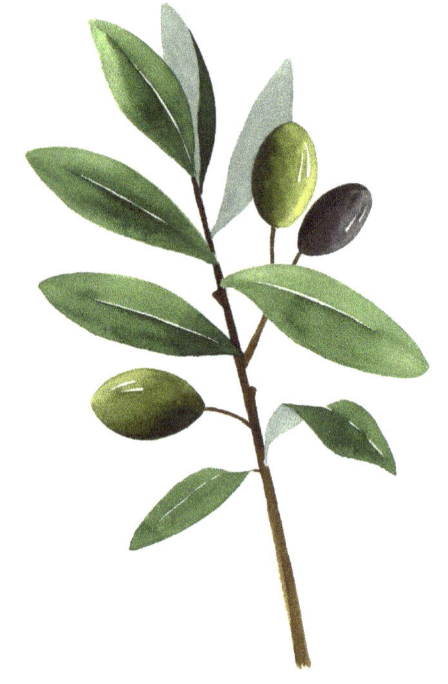

SKETCH THE OLIVE BRANCH

1 Draw a line slightly slanting right for the stem. Draw two leaves on the left side of the stem and one leaf on the right, as shown. The leaves' curved center vein indicates a slight curl.

2 Draw an olive below the leaf on the left. Draw two more fruits behind the leaf on the right. Add highlights to each fruit as shown in the dotted line. Draw guidelines for additional leaves on the top and bottom of the main stem.

3 Draw the additional leaves at the top and bottom of the stem. Note how the leaves curve, showing the undersides.

Draw the rest of the leaves positioned at the top and bottom of the stem. Draw the backside of the leaves marked with dotted lines. The guidelines on each stem are necessary for painting, so do not erase them.

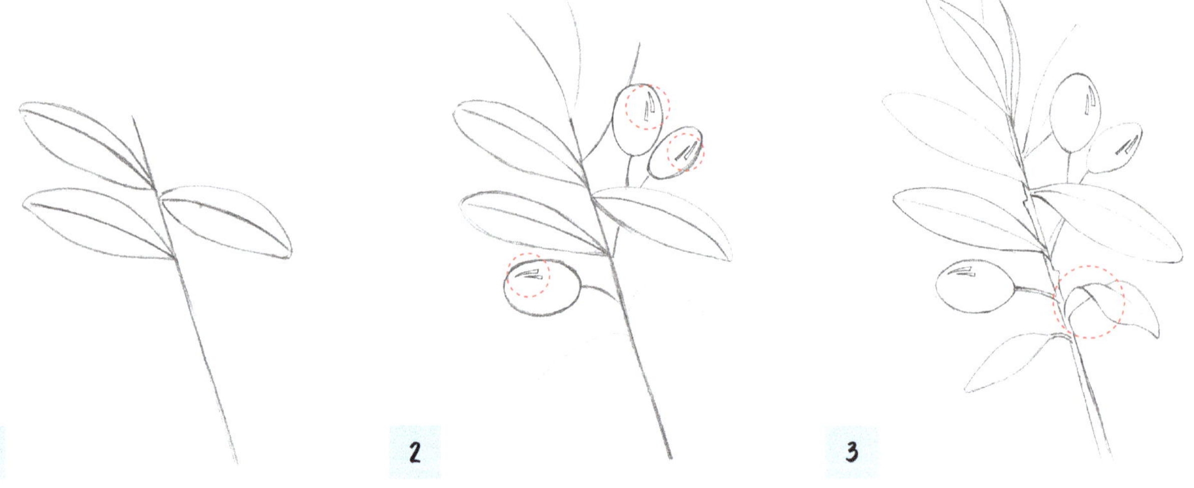

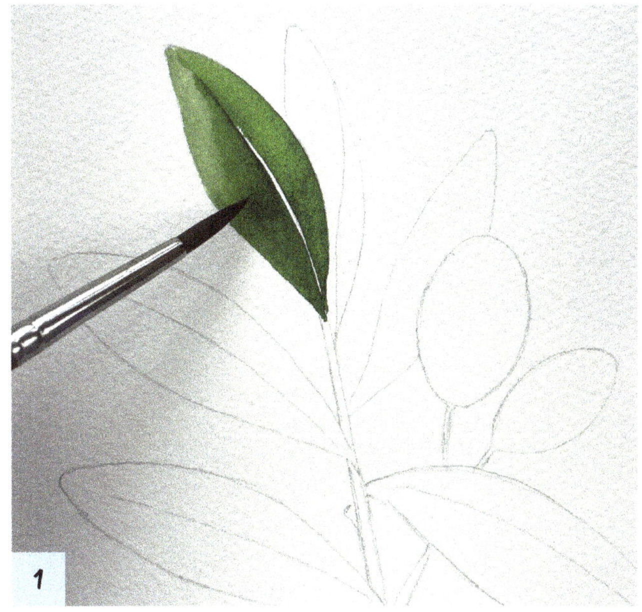

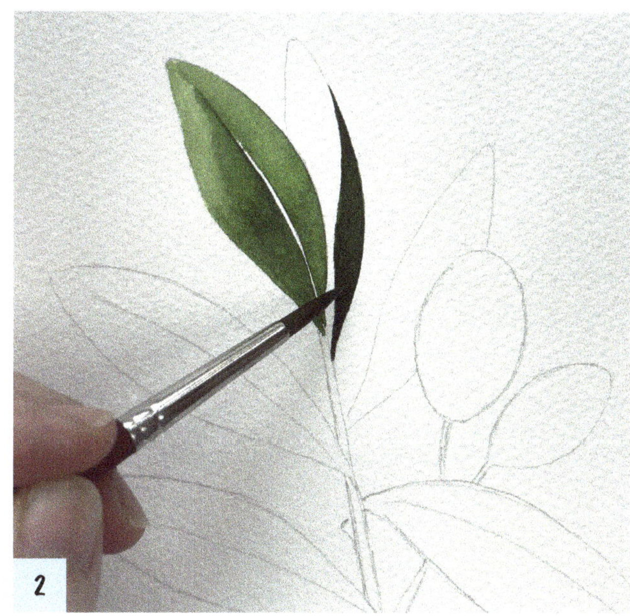

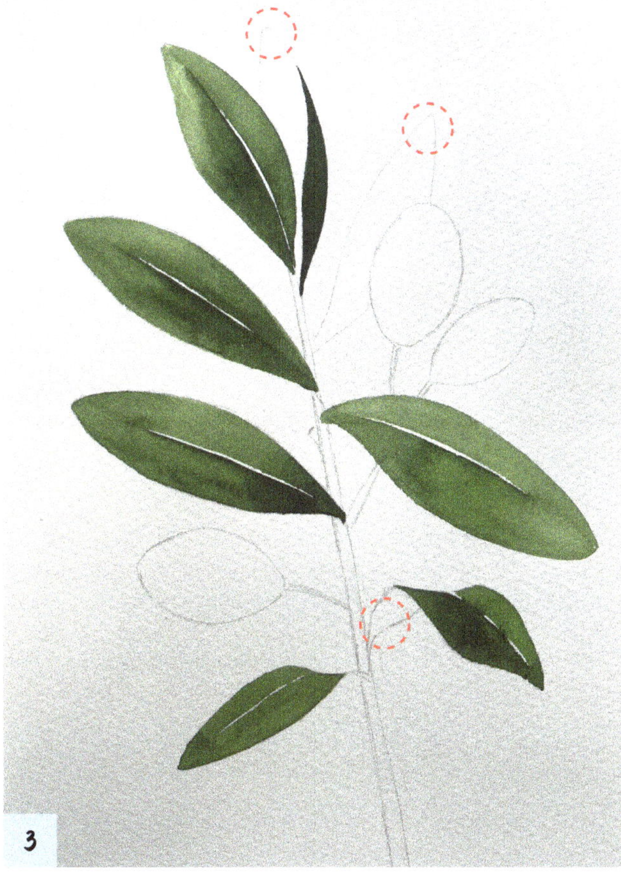

PAINT THE OLIVE BRANCH

As you paint the leaves, make sure not to color the midrib line at the center—leave it blank or white. In this portion of the lesson, you'll learn how to create highlights on the surface of the olives. All of the painting will use the wet-on-dry technique.

1 Add color starting at the top of the stem where it joins the leaf. Working wet-on-dry, color the beginning of the stem and leaf in Level 4 density Hooker's Green. As you approach the end of the leaf, use the paint in Level 2 density to create a gradient. Make sure the color isn't as light as Level 1 density; if it's too light, there won't be enough difference between the leaf and the white midrib.

2 Use Level 5 density Hooker's Green to color the front side of the top right leaf.

3 Color the remaining leaves following the instructions in step 1, except for the leaves noted by the dotted circles.

(continued)

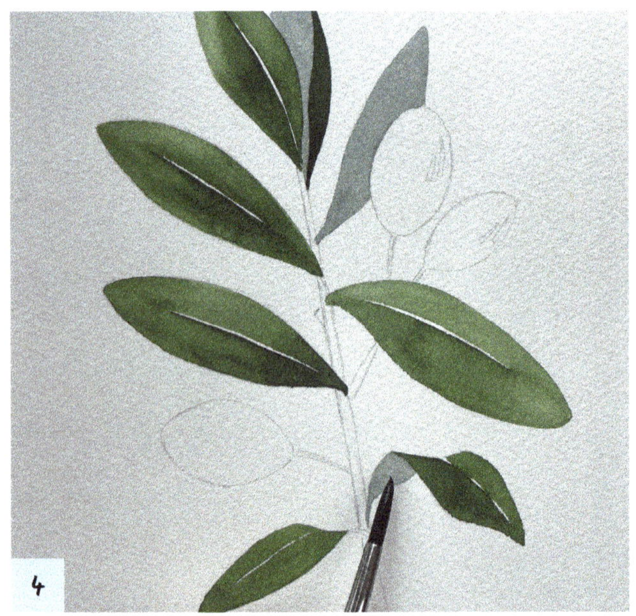

4

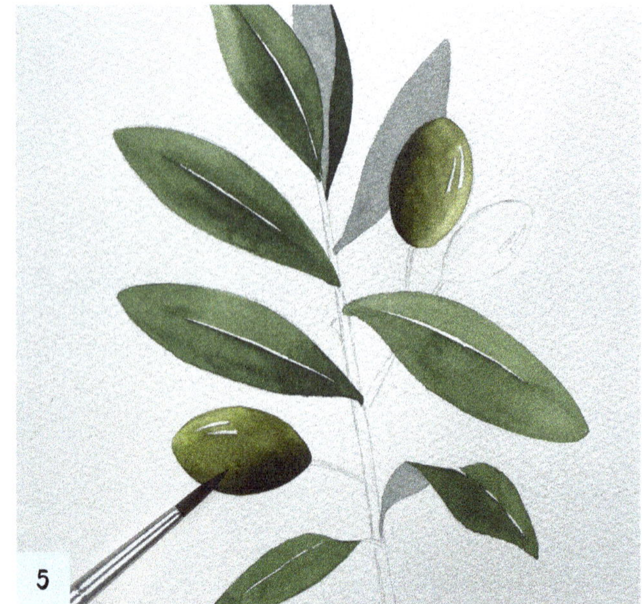

5

4 Mix indigo and Hooker's Green in a 3:1 ratio to create green-gray. (If you don't have indigo, mix Hooker's Green, Prussian blue, and black in a 1:1:1 ratio.) Paint the undersides of the leaves that show that portion with Level 2 density green-gray.

5 Paint the two olives, as shown. Apply Level 5 density olive green to one side of the fruit (the shaded side). Create a gradient as you move the brush toward the highlighted area, using Level 2 density olive green. Don't color the highlighted area.

6 Mix a 1:1 ratio of sepia and clear violet to create dark violet for the remaining olive. Apply Level 4 density dark violet on the left side, creating a gradient as you move toward the right with Level 2 density paint. Don't color the highlighted area.

7 Paint the stem with Level 4 density burnt umber to complete the painting (see finished image, page 116).

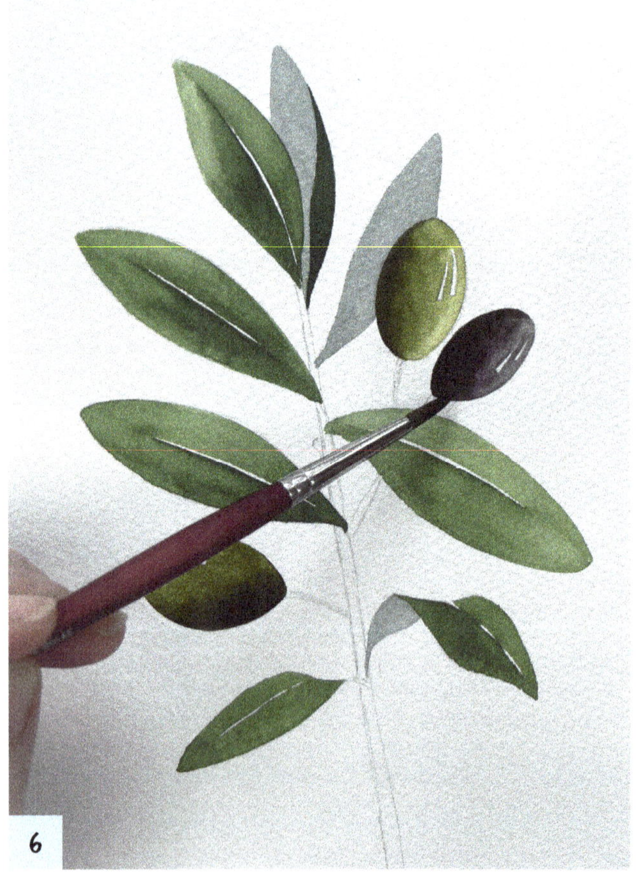

6

Potted Pilea

The pilea is another plant suitable for beginners. The structure doesn't become complex even when the angle of the leaves change since the basic leaf shape is a circle. Despite its simplicity, your drawing and painting will look beautiful.

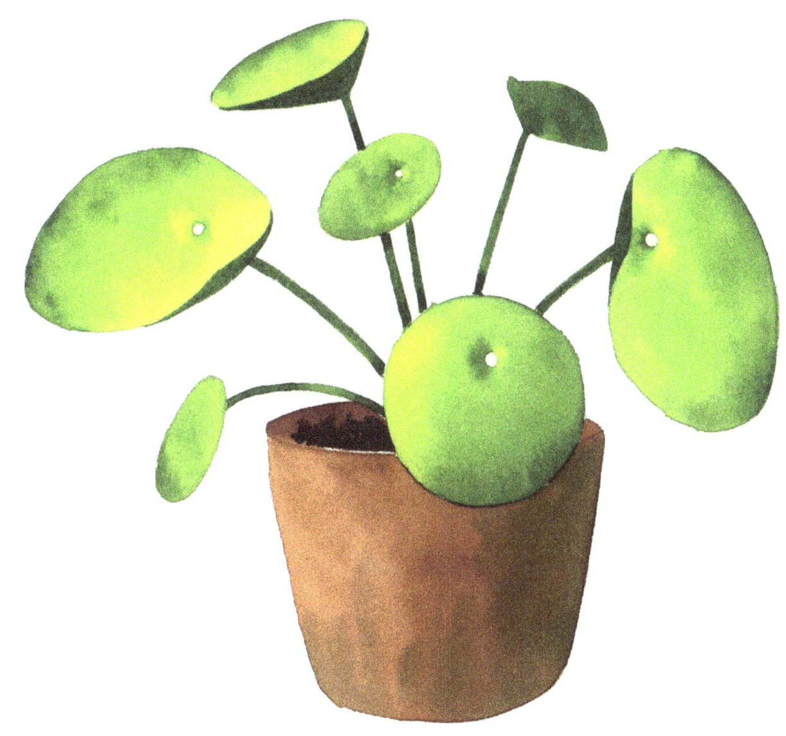

SKETCH THE POTTED PILEA

1 Draw a basic pot (see below). Draw a large circle (leaf a) overlapping the top-right portion of the pot. Draw a long oval (leaf b) near leaf a on the right side of the pot. Draw a long oval (leaf c) on the left side of the pot. Leave space between leaves a and c. Draw guidelines as shown on the oval leaves to indicate their angles.

2 Draw small ovals for leaves d and e between the larger leaves. Leaf f has a cone shape with a wide horizontal top due to its angle. Leaf g has a fan shape. Add tiny circles in the positions shown to indicate where the stems attach to the leaves.

3 Add details to some of the leaves by adding curves that reveal the underside. Draw thick stems that connect to the small circles on the leaves.

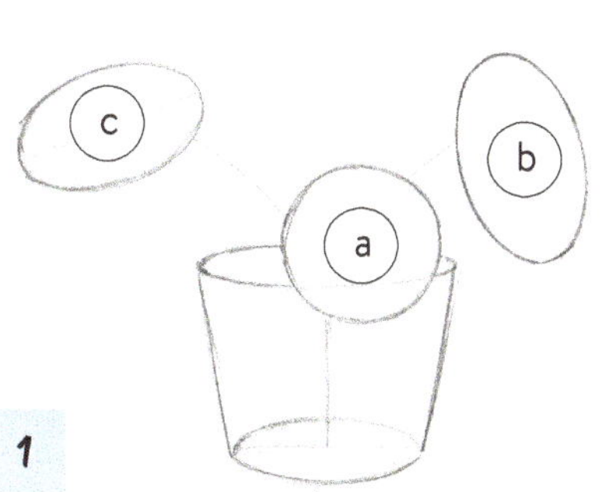

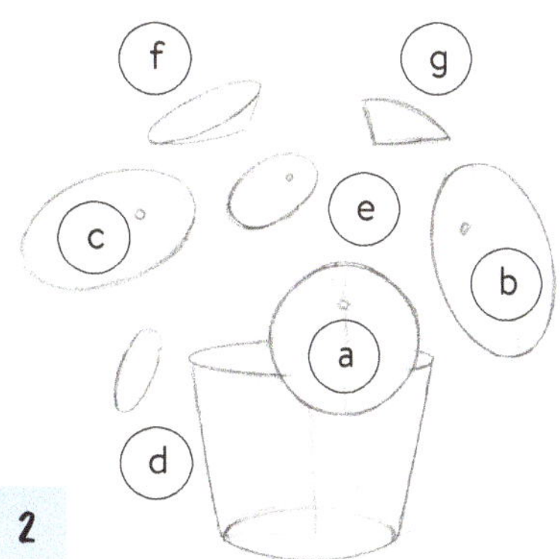

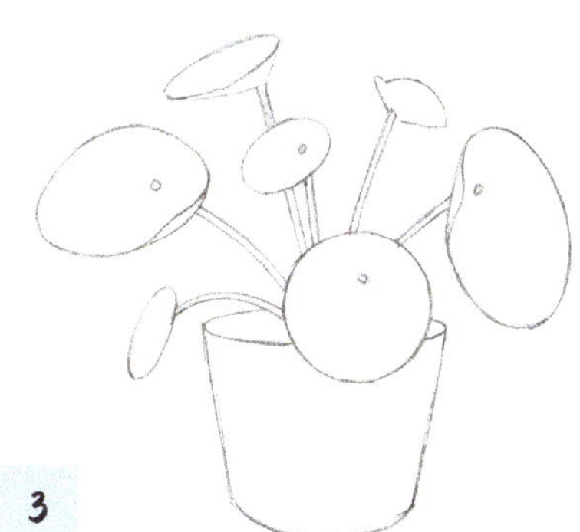

PAINT THE POTTED PILEA

Sap green is the only color that will be used to paint the leaves. However, you'll be able to create several shades by changing the density level of the paint.

1 Begin by painting leaf a. Working wet-on-wet, brush water over the leaf except for the tiny circle near the top. Apply Level 3 density sap green to the right side of the leaf, creating a gradient as you move toward the left. Be careful as you paint not to color the tiny circle.

2 Apply Level 5 density sap green at the left edge of the tiny circle using the tip of the brush. Use a thin stroke.

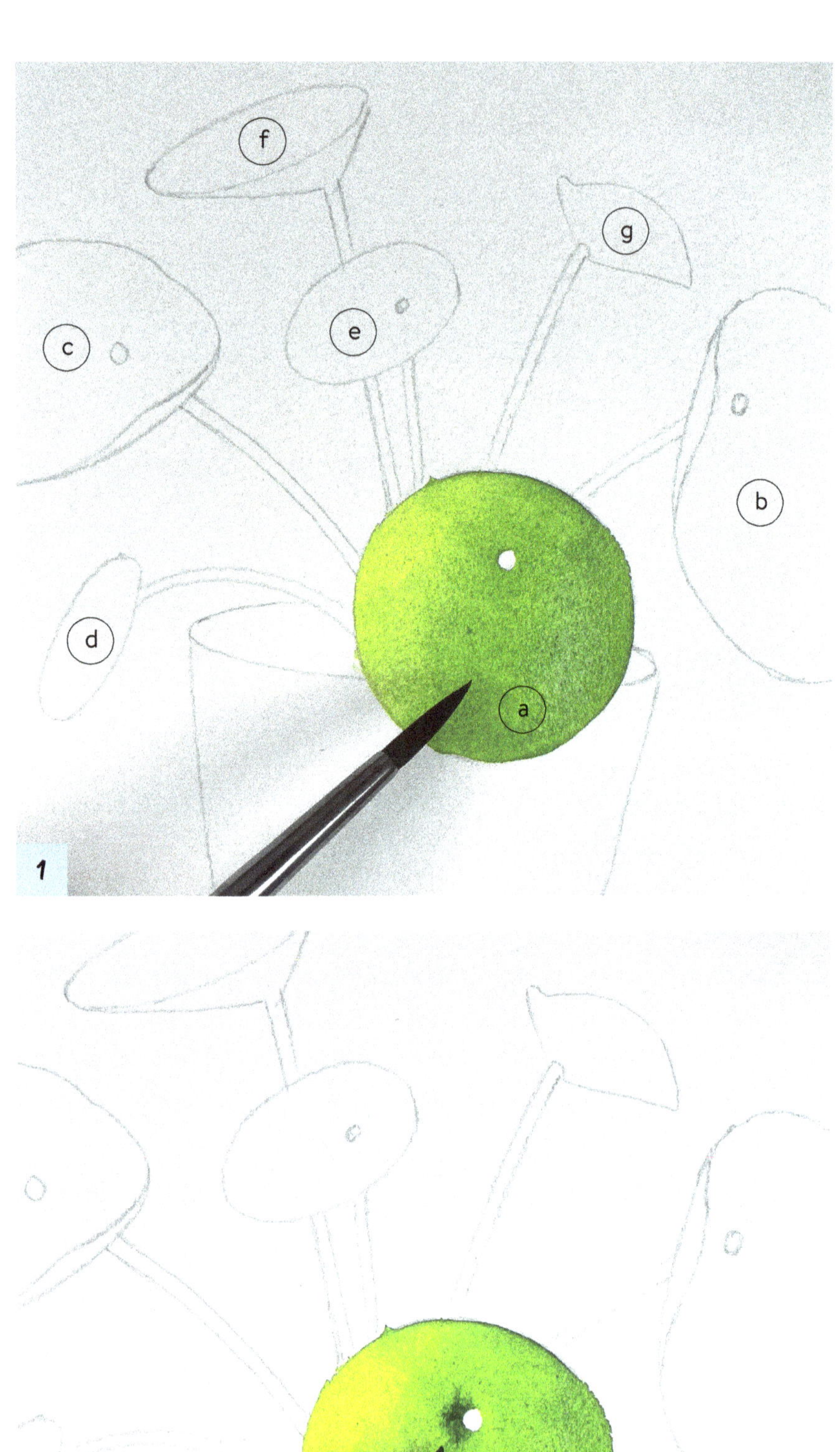

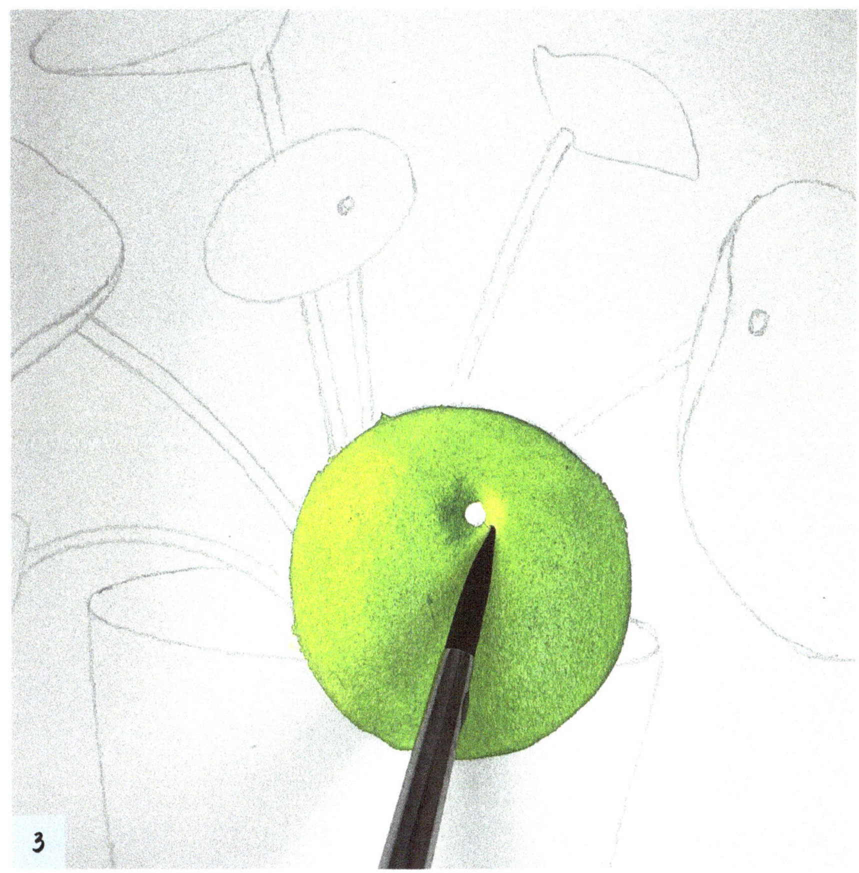

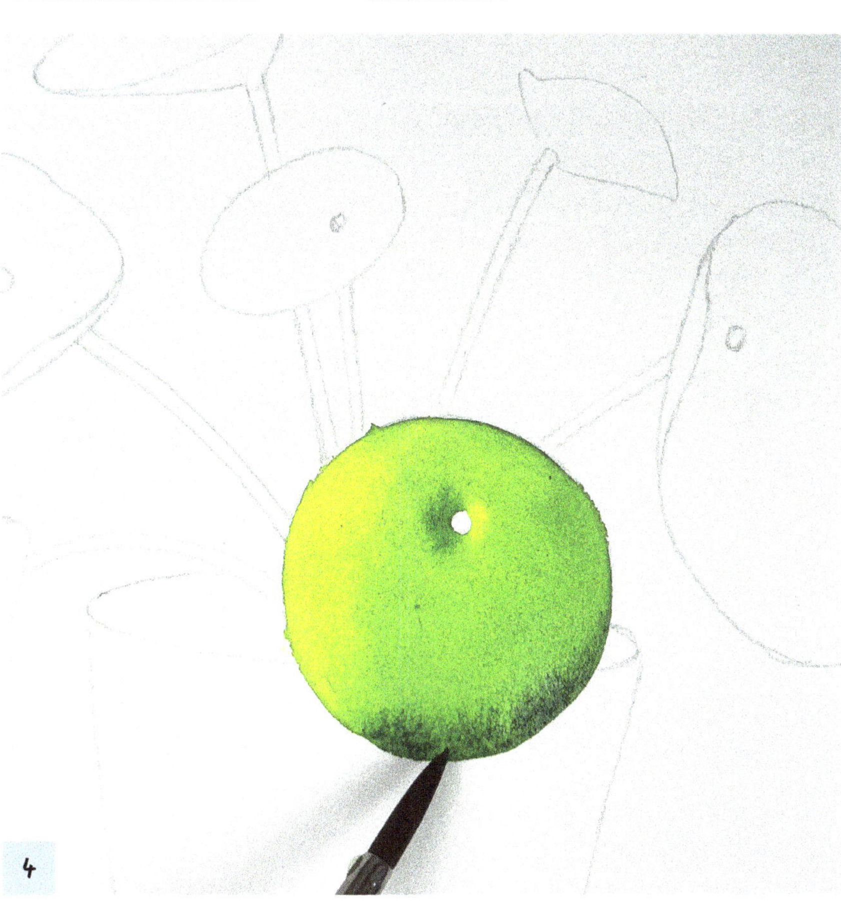

3 Wash the brush and remove any excess water. Wipe away the paint on the right edge of the tiny circle using the brush. Repeat to remove additional paint, creating a brighter highlight. This technique creates a noticeable three-dimensional effect.

4 Color the bottom-right edge of the leaf with Level 5 density sap green to shade the leaf.

(continued)

5 Repeat steps 1 to 4 for leaves b, c, and e. However, when coloring leaf c, apply Level 3 density sap green to the left side of the leaf and make a gradient.

6 For leaf f, apply Level 3 density sap green on the upper part of the leaf and make a gradient downward. For leaf d, apply Level 3 density sap green on the left bottom of the leaf and create a gradient upward. Paint the underside of leaves and stems with Level 5 density sap green.

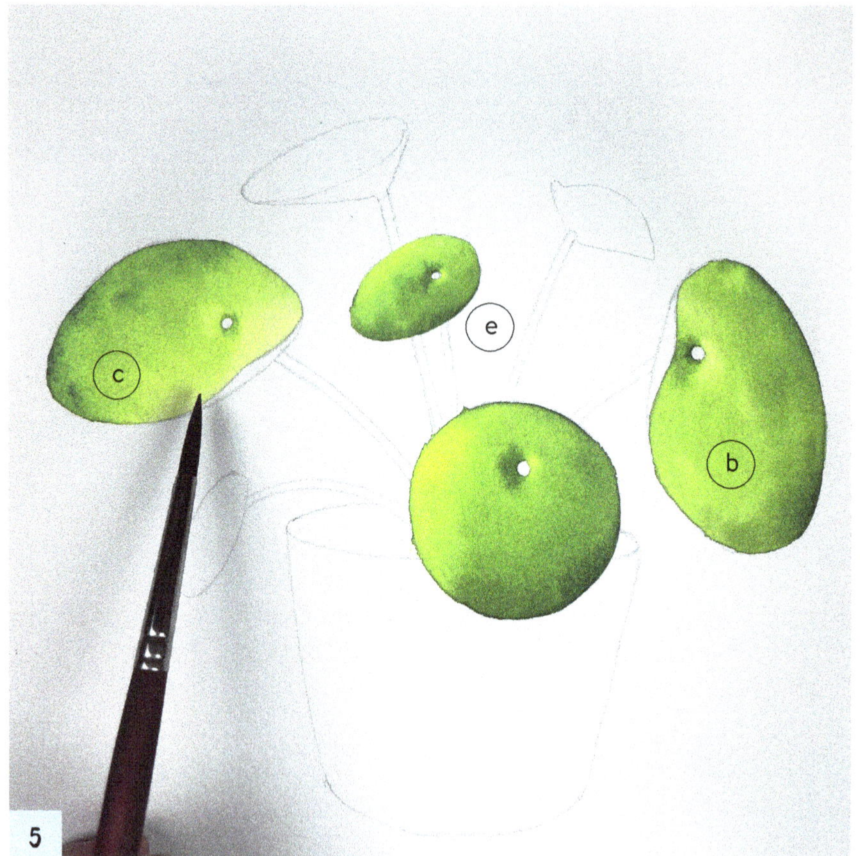

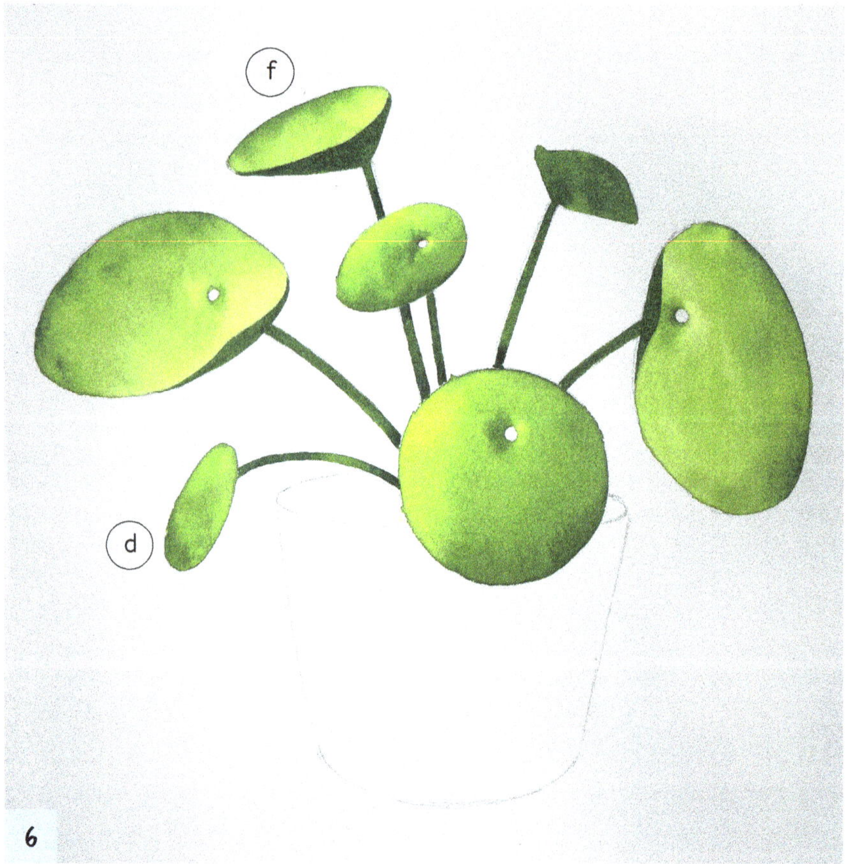

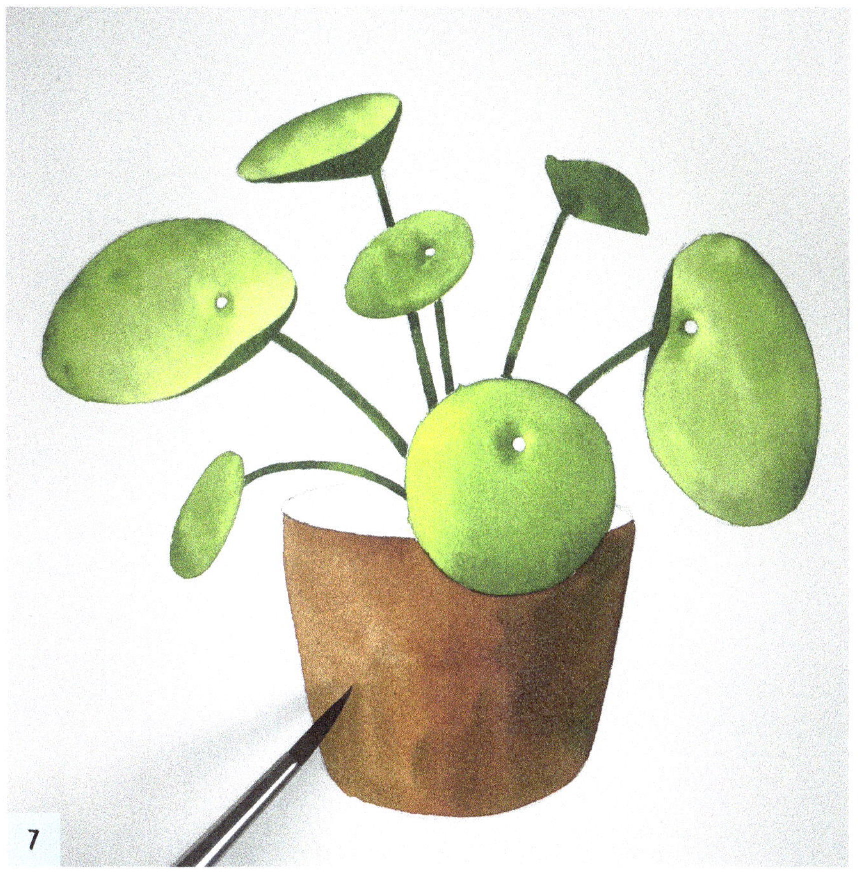

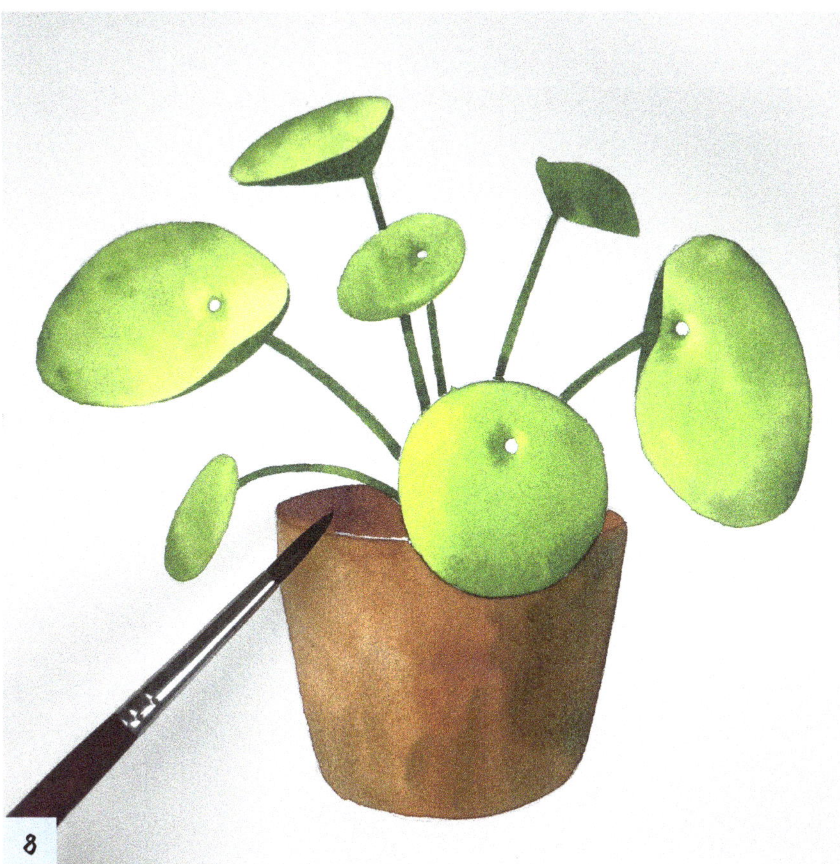

7 Working wet-on-wet, brush water on the front side of the pot. Color the right side with Level 3 density burnt umber. Create a gradient, making the left side brighter than the right. Paint the right third of the pot with Level 2 density Cerulean Blue (sky blue) and paint the left third of the pot with Level 2 density Raw Umber.

8 Working wet-on-dry, use Level 4 density burnt umber to paint a flat layer for the pot's interior. Leave a thin unpainted border between the interior and the exterior of the pot.

9 While the paint in the interior of the pot is still wet, create random brushstrokes using Level 5 density sepia to mimic the look of soil (see the finished image, page 119).

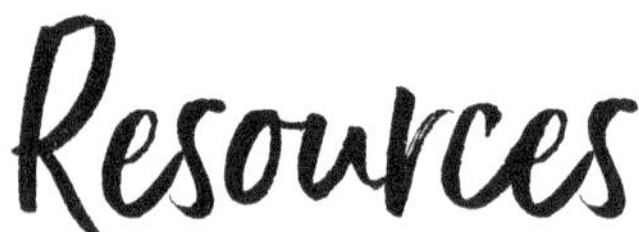

Resources

WATERCOLOR

Mijello Mission Gold Watercolor: mijello.com

Holbein Artist Materials: holbeinartistmaterials.com

BRUSHES

Princeton Artist Brush Co.: princetonbrush.com

PAPER

Fabriano Artistico 100% cotton cold press paper: fabriano.com

Saunders Waterford 100% cotton cold press paper, manufactured by St Cuthberts Mill: stcuthbertsmill.com

Canson Montval watercolor paper: en.canson.com

Bockingford watercolor paper, manufactured by St Cuthberts Mill: stcuthbertsmill.com

Fabriano Studio watercolor paper: fabriano.com

Canson Drawing Pad, 9" × 12" (23 × 31 cm): en.canson.com

OTHER SUPPLIES

Winsor & Newton art masking fluid: winsornewton.com

Arteza masking fluid brush, size 1 round and size 1 liner: arteza.com

Faber-Castell HB pencils: faber-castell.com

A FEW FAVORITE PLACES TO FIND FLOWERS

BOTANICAL GARDENS

Botanical gardens are perfect places to observe various plants, including wildflowers and huge trees. You can discover seasonal flowers as well as rare species and various cacti, which are great sources of inspiration. I frequent the South Coast Botanic Garden in Palos Verdes, California (southcoastbotanicgarden.org). I often take pictures when I'm there and save them on my computer to use as sources in the future.

PARKS

You can encounter many varieties of plants in nearby parks, and the same plants can look different depending on the season. Try taking pictures instead of walking past them—they'll make great material for your sketches.

PLANT NURSERIES

You can purchase potted plants and seasonal flowers at plant nurseries. I visit them often to purchase or simply observe the greenery. These are good places to see indoor plants you can't find outside as well as various flowerpot designs.

GROCERY STORE FLORAL SECTION

Most grocery stores have a floral section where you can observe different seasonal flowers. You can also purchase small plants and arrangements.

YOUR NEIGHBORHOOD

Neighbors' lawns can sometimes be wonderful sources for flower sketches when you're out for a walk. There have been times when I found the exact flower I needed on someone's lawn, and these instances were honestly some of the happiest moments I've experienced.

ARTIFICIAL FLOWERS

If I can't find the real flowers I need, I'll occasionally purchase artificial flowers. Many are well made and almost indistinguishable from real flowers, and they're easily accessible. A big advantage is that artificial flowers don't wither, so you'll have ample time to observe and sketch the angles you want.

Acknowledgments

Without my family and friends, I would not have been able to complete this book. I know I can't explain it all in words, but nonetheless, I'd like to express my thanks to all those who have supported me along the way.

My daughter Jia and husband Hoonju: Jia, my love, this book is dedicated to you. I often had to make this book a higher priority than you when you had just been born, yet you were so patient and good for your mom throughout the project. I'm forever grateful for you and blessed to have had you along for the joyful ride of creating this book. My most faithful supporter, Hoonju: If it weren't for you taking charge of caring for Jia and the housework, I would not have survived this project. Your moral support, thoughtful listening, and words were what kept me going. Thank you.

The team at Quarto: All my thanks goes out to the team for making my dream come true. Publishing a book is something so many people dream of achieving, including me. But I didn't think it would become a reality. To my editor, Jeannine, who has supported me to the very end with unlimited positivity, encouragement, and patience, I cannot thank you enough. It meant everything to me. To the art team and marketing team, thank you so much for lending my book a professional hand and turning my work into fantastic pieces.

My Instagram followers and online media platforms: Because my followers have consistently loved and supported my artwork, I was able to make it this far. Your interest motivated and presented a new path for me. Buzzfeed, as well as other online media platforms, introduced my art, which was a catalyst for an increase in my followers and the growing popularity of my three-step sketch method. I hope all that love has translated into this book and that it will be helpful to anyone learning how to draw and paint.

My parents: Mom, you're always my first like on Instagram whenever I post my art. Dad, you worry about my health more than I do, telling me to exercise and do stretches. You two never fail to make me laugh. Thank you for being so proud of your daughter.

Friends: To my book club members, K, S, and Y, who are always bright and joyful, thank you. To Y and D, who were a huge help in taking care of Jia while I wrote this book: You were my village and community. Thanks to you, I was able to wholly focus on working on this book. To Allan and Jake, I am so lucky to know both of you. Thank you!

About the Author

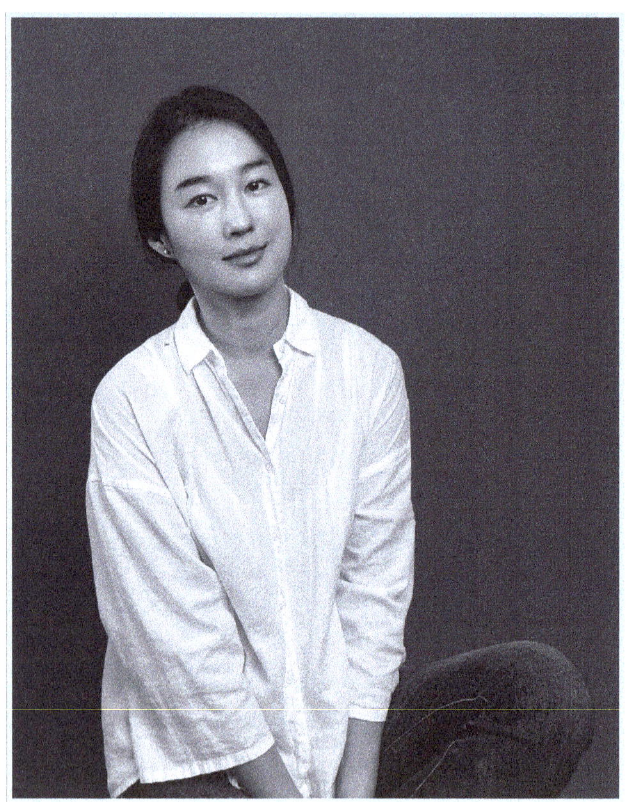

Kyehyun Park is a designer and illustrator who was born and raised in South Korea. After obtaining her bachelor's degree, she worked as a graphic designer in South Korea and New York City, then received a master's degree in animation and visual effects with an emphasis on 3D animation from the Academy of Art University in San Francisco, California. As she studied the 3D environment, which deals with animation backdrops and virtual reality for games, she developed an interest in the environment, specifically in plants and nature. Kyehyun is currently collaborating with companies and artists from various fields and runs a watercolor workshop for Korean and Korean-American adults in Los Angeles. Her Instagram account features her flower sketches and watercolor process videos. Kyehyun lives in Los Angeles.

Index

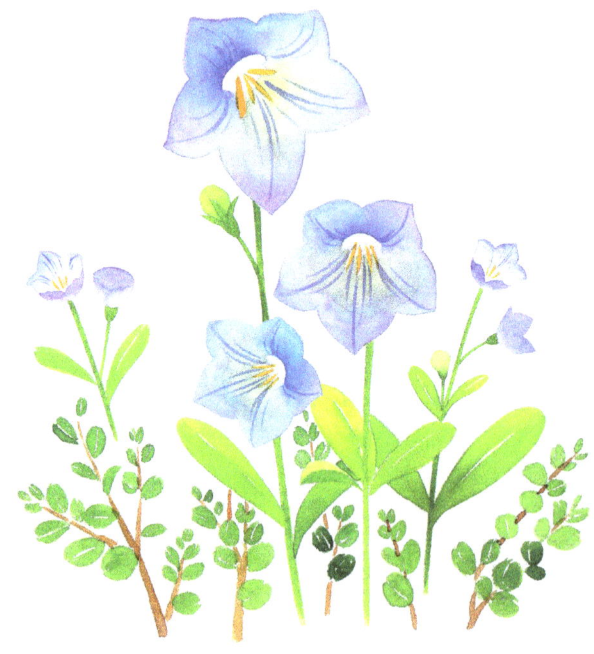

www.ingramcontent.com/pod-product-compliance
Lightning Source LLC
Chambersburg PA
CBHW060856180726
48173CB00003B/7

9780760373309